DAVID PHAYRE
3104 N. E. 9th ST. #F
FT. LAUDERDALE, FL **33304**

Also by Gloria Emerson

Winners and Losers:
Battles, Retreats, Gains, Losses
and Ruins from the Vietnam War

SOME
American
MEN

6   '88

Gloria Emerson

SIMON AND SCHUSTER
NEW YORK

Designed by Barbara Marks
Manufactured in the United States of America

1 3 5 7 9 10 8 6 4 2

Library of Congress Cataloging in Publication Data

Emerson, Gloria.
  Some American men.

  1. Men—United States.
2. Masculinity (Psychology)
3. United States—Social life and customs—
1971–
I. Title.
HQ1090.3.E46   1985   305.3'1'0973
85-19576
ISBN: 0-671-24588-0

Parts of the "Work" section, under the title "A Month
of Sundays: Living Without Work in Lorain, Ohio,"
were originally published in *Vanity Fair*, April 1983.
Excerpts of the poem "Anna Grasa" by Bruce Weigl are
from *A Romance*, published by the University of Pitts-
burgh Press, 1979.

AUTHOR'S NOTE

The interviews in this book were done over a period of seven years and in nearly all cases permission was given to use real names. An immense debt is owed to a clinical psychologist, Dr. Robert May, whose own book, *Sex and Fantasy: Patterns of Male and Female Development*, published by Norton, 1980, is a remarkable and beautifully written book. It is Dr. May who is quoted on page 151. Much of what I already knew, and did not realize, became clearer after reading his work and gave me the courage to push on. Working in a profession for so long monopolized by men, I must have begun this book fifteen years ago. In Dr. May's book and my own, the expression "do or die" appears. I first heard it spoken by two young American soldiers in Vietnam struggling to push back the very real possibility of their own destruction.

Gratitude is also owed to Jean Brown, Mary Jane Nolan Kelly, Henry Ferris, and Peg Haller.

For Sylvia Wacs
and
Matthew Naythons

CONTENTS

PROLOGUE

This is how peculiar an American man can be: At a ceremony in New York to honor various writers whose new books were being given an award, among the winners was the man I had come with, my dear friend, perhaps the most fearless one I have. He does not like to go to such occasions by himself so by now I have watched him win seven awards. That night after his acceptance speech—warning us how much worse our government had been than he was ever able to write or we were meant to know—I went to his side and said how proud of him I was. "You are always proud of me," he said. It was not the response of a humorist or a boor, only the remark of a man still uncertain how to behave and quite unable to comply with other people's idea of decorum.

He is nowhere in this book except here, for the men in these pages have more ordinary lives, are not famous, and the risks they have taken, or refused, are quite different. This is a book suggesting why some men of different generations and class behave as they do, how they defend themselves and have made their own trails, what they fear and what they believe is required of them.

The men chosen for this book are those whose thoughts about themselves and their own lives provide a range of expressions of masculinity in this country, for better or for worse. Not all their memories or actions need elucidation by me; what is mysterious or never quite clear must simply be that. Writers should know when not to intervene, for very little in any life can be tidily explained and its seams made straight.

In a decade when so much has changed at last for American women, it has been odd, and even unsettling, to keep making discoveries about men during a time when they have been denounced as childlike, brutish, inchoate, unfeeling, bullies, and deficient in both decency and imagination. (And I have grievances of my own.)

It seems now as if all men were strangers until my late thirties when, as a *New York Times* reporter covering the war in Vietnam at its oldest, I saw huge numbers of American men as few women do: in unimaginable misery and peril. Trained to kill, and facing the greatest disgrace if they faltered or refused, they were often only adolescents with no choices left. Ordered to move forward, when it could mean their own mutilation or death, they obeyed, knew no mercy, and gave none. If they wrote their mothers, the loving ones lied. Our lives would all be changed if you, too, knew the sorrow they have swallowed for so long and the mutinies that have filled their dreams.

This is not a book about them, but perhaps they are the reason I began it, for no other American men had ever spoken to me as they did. Knowing them, all camouflage between us put aside, taught me not only how to speak to other men but how to hear what once I might not have heard at all. It is not that all the men in this book have gone to war, but there are some in these pages, like the veterans whom I love, whose deepest hopes for themselves have also been lost.

Looking for men in this country is hardly difficult. They are not afraid to talk to a woman, as we are to talk to a strange man, but some were so shy or suspicious, while others saw their lives with the clarity of men staring in a deep sleet, that I let them be. The ones I interviewed, by chance or by design, I often met while traveling in this country or abroad, often on assignments for a magazine or to give a lecture. One conversation began in a grocery store in New Jersey when I asked a man I mistook for the manager where the dry mustard might be found. In Ohio, standing in a food pantry where free boxes of groceries were, and still are, handed out, I spoke to an unemployed man because his face, although young, told you precisely how much had been taken away. Deprived of work and wages, of all command of life, he had begun to wither as if invisible transfusions of blood and bone were being taken from him every minute. He came in that day with his wife for the groceries, with two children whose round and pleased faces made those of their parents seem even more forlorn. That year, when there was so much he needed and least of all my questions, the desperate man obliged himself to speak, a generous thing. The others in this book include a student in a class I once taught, a young friend's uncle in Queens whose health was then so frail he could not easily speak for more than an hour, a man I met in a diner who was in a bad mood, a correspondent from *The New York Times* who was assigned to Africa and was not grateful, and a doctor from California who helped save my life in a Bangkok hospital when I had begun to die.

Growing up in an era when both men and women were required to assume such deep disguises—they would be stoic and do their duty, we would make ourselves small and obedient —none of us knew better or how to seek release. Subversion was too lonely. If justice is the fulfillment of a person's truest self, many went without it.

Some things have changed for American men but not that much for all of them so they must only pretend. The most gentle boy knows what might be expected of him in case of attack, if war comes or if some particular chaos is coming closer. He is to stand up to it, not hide or flee. Always humming behind him is the American music played for men and meant to rouse them. Be All That You Can Be . . . The Marines are Looking . . . Once I believed, as who did not, that Americans always had a freer hand, could take life in larger, more rapid steps, although, as they used to say, it was a man's world, I had no way of understanding there might be penalties for them to pay. Even now what many women most dislike about men—their hardness; their lack of the generous, quick response; the distance they keep; their faces that so often seem shut; the things they find difficult to say; their tendency to tell women when a decision is required, "We'll see"—is often the result of the old stances they are certain they must assume. In a country whose insistence on delusion seems without clear limits, the old definition·of masculinity still persists. And it persists because of hidden permission and unspoken expectations.

Prologue

At a time when women, with good reason, are asking men to make known their most guarded feelings, when we want them to love and raise babies and remember our birthdays, it is also required that they be the ones to rescue people in a burning building. And startle the dragons when they are heard in the dark. There are new words for men who strike us as not up to any of it, men who may be too timid or uncertain or frail in some way. The words are jokey, to be sure, and may not last long, but they are a warning to men of the ridicule reserved for those considered epicene. It is exactly this that most men fear.

Certain that I would be startled by nothing that the men in this book said, I was once more wrong. What surprised me was that, so many years after the end of World War II in 1945, some of its former combatants still feel that war intruding in their lives. What also came as a surprise was the unmistakable, if slight, melancholy settling on men well into middle age, as if they could not help but see themselves dim and weaken. So many women I know who are as old or older seem more vigorous than ever.

And most of all I was astonished by the intricacy of their memories and by the vast, secret ledgers they keep on themselves while often passing as plain, practical, busy men not given to introspection, one eye on the world. Some men pull off a close escape from life and know why.

What is most deeply hidden from view is the great tenderness many men, more than I thought, feel for their own fathers. "It is his face I see each morning when I shave," a friend once said to me, missing the man who died when he was twelve. Stuffed as we are with our daily rations of psychoanalysis-publico, it is not a revelation how the harsh father damages the male child. What is not so apparent is how the father who loves his son and makes it known, even in the sorriest circumstances, lifts the child to a privileged order from which he can never be expelled.

DISORDERLY
CONDUCT

*O*n the streets over the week-
ends a greater number of fathers, as various as they have always
been, are carrying babies, pushing strollers, leading children on
walks, and giving them lunch in places that serve hamburgers and
pancakes. It is proof, of a pale kind, that more men are helping to
raise their children. The fathers seem suitably affectionate and
alert to possible danger and the children's misdemeanors: a reckless driver, a glass of water spilled on a cheeseburger. In the post
office, where the line is long, a child, perhaps two years old, wan-
ders among our legs and, by its rapture with the silly red chain that
keeps the line from sprawling, brings smiles. "What a nice girl,"
says the woman with three packages for Canada, bending down to
the child, who is holding the edge of her coat. "What a nice girl
you are." The father draws the child back and tells her it is a boy.
Parents are still apt to correct people who do not correctly guess
the sex of their children as if the child might hear the mistake and
be harmed. It is they who care and who want no confusion about
it from the start. Pink is not for boys.

Now there are some men, well into their thirties, who are more
anxious for their sons than they are for their daughters, a peculiar
reversal in paternal attitude, almost a breach of contract. Such a
man is thirty-six-year-old Steven Trimm, whose only child is a
daughter. Mr. Trimm works in a psychiatric hospital where, among
his other duties, he conducts poetry workshops for patients. He

believes the workshops are of immense benefit. On the telephone late at night, when certain sad men stop speaking as if they were on a military radio, he talks of this daughter, named Arielle, who at the age of three years and eleven months sang out a poem for him which her mother wrote down. "Some Thing I Like" was the title. Some of the melancholy shakes from his voice as dust lifts from a flapping blanket when he speaks of Arielle. His own life was an old case history by then: at eighteen, wanted in a war, he refused. His defiance and open opposition to this war meant going to prison as a draft evader or fleeing the country. He fled, living in Canada for five and a half years. In the early days, an older man advised him to go in the army, what the hell: "Think of all the benefits you'll have after as a veteran." His years of exile and principle had been expensive; some men who knew his history found it very disturbing, while a few were admiring.

Mr. Trimm said he was sure that he would be a different father if a son had been born to him. "I would have to attend to the fact that he would be under greater pressure to conform to certain very strong stereotypes," he said. "He would need more protection."

And there are others who say the same, for one reason or another, but are not certain how to follow their hope of sheltering a son from the larger world, of teaching him what to resist, and why, and how to bear the consequences. The country conspires against them, the culture is deceiving. Children are expected to be successful; the successful boy will not refuse to fight because he is afraid or sees that a fight is senseless. It has always been accepted that boys whose fathers do not wish them to back away from the world will get into spots of trouble and even misbehave. The need for risk is in the blood, a man tells me. The disorderly conduct of a young male is often admired, expected, endorsed, or found normal. It is often considered far better, even when punishment is incurred, than the behavior of the male child who is too cautious, who tries too much to please, and who hopes not to be noticed. This is the child who is suspect and who inflicts the deepest blow on the father longing for the charged-up son.

Parents let a child know in a multitude of ways what they do not wish the child to become, sometimes in code, and sometimes by drumming lightly to a humorous theme. "My mother was always afraid I'd grow up to wear a big, heavy coat and little, round glasses and read a lot," said a young man in New York who was raised in the South. His father, once an athlete, was a tennis instructor who did not much fancy this grown son. The father's silence was more punitive than the mother's whimsical warnings. The mother often said that as a little girl she had known another child whom she detested, and the precise portrait—coat, specs, books—was of this very boy. Returning home for a visit one winter in his heavy New York coat, wearing his small and round glasses, in the suitcase new novels which he planned to read, it was hardly a surprise to the son when his mother said, "Oh, it's all coming true." She feared, perhaps, what she had always really dreaded: the son becoming a northern intellectual, a fugitive, moving farther away from her. She relented in time and found his little glasses not so awful after all. It was the tennis-father who by saying nothing at all, as usual, made the son know how regrettable it all was and how puzzling to him.

Not strange at all are men raising young children by themselves, as women have done for so long, men who do not doubt their resources as parents but are worried by a world that could sabotage all they wish for their young and even deform their children, once grown, in irreversible ways. Such a man, a history instructor at a university whose wife died when their baby was slightly more than a year old, names his eight-year-old daughter in a letter and makes clear what distresses him: "It is that Christina may not be able to find a man who will have been raised to love her in some new, less obsessive, less subordinating way than has been customary among us."

It is common enough for fathers, alone or not, to be anxious about whom their small daughters will someday choose to love, but men raising sons rarely speak of such distant alliances and never say they hope that somewhere a girl is being suitably raised whom their son might someday care for.

When younger, the daughter of the history teacher often moaned about little boys her age, those horrors, always making such a racket and pushing each other down. The father could do nothing to make her see why they carried on like this or how it might be so different.

He would wish it noted that children's toys considered the most successful in sales showed how The Enlightenment had not come: violent "action" toys for boys and lovable dolls for girls. And *The Wall Street Journal* noted that the GI Joe "action" toy line, among the top sellers in toys and games, included a cast of heavily armed soldiers "each with a distinct violent personality sketched on the back of its package." None of the major toy companies still bother to make guns. Guns are too simple. The manufacturers of the GI Joe line have an aircraft carrier, seven and a half feet long, for one hundred dollars. The toy accommodates one hundred GI Joes at three dollars apiece. Only poor children are given guns; the more privileged may have arsenals and armies and airstrikes.

In the last class in June, thirty-nine-year-old Michael Hamburg, an unusually attentive and passionate teacher of adolescents considered to be problems in one way or another, asked the students in his course called the Writing Lab to say how much money they thought they were worth. It made them a little giddy, for they did not see where he was leading them. One by one the students sang out something; they were not a group that lacked spirit or opinions about themselves. His intention that day, as on many others, was to make them see their own value and see how, without self-respect, they might put themselves in peril. At first there seemed little difference between the boys and the girls, exhilarated as they all were by the naming of vast sums, but later, when they were assigned to write letters, then they divided. But the first topic was money. Susanna, who distrusts words, said her worth was "nothing." She did not mean she was without value, only that it transcended any known sum; another girl, too, thought her worth was "infinite." Norma came out with twenty million dollars. Thomas, who does not rush, settled for a million. Nicole only said "a lot, a lot," and someone else rolled out one hundred trillion for himself.

James asked Mr. Hamburg if he meant what they were worth right *now*, twelve adolescents in a small yellow room, windows opening on an old, not unpleasant city wall, all of them at seven small tables making a lopsided circle. Only four in the room were males. They were studying at the Satellite Academy, a small alternative high school—one floor in an old-fashioned office building in the heart of Wall Street—for those whose work or aptitudes or attendance made them no longer suitable for the city's traditional high schools. The students called all their teachers by their first names. Michael Hamburg, who once wrote a thesis for a master's degree on the religious transformation of Aldous Huxley, wore blue jeans. The class dressed as the young everywhere dressed on a day of greasy city heat; poverty could no longer be assumed from what was worn. Some of the young women had tropical colors on their eyelids and were clearly careful of their long nails painted silver or red or green. One girl had pictures of her baby.

Mr. Hamburg, who has been teaching the young not viewed as promising for sixteen years, himself a student for twelve years of the Japanese martial art called Aikido, "the way of joining spirits," then began to gather in the class, who had been greatly excited. They went back to reading aloud the novel by Richard Wright called *Native Son,* now to those pages describing how the black elevator man named Shorty would make money by taunting and begging white men to boot him in the rump. The class then considered why Shorty did that. Thomas was unhappy about it. "A poor person will do that," a girl said, quietly. Another girl wanted to know why this Shorty called himself a "nigger." A boy said, Okay, he would kick the shit out of Shorty because Shorty was degrading himself and deserved it. For a little while Mr. Hamburg spoke about self-respect and pride, about masochism and self-hatred, and explained how racism could deform people. Then he asked all of them if they would consent for a very large sum of money to commit one act required of them in return, not knowing in advance what it might be. "I wouldn't sell me for anything," said Susanna, who got the point. The prettiest girl in the class, Mercedes, who was so proud of her baby, thought the idea farcical and laughed. She said she would do any foolishness, perhaps walk down Fifth Avenue without clothes, for a lot of money. Well, *one thing* and that's it, said Mercedes. Nicole said no. "What if it is something good to be done?" a boy asked, but they all knew better and assumed it would be heinous. Mr. Hamburg asked where a person should draw the line between something that adds to their dignity or an act or attitude that takes away from it. Such a genuine and interesting inquiry made the class silent, heads seemed to lower, a sigh came from someone.

You may think it a simple lesson to bestow on such young Americans, that perhaps teaching self-respect to this group might be no more complicated than instructing children how to pray and then, because their eyes are shut, their hands pointed up, assuming success. Mr. Hamburg was poor in the very illusions that made sense of the country for so many others, including the belief that the impoverished need not sit in the slime if only they worked harder, were neater with their garbage, had fewer babies, and did not act depressed. He did not choose to speculate on the future of those he taught. Nothing convinced him that Americans loved their own children or cared much about education for other people's. He thought his was not just the vague judgment of the liberal: a deterioration in ethical behavior in business and on Wall Street, in the corporations, the economy, and even the public at large was the subject that year of an article of more than four thousand words in a respected newspaper.

Then he gave them twelve minutes to write a letter about unfinished business, as Mr. Hamburg put it. "We did that already last week," said a boy. But they had not. This letter could be to someone who had died or disappeared, who had moved away or who was around every day, Mr. Hamburg said. They were to write what had never been spoken but was in their hearts and needed to be revealed. Gabriella wrote a letter to a cousin who had been a mother to her: "No matter what, I never got a chance to tell you how much I loved you." Jesús wrote a poem to a girl he had not yet met but intended to fascinate.

Some girls kept writing of a different lost love. Two of them wrote to their fathers who were gone for good now, letters of longing for an outcome that was not to be. Demetria read her letter aloud, with difficulty: "As a matter of fact it's been almost eight years since last we saw each other. I was nine years old when it all happened. I miss you a lot, although we never got to know each other like I wanted to. I still miss you. Although I remember you always used to beat me because you didn't want me to go outside and have friends, and that really hurt me a lot. I also remember the times you made my mother suffer by coming in at 2:00 or 3:00 in the morning and being with your friends, hanging out with women when you should have been home like a real man should. I always hated you for that and for always beating on me. You never used to lay a hand on Rosita. . . . Since you've died I know I've done a lot of good things and bad things. But I really wish that we would have got to know each other. . . . I was always so afraid of you. I figure maybe if you were alive you probably would never have changed. Now my mother is happy and I'm glad. Sometimes I wonder if you're in heaven or hell. Love always, your daughter."

The class heard. But none of it was new to them, none of it was new to Mr. Hamburg, though he looked distressed when Demetria started crying as her letter came to its end. "Do you want to go outside and wipe your eyes?" he asked in the odd way men have of hoping to console women. She chose to stay put.

Another letter to a dead man from his daughter was read: "I always felt funny talking to you. It wasn't that I didn't love you, 'cause God only knows how much I do. Even though I know you felt I didn't 'cause I hardly talked to you. And I know Anne Marie was your pet in a way 'cause she always talked to you and showed you affection. But I also know you cared a lot about me by the way you kept me strict. I used to hate it but now that I'm old enough to know better I feel I turned out to be a good, respectable person. And I thank you for that. Maybe I didn't show you enough attention, but I was afraid to. And the only time we talked was when it was about wrestling, boxing, racing, and other sports. We never had a father to daughter talk. . . . I love you and I miss you."

To a visitor once deeply moved by the letters, and their power, Mr. Hamburg only said that the fact that the students had problems with literacy did not mean they were illiterate.

The letters read aloud by the boys were fierce, belligerent, and often aimed at their best friends. They were without generosity. One began: "To my friend Al you are a jerk." The writer complained that Al always wanted him to pay for things and that Al wouldn't work as he did, Al thought he was above work. Another letter, rich in fury, began "Dear Rick," its denunciations swelling like chords played on an organ. "I hate it when you bullshit all the time. When you tell me stories about how you are workin' when I know you're not. I hate it when you lie about girls. It sounds like all the girls in the world love you when I know they don't. Like one time I know these girls and you were telling me this bullshit story about them. That all the things they were doing to you, that they were in love with you. When I know them better than you did. They tolled me everything. Because they were my friends and they tell me everything. I tell them everything. So that's why I call you Capten Bullshit because you lie to me you lie to your parents and mine, also you lie to all of our friends and girlfriends."

The first boy was asked by Mr. Hamburg if he would send the letter.

"I don't want to mess up the friendship," he answered.

When asked if he would send his letter to Rick, the second boy declined too. It wouldn't do any good, he said. "He would feel a little bit depressed, but I don't think it would soak into his head," he added.

Neither expected their friends to change and by sending these letters too much could be undone. The boys understood that if they humiliated these friends they might well be humiliated in return, and that was too great a risk. It was to be avoided, although neither young man was exactly clear on what was being so carefully avoided.

It was a masculine response: they wished to avoid a confrontation, as if their own anger was dangerous to them and might threaten the self-control they wanted to maintain which they believed made them different from women, who were permitted to be emotive without disgrace. And women were not inclined to use their fists, only hitting children sometimes, but not to knock them out.

In that June they had begun to understand that for the rest of their lives it would suit them best to be evasive and remote. They already understood the danger of being too open with Al and Ricky, that the huge nervous expenditure of telling the truth held in those letters might provoke the most dreadful retaliation. Al and Ricky might well say the world saw them as vile creeps or tell them what girls were really saying about them or worse, if anything could be worse. They did not want that kind of trouble, already having learned it was safer not to expose themselves. This made them frailer than the girls wanting to be held in the ghostly arms of their fathers, who had other fears no less grave but different.

What they feared was what grown men almost always wished to avoid as well: a confrontation in which they would have to come clean, hear themselves shout or get nasty, listen to what came back, do battle with words they could not trust as weapons, and probably be defeated. At their age they already knew this almost never worked, and there was this too: what if tears came? In the classroom Mr. Hamburg would be calm and kind but the girls would be watching. Pity was what they could not tolerate; they did not want to feel or receive it.

It has been put forth that the reason that women are less secretive about their emotions, and more attentive to feelings, is because centuries of restrictions placed on their lives left them not much else to talk about. Some women say, rubbish, such reasoning is delusive and speaks of the cultural conditioning of children. But there is this: a woman is not ridiculed or seen as a disgrace because she articulates what she feels, when she complains of being tired and then more tired, real or imaginary ailments, all injustices, when she behaves impulsively or makes known that her truest dream was once to be the littlest Rockette at Radio City Music Hall. If her life is meager or balked, someone will listen but never deliver the admonishment: "Be a woman. Bear it." If she sings her hard songs, loves and is not loved back, is cheated and ignored, she is not reviled for slipping beneath a standard of behavior that all women are required to observe. It is not unusual for women to speak of wanting and needing happiness; that word may be used by us.

Men, who also want and need the same, are more careful with their laments and see visible emotion as a form of surrender. They conceal and muddle and evade, turn sly or joke or provide answers that are only twigs pointing nowhere. Or they retreat. They do not wish to appear helpless or silly or as if they were men tossed about, even when their lives are hateful. And often they can be strangely fragile and cautious when a leap is called for, the cold stare and the hard question for once not excessive.

Men who are older are not different, even those who have seen the most sickening things.

Some time ago, in the kitchen of a small house in upstate New York, four men sat at a kitchen table hardly big enough for such bulk, speaking on a matter of immense gravity. There were wives on their feet, for coffee was being served, and cake, while a child reeled and thumped from room to room, dismissing forever the idea of bed. The men had once fought in Vietnam, but the war was not exactly the subject that night; there was nothing left to say about it by then, the tomb sealed above us, the air old and rank.

And I sat with them at the table because long ago I had chosen to be pulled inside their war—knew the terrain, who had died, what else was gone forever—and was therefore not like their wives. For the time being the men treated me almost as one of them.

A betrayal had taken place, it needed examining. How

strangely animated we were in that kitchen, talking about the culprit, the man without honor—a terrible man, one to be pitied, another victim; the shock of it; the covenant among the veterans, weakening now, which he sabotaged; his lies of the greatest importance, or none at all. Only one man in the kitchen showed impatience with the condemnation, thought the lying only a small mess, not a sin, not an outrage.

All of us knew the man, who had been lying with some success for a number of years and could still be at it for that matter. Describing his capture by enemy troops and the abuse inflicted on him as he lay naked and bound, curled like a child, the details he used to give so slowly were ghastly and precise. None of it had happened, ever. But he had claimed to have been taken prisoner in an interview that was published, then had been exposed when the records were checked, had confessed more calmly than one might expect, and became a brief embarrassment to the veterans' organization to which he and the men in the kitchen belonged. Men who had seen the fighting despised him for this theatrical little fiction; others saw him only as more damaged goods, impaired not evil.

The former marine, in whose house we gathered, knew fury because, he said, the Vietnamese had been lied to so often it was unforgivable that one of their own, who was trusted, would turn out such a story. The culprit had been summoned at a state meeting of the veterans' organization, been called to account, remained composed, spoke briefly in his own defense, admitted the wrongdoing, and apologized. The others fell silent, unwilling to reproach him; only one or two spoke out on the harm that had been done.

The man whose wife was making us coffee had been at the meeting and was enraged when the other veterans, after all their oratory, had nothing to say to the liar. They behaved like cowards, which was worse than being a liar, he told us. It was the time to stand up but they sank. At this meeting a vote was taken, in another room, and then the disgraced man was asked to resign. But to show his contempt for the veterans who did not speak out, he voted, the only one, to let the untruthful veteran keep his membership, our host said.

"After the vote I went up to him and shook hands and said to him, 'Look, it was nothing personal,' " he explained. "The guys at the meeting couldn't do it to his face, but they were willing to sit in judgment behind his back when they voted. So I had more respect for him than I did for the men who betrayed themselves. When we shook hands after the meeting we stared into each other's eyes for about thirty seconds. I saw those eyes and knew then he was crazy. That's all. Maybe something terrible did happen to him in Vietnam and all he could do was invent the equivalent of it."

The wives then seemed to go away, the child found sleep somewhere. Surely what had happened at the meeting was that the men present had not wanted to play colonels at a court-martial, to pass sentence and risk seeing the prisoner pale and twitch. All knew what it was like to be at the bottom. It was dreadful business, that meeting, which no man there could relish. Embarrased, or made so uneasy by the sudden sympathy they must have suddenly felt, perhaps remembering some disgrace each man had himself once known and the bogus stories of war others had told without being caught, they lost their nerve and were glad of it.

But the man telling us all about the meeting—in whose kitchen we sat, warming the room with our scorn and voices— could not admit that even he wanted, at the end of it, to be kind. Nothing personal, he said, putting his hand out.

The denunciation that kept up came from me, in installments, because I too had been fooled by the lies. Once I had listened to all of his stories for a few hours, I felt saddened and respectful toward the man who had survived so much and felt such torment. Not once was it clear he was putting on a performance, watching me to see my degree of belief, as an actor might work a difficult audience. The men in the kitchen were not as angry or shocked as I was. For them there were worse things, deeper betrayals, more vile plots. Nothing personal, my friend said to the expelled man at their meeting, when that is exactly what it was.

When the Writing Lab came to an end, no one plunged for the door, they ebbed out. It was curious how the Satellite Academy appeared to be such a peaceful place, as if the students, unwelcome in so many schools, enjoyed a secret safety here and no longer needed to submit to mysterious judgments, to tests whose validity they did not understand any more than the questions.

At graduation the valedictorian, a girl who had known a fierce struggle to win a diploma, spoke movingly and was heard to say "youse." No one was upset.

Not given to psychiatric evaluation of his students, since this was useless to him, Michael Hamburg nonetheless understood that to many of them he was something new. They had not ever known an adult man like him, a grown man not taking orders all the time or waiting to be told what to do or be. And nothing the strangest or most forsaken child could say would shock him. He was not only calm but even happy as their teacher, pleased to be in that room with them, always remembering their names and much else. He was not in the least afraid of any of them, as others had been. They did not displease him.

"The males in their lives are inadequate in many ways," he said. "They are not there. They are not supportive. They are abusive. Not to be depended on. In my role they can depend on me. You have to be like a counselor and help them open and stay open."

He knew when there were pupils who did not want to leave him or the school. "I can't live with you all," he would say. "You have to take a piece of this with you."

His own adolescence, so different from theirs although not without strains at home, had been made darker by his failure to understand high school geometry. He could not make sense of the theorems and the equations. Even now, that defeat so old and shriveled, he says of his ordeal that it was scary. It was taken for granted then, as it is now, that such bright boys would always do well in math. None of his friends suffered from this peculiar allergy to geometry. What raised him up was a talent for languages: he came to excel in Latin, French and German, Russian and Spanish. Music and science fiction were as important as meals, more so. He went in many directions for some years.

Sometimes, as with the boy Phillip, he needed to teach students how to focus. Phillip, who was unusually large, could not sit still or concentrate, claiming he was hyperactive, pleased to have that bit of jargon at his command. Mr. Hamburg thought Phillip unusually immature and scattered, tendencies aggravated perhaps by his mother. There was no father. Phillip taxed adults with his constant twirling, but Mr. Hamburg, who sometimes even put his arm around the boy and other times would speak to him firmly, achieved some success. At graduation, attended by his mother, grandmother, and girlfriend, Phillip exulted and said he would never forget the word *focus*. It was a standing joke between them. Mr. Hamburg hoped that Phillip might qualify for a job as a sanitation worker.

Not all the students, of course, lacked fathers. Thomas who lived with both parents, had a summer job working in the liquor store where his father was employed. In the classroom he seemed too dreamy and kept halting. Thomas's problem might be organic, Mr. Hamburg could not be certain. "I am not a psychologist and I am not a diagnostician," he said. "But I think a person's relationship with the mother often reflects our self-image, and the relationship with the father sets a lot of the tone for how we relate to the world."

It was thought that about 8.4 million women lived with a child under twenty-one without a father in the house. Often this was by choice. Middle-class women with careers sometimes refused to marry or live with the man who fathered their child because they did not want to be attached, beholden, dependent, or obliged to love him. Men were now considered a burden to some of these women, almost a luxury they could not afford on a permanent basis. Men were no longer solutions to life.

In the new epoch, the white male worker, the very symbol of American labor, now no longer made up a majority of the work force. He was outnumbered and, furthermore, in some danger if his job was in heavy manufacturing. The eclipse had long since begun: The United Steelworkers of America in a letter said unemployment figures for their members had risen to 35.9 percent by February 1983. There were 327,200 steelworkers in 1981 and by September 1983 only 207,500. It was predicted by the Bureau of Labor Statistics that women would account for 64.5 percent of all new workers in the coming years. A professor of sociology said economic changes and the growth of service industries meant the emergence of a need for workers different from the blue-collar male. Once the American archetype had been the farmhand, then the factory worker, now the clerk. The clerk has no gender. Women needed day care centers for children and parity with men and often had neither.

The women's revolution has only begun, a man said in *The*

New York Times. The gap in longevity between men and women was widening; women were expected to live until seventy-eight and men until seventy, but the chance of a woman being destitute in old age went up to sixty percent.

Feelings were a major industry. Psychologists came to be its bankers, their speech slow, cautioning what withdrawals and what deposits were of benefit, their opinions ceaselessly quoted, although psychiatrists too were now less shy about making comments for public consumption, as if this might show their congeniality and importance at the same time. It was they who were believed to be in command. Much was said about stress and coping, and then more, as if the subject were inexhaustible. Stress management, as it is known, became dear to the hearts of all those whose most punishing worries did not often include how to get food and how to keep alive. A psychologist at Indiana University put forth the theory that men may suffer more biological punishment than women from "prolonged negative" feelings and that this could explain the findings of a marital research project that, in stressful times, women tended to keep confronting their husbands to get at the root of a problem. The men, instead of responding as the women wanted, became conciliatory or, if that failed, even withdrew. Ordinary women, with an understanding of their own about male psychology, will tell you that it seems as if men don't like to be upset or angry because they do not believe the problem will be resolved this way and do not like scenes which could provoke them into impulsive behavior which later they might regret because it would weaken them. And they often did not have the words to make their case. "When Ida and I had our last fight I broke the plug on the toaster oven," said a man in Chicago. "I lost my self-command."

No subject was quite as alluring as the perilous condition called stress, and stress-related symptoms; it was favored over depression, which men do not like to admit, and over dieting. It was largely an affliction claimed by the powerful and the driven. Aside from contributing to six leading causes of death in the United States, stress, *Time* magazine pointed out, could aggravate such diseases as multiple sclerosis and even trench mouth. The article made no mention of the subhuman condition of exhausted soldiers on the Western Front, who suffered this trench mouth because of *Fusobacterium fusiforme* and the spirochete *Borrelia vincentii*, which caused ulcers in the mucous membrane of the throat and mouth of those who were unable to brush their teeth or eat decently and who did not expect to live for more than a few weeks, if that.

For all that has changed, it is still a matter of life or death for some American men to lead impatient lives of immense exertion and then even more a matter of life and death to slow down and do less and behave with a sweetness they know nothing about. Their behavior is widely known as Type A, its most prominent characteristics being a feeling of urgency, easily aroused hostility, and constant competitiveness, those very characteristics the country most favors, admires, extols, expects, and rewards in a country where the whip you hear is the whip you hold. Type A's have the tendency always to play to win, even in a game with children. They distrust other people's motives, hurry or interrupt the speech of others, have trouble sitting and doing nothing, often try to do two things at once, and talk with their hands or pound their fists for emphasis. Type A's are susceptible to heart disease, their behavior considered a risk factor, and always of considerable interest to cardiologists. In a federally financed study of men who had already suffered heart attacks, one group was given counseling on behavioral changes in up to forty-four sessions. They were to learn new habits and responses. In daily drills, instructions seemed simple enough: "Do something nice and unpredictable for your spouse" and "Admit to being wrong even if you are not" and "Play a game and plan to lose." They were to smile more, even at strangers.

Such advice is not easily understood even by men who are not Type A's. "Women hate it when you smile at them in the street, and who wants to smile at men?" asked a man in Rochester. He did not want to lose in his weekly volleyball game, he did not want to say he was wrong.

Avoid other angry A Types.

Listen to someone talk without thinking about something else and don't say anything until they are done.

Men all over were expected to change unless they were elderly or ill; some did, others tried, there were those who could not. It was put to them, usually by women they knew, to release their feelings from such deep clamps, to see that the vague congeniality affected so often was as useful as a concrete overcoat. With good reason, many women let men know they were stifled, repressed, without imagination or a sense of fun, unfeeling, self-centered, prone to egoistic domination, tone-deaf to the notes in other voices but the accusations often hid the charge that they were only distant and inattentive. You did not really know what they were thinking. They are always in disguise, themselves in secret.

The ground has been gone over and over: the terrain is rutted, torn, discolored. Here has been dumped the cold and lamed father who did not show his daughter she was prized; over there the husband who did not speak; the teacher who did not urge the little girl to study medicine; then the selfish brother; and the man who could not hold up when the children were young, he working nights, his wife days. Somewhere is the male parent with a work-horse of a wife who could not be trusted to see what is only a small and decent duty: one day every week buy a chicken, cook it for dinner, and then clean up. Their sin was they knew no shame. To a generation of women it was as if all these stunted and ungenerous men came from a different country, so that, needing only swagger and superior upper-body strengths, they had only to go forth to have their way in the world, as easy as kicking tin cans on a country road.

Every twelve-year-old boy knows what must be done to make it as a man, what it will cost him to be an American: the lessons seep through the skin forever. Money must be made, nothing is as masculine as this. Men whose wives make more money than they do praise the women while making sure it is known that the work they themselves are doing is exceptional, requiring a gift or a loyalty to an ideal or iron will. What cannot be permitted is more intricate: timidity, squeamishness, kindness toward too many people, a habit of pleading or the look of pleading, an excessive concern for mercy and justice except when confined in church, a tendency to dither, and the habit of asking for help, even if it is only for a few directions when driving. A pretense must be maintained that the man working for another or an unseen group is not submissive but rather obeying orders from a high command. Language is a camouflage not intended to reveal or clarify; many men are suspicious of it. A drunken man does not disgrace himself. Humor is acceptable at all times; the witty man will never be found out.

"I'm sleeping with the light on, I don't know about you," says the veteran in Saratoga Springs. We have both watched a documentary on war, wondering if among the dead faces our own will be there. I have called him to talk, an old friend who is often expansive on the telephone, unlike so many men who cannot yet converse, who use it only for communiqués. He makes the joke but we both know how that night will work on him. There are secrets everywhere: a dentist in Hershey, Pennsylvania, says that on some days of the week he wishes he might just stay home and be quiet. He envies his wife but she is not to know this.

"It's getting harder to find your way around," writes a man in Georgia, the letter five years overdue, as if it was beyond him to describe the obscurity all around. "When I need to be alone I have to go in the shower," says a woman with three children in California, making it clear how daily life was going.

Sometimes, despite the wide disorder, a story of sturdy perfection, of happy compromise, of civility, passed before our eyes. "I couldn't resist writing to you about my husband. We have a five-year-old daughter named Shannan. I work full-time as a parole and probation officer and my husband, Jim, works full-time as a fire-fighter. However, he works twenty-four hours and then has forty-eight hours off. During his two days off, my husband is Shannan's sole caregiver. . . . On his days off my husband bathes and feeds Shannan, changes her diapers, makes up her bottles, takes walks and plays with her, and makes sure she has a nap. . . . And when she was born he even took a month off from work to help with the adjustment of having a new baby in the house. So I rate my husband an A+. My daughter and I know that he's a Superdad!" So wrote Parole and Probation Officer Shaun Leary Wahl of Fire-fighter Jim Wahl to a magazine for working mothers who asked its readers to rate their husbands' role in caring for the children.

So profound was the distaste for aggression in women that women with conspicuous careers in fields once forbidden were not to be called aggressive; a nicer word would do. It was *assertive*. The buccaneers in America—women among them, dressed in blue or black or beige suits of their own—still have a battle language all must speak: territory is to be seized, the line is to be held, dues must be paid, a campaign would be on the high road, we will hit the ground running. It is to be denied that profits put people in peril, cause the deaths of workers, or deform humans, because that would not be nice. Corporations wanted people to see that they were nice. So in a lawsuit against the Monsanto Chemical Company brought by seven men, former workers, who claimed their health had been affected by exposure to dioxin and other chemicals while the company knew of the great risks, a Monsanto attorney named Charles Love III said not so. The company was "made up of people," the attorney said. "It is not a cold, heartless thing." The attorney for the plaintiffs, claiming that Monsanto had figured the cost of injuries, said: "They calculated how much the sickness costs and found it costs them 4 cents per pound of finished product."

It was not shocking news by then, it was commonplace, old stuff.

In the summer families starting vacations waited for flights with their children. The fathers, picking up the babies, often lift the infants far above their heads with straight arms. Raised, the children at last see the world differently and are surprised by joy. The mothers do not take the child up so high, keeping the baby at the shoulder, the breast, the hip or in the lap. In the stroller the children see feet, roots of trees, pavements, litter, car wheels, perhaps a squirrel. Sometimes a father throws the baby in the air and catches the child, who is ecstatic.

On vacation the teacher Michael Hamburg, his own son almost three, was in the Berkshires, intending to finish the house he had built. With his old eight-inch telescope he saw the rings of Saturn, he saw double stars and galaxies. He saw exploding stars which were gases that glowed.

The twenty-year-old son of a New York editor hitchhiked from Santa Monica to Denver where he was to pick up a car and drive it east for a fee. His father's money was hidden in his sneaker. The father explained that he wants the son to know how to survive in life, as if hitchhiking might prepare him for life as a banker, a television producer, a historian, a proofreader, a plumber. "He really likes being on his own," the father says, and there is no reason to believe it is not true.

More haircuts were given to the small boys left alone until now so they would not be mistaken for girls when taken on a trip to see grandparents.

A twenty-six-year-old man, who became a registered nurse, recalls that on completing his studies his father asked, "But what will they call you?" Unbearable was the idea his son would answer to "Nurse!"

On television, a startling sight: the wracked and narrow faces of women engaged in struggle and who, if you could not see what they were doing, might appear to be in trouble and needing help. It was not the case. They were running the 26-mile, 385-yard distance in the Olympic marathon, the first women allowed to run in the history of the Games. The sight of women knowing such exhaustion, the terrible effort, was peculiar and unsettling to some people, but not to all. With men it was an old story, no one cringed or turned away at the sight of a man in pain.

No matter what the fine exertions of women—the old restrictions that hemmed and pinched their lives now torn out and reviled —it was still expected of men that they move out in the world and do something. Do something, anything, to an idea, an adversary, a business, an industry, the land, a machine, blank paper, to the world.

Stona James Fitch, class of '83 at Princeton University, thought this was fine by him; the men in his family did not sit still and wait for the world to tell them when to advance. Mr. Fitch was fired up. By his side some classmates often appeared docile and obedient when in fact they were only more studious and circumspect. Even after he graduated there were students who still knew his name and said of him yes, he was a legend. Women three years his junior still knew what a charmer he had been and which girl still smiled when hearing his name.

Not only did Stona Fitch revolt against the dullness of a student's life, but he was both witty and inventive in his disorders, carrying on in the highest tradition of the reckless, defiant, poetic American male. It was not the ideal era, of course, to be inattentive in class; by 1982 the university needed $11,648 a year for tuition plus room and board, a 14.7 percent increase over the previous year. The tuition kept rising. It made some students solemn, as if they were mindful every minute of the cost-benefit calculations of their parents.

At this time no one was rebelling; the intent was to please. Asked what was preoccupying him and his friends, one upperclassman answered: Jobs and hair. He meant finding the first and the fear of losing the second. Mr. Fitch and his followers had their minds on other things.

So there were days when by himself Stona Fitch provided a one-man mockery of the violent and foolish world waiting for all of them, as if he already knew how dangerous and absurd life could be and would warn the protected. He was often violent to things but never to other people, endearing himself to other young men whose mothers wanted names put in their tennis socks.

It was not just a matter of calling attention to himself, as male children will do by being defiant or mischievous, sometimes succeeding more than they bargained for. Stona Fitch did not wish to be squashed or captured by the conventions and expectations of nice people. He had a horror of it. What was at stake, he felt, was his right to experiment with his own self before his freedom might be gone and he'd be a man like all others, sinking slightly each year. He was amusing himself, too, in one tableau after another, an audience there or not there. Some young men at the university envied his bravura, his writing, the notoriety gained, and the number of women so clearly captivated. To be with him and to have his attention was to be at risk, of course, but it was exhilarating. If it is true that one reason young people fall in love is their need to confide their huge uncertainties—which is exactly what older people are no longer able or willing to do—he was a magnet for pretty girls, clever too, who wanted to bare their hearts, and see his own as well. He did not believe in them.

That he could be cutting was not important; almost everyone could lay claim to that, or be accused.

The university was long accustomed to trouble, to seizures of ferocious behavior by young male students. In the fall of 1930, for example, undergraduates after a football rally tore down a statue and rocked a public bus on Nassau Street which was carrying passengers. The Dean of the College, Christian Gauss, remembering *Gulliver's Travels,* called it "yahooism." Two ringleaders were punished. There had always been students who made a career of getting into trouble, but in the great, almost gloomy calm that now prevailed, Mr. Fitch did not know this or that he was really not so bad.

When *The Daily Princetonian* gave a party to attract more students to the staff, Mr. Fitch put on an army uniform, dark glasses, grimaced and raised a machete as he sat at his desk for the picture that ran with his copy in the student newspaper: "Go interesting places, meet fascinating people . . . and slander them. Become a tough, hard-bitten journalist, or a business mogul, but first come to our house for both the news and business staffs. . . . No lie, GI." Very few students wore Woolworth T-shirts with traces of crude oil spots on them from a summer job, or had his thick sideburns or such a manner of speaking. He had a twang and a slur, always talking rapidly, his sentences not honed in the neat way of the Easterners.

Sometimes it bothered him to be with so many young people so properly dressed, of such moderate metabolisms, careful children calling home once a week with a new report of how it went, some of them with names he would have once thought fictitious, with Roman numerals at the end. He said he minded what he considered to be their coldness, their caution—their comportment a puzzle to him—so it was obligatory to be as different from them as he could.

A number of people, not maliciously, asked him what he was doing at Princeton, as if the air there might be too thin for his lungs, the place too proper or confining, the campus too adorable. In the beginning he used to feel disgusted when students thought he was a Virginian, or some sort of Southerner, not knowing the difference, when he was from Cincinnati, his father's family from southern Oklahoma, and furthermore had what he called a clot of relatives happily rooted in Arkansas. "I'm from backward people," he said to one professor, grinning, not meaning it, making exactly the opposite point, but no Fitch had ever gone as far as Princeton. Presented to the New York mother of a young woman also at Princeton, he learned later that she thought of him as a nice Midwestern boy because he turned up in the city wearing jeans and boots and his lizard belt. He minded hearing that, but more disturbing was the young woman's revelation that her mother had been married four times and it was not certain who her real father might be. Stona Fitch, not easily shocked, found that hair-raising, and felt grateful for his own stock, which he considered a long line of strong, resourceful men, a memorable female here and there.

His great-aunt Mrs. Irma Giffels of Springdale, Arkansas, the family historian who always said she had enough material for a book and no time to write it, knew that John Fitch came from Scotland to Virginia at the beginning of the nineteenth century and that her own great-grandfather's mother was part Cherokee Indian and named Kate Hands. He had a photograph of Aunt Irma's own father, Catlett Franklin (Dick) Fitch, which he loved, although nothing much could be deduced: a handsome man, still young, who had waxed the ends of his mustache, put on a suit and vest, a watch chain too, and sat patiently, hands on his legs, unsmiling, until the record was at last made. It might be said that here was a man you would not willingly provoke. "The roots of the name Stona escape me," Aunt Irma wrote him. "Am sure it isn't a family name. Mother once told me that she got my name out of a story book about a Lady Irma, which she read while recuperating from bringing me into the world. I have no middle name. Am sure she hoped I would be a lady." Come and visit, she wrote. A great-grandfather had been named Stona, and the eldest sons thereafter usually were, others being christened Larkin and Virgil, Thad and Sterling.

"I've always felt those faces behind me," he said.

It did not matter at Princeton that he was on a National Merit Scholarship and nearly always pressed for cash; more than forty percent of the students were receiving some form of financial aid. Worried by the prospect of reduced federal aid to students, the president of the university, Dr. William G. Bowen, said at a graduation that there were signs that the university risked "reverting to a situation in which educational opportunity is more a function of family circumstances than of qualifications." Thirty percent of the students had attended public high schools. Mr. Fitch swore that a good many students had been selected solely because they were beautiful, which the admissions office would have sternly disputed.

The Central Intelligence Agency recruited on campus and ran ads in the *Princeton Alumni Weekly* for those interested in serving as Intelligence Officers. There was huge excitement when, for the first time in fifteen years, the Princeton Tigers defeated Yale in a game seen by 20,303 fans in Palmer Stadium. The win was nailed down with only nine seconds left to play. Several players psyched themselves for the game by shaving the letter *P* in a pattern on their chests, *The Princetonian* reported. "Their Finest Hour," read the headline.

At the end of his junior year, during an unexplained epidemic of haircuts, he had a good deal of his own blond hair taken off, even the sideburns, and suddenly appeared younger and smaller.

But still he did not look or act like anyone else and he never felt that this would be possible, or of any benefit.

He was always afraid of being bored and, worse, felt cheated that others did not feel this way.

"At this time, in this country, at my age, we are very much a blank generation," said Mr. Fitch. "It's very self-centered. People aren't as giving and aren't as willing, are not as reckless. There's a level of complacency in my generation that sort of sickens me, makes me kind of worry to see it happen. There are whole squadrons of people here—Lacoste shirts, corduroy jeans, names longer than they are—and an incredible coldness too. I could see it right away, the amount of writing and poetry that comes out of here is minimal. People need to feel some sort of wholeness—either pleasure or pain, either way—to put it right. You don't feel that here."

What made him so different was the rancher-style black tie with the silver head of a steer on it, the stories he told so rich with threats of danger and disgrace. Few other boys had so often seen their lives hang by a thread. One summer, while he was driving a truck whose brakes failed, death was defied once more, only the air-conditioned huge tubs of butter in back got jolted and messed up. If you wanted to know what the main street of Wetumka, Oklahoma, looked like, he had a color postcard of it which said Gateway Eastern Oklahoma Playground. He laughed a good deal and liked to huddle with other people in hallways or small spaces, entertaining himself and all of them. He had a black suit and seemed to own only very narrow neckties and none of the expensive sweaters others wore, which he scorned.

One January when the cold caused trouble he did not wear a muffler or a down jacket or gloves, as if shivering was an acceptable, interesting state. He always put on a gray and white herringbone overcoat, slightly too large in the shoulders, perhaps once the possession of a banker or businessman, which Mr. Fitch paid five dollars for in a used clothing store at home run by the Salvation Army. In a pocket he found a gold wedding ring, eighteen-karat, with the inscription "SRS to JVZ 10–25–69," which he would not have dreamed of throwing away. He wore it on his right hand, out of respect for the bond between two people he would never know. He was attached to things from the past, preferably his own, or reminders of what other Fitch men had done or seen, as if these could make him part of a world he had been denied but wanted to love. He was a collector, a pack rat, taking certain of his possessions wherever he went. In his office at *The Daily Princetonian*, where he held highest rank, the life and longings and bravura of Mr. Fitch gave the elegant little room a suggestion of dementia. He was chosen chairman in the shortest election held in the newspaper's ninety-four years; his elation was so extreme he behaved for a little while like the writer Hunter Thompson, his literary hero, whose excessive eccentricities and paranoia were so much an inspiration. Stona Fitch made a statement, he had his picture taken.

"I have sold all my worldly possessions," Mr. Fitch said. "I will live in a small cubicle, drinking only fresh fruit juice and eating raw fish. In this way, I will purify my body for the work at hand." During his triumph, he found time to visit one of the runners-up in the election who needed bucking up. He went, as he so often would do, to persuade the loser very little was lost. His tendencies were always kind and sometimes he seemed patient, even protective, of other students who were shy or uncertain or confused. Someone was always distraught or wretched. His intention all along was to make *The Prince*, as the students called it, a better paper, less childlike and collegiate.

Looking back at old issues with the headlines "Vietnam Situation Prompts Dispute on Current Policy, Student Power Struggle Reaches Nassau Hall;" "Anti-War Strike Begins: Majority Cut Classes; Campus Social Facilities Curtail Houseparties," he felt wonder and a slight sadness that he would never see or feel such passions and anger.

There was a fire-bombing of the Princeton Army ROTC offices, an editorial called for a campus recess so the students could campaign against the incumbent President to stop "the nation's war sickness." It was very cold, this news, in the year he devoured it.

He began running stories critical of United States aid to El Salvador, of Washington's support of the regime, and wrote a story himself on the delegation of four combat veterans who made a return to Vietnam to face the old enemy, to become friends, to call for recognition of that government and American reconstruction of the damaged country. And to finish off the war at last by facing the children they had been when sent to such a place to do the killing.

He knew how to talk to them; he never wandered or wavered as a reporter.

The Vietnam men had been as young as Stona Fitch or his friends when they were sent off, ready for none of it, and he was shocked by that. His own father had been in Korea and seen the wounded close up, over and over. He said very little to his son, keeping the silence that most men prefer, any description of what they once saw, sometimes still can see, far beyond their power— wounds and the different shades fresh blood can be, the noises made by men that great pain invents, the questions asked by the casualties on stretchers who did not want an answer as much as the happy lie.

In all his years at school he learned nothing about the war of his father or the history of Korea.

It was not his intention for a minute to lead the comfortable, contemplative life. In his sophomore year, writing a paper on Nathaniel Hawthorne and the importance of "The Customs House," used as an introduction to the novel *The Scarlet Letter*, he typed most of it on his knees, working on a small, low coffee table in the living room of the suite he shared with two Virginians of old families, both his good friends. He worked like a man under siege who could not possibly straighten up, his bones locked, as if this was the honorable way to do justice to Hawthorne, whom he now admired. On Friday from midnight until 2 A.M. he did a sixties rock show on the students' radio station, not talking very much, and was considered by his peers to be a video game wizard. His marks were decent; they had to be, for two failing grades in a semester meant dismissal. He usually seemed short on sleep, food, time, even oxygen, somewhat pleased by the occasional stagger of exhaustion.

"I could go through Princeton, just take the usual English courses, not do much of anything, get to bed at nine o'clock, get up, have breakfast," said Mr. Fitch. "I make my schedule incredibly hectic because I like it that way. I very much feel that I should challenge myself, and I do." He always had his father and grandfather in mind. The older man, roly-poly, tough, a chatterbox, had gone from Arkansas to Oklahoma at nineteen with no assets, and started a small cattle ranch. It was to Wetumka that Mr. Fitch had been sent each summer until he was thirteen. His father had played football at Wetumka Senior High School and, at only seventeen, the son thought, had been the valedictorian of his class; just behind him were a younger brother and sister, both terribly bright too, who also became valedictorians. No Wetumka boy had done better than Stona Fitch's father, who was manager of manufacturing for a multinational corporation, one of the few men in the Midwest to reach that level without an engineering degree, a man who had risen up the chain of command, loyal and uncomplaining.

He wanted to live up to them, to be at least as good as they were, to have his own engine work like theirs. It was the only acceptable way of showing love, to pay his respects without having to tell them so. Such things were not openly said by the men in the family.

"My grandfather talks all the time," Mr. Fitch said. "He runs a stream-of-consciousness monologue. He will go to turn off the water and suddenly bring up the strangest things. There will be paragraphs coming out, it's almost like something out of Faulkner, he will just babble. He'll bring in a whole dictionary of Oklahoma expressions, quirky little words. For *cheap* or *stingy* he will say tighter than skin on a grape, than bark on a tree. He races at high speed in a sing-song voice. He and my grandmother are well liked and respected. They didn't have much education but they are smart in lots of ways. They are not the kind of poor whites that you see in Oklahoma a lot, in all those small pathetic places. They know better." After the summers in Wetumka, he was sent at thirteen to a wilderness camp in the woods of Minnesota. Later he became a paid canoe guide for a company called Canadian Waters during high school summers and lived in a trailer by himself.

The day of the monstrous storm he was by himself in the woods, sleeping in a pup tent, having paddled there across a small soft lake named Hegman. Shortly after the wind began its rampage the jagged chunks of hail astonished him and so did the sight of the furious little lake. When the top of the old red pine was sliced by lightning—making the sound of a rifle—he thought he was hit, too; the lightning sent a deep buzzing through him, a ghastly and new noise. He lay pinned under the top of the tree and was certain that someone was pushing on him. Trees were on fire across the lake. He fainted and not until after he revived understood how much his head hurt or how his eyes would no longer obey. No one was coming to help. It was all more difficult than anything he had known: wriggling out from beneath the pine, holding the car keys, getting his canoe back to earth, paddling across the lake, then carrying the canoe to his car and tying it on top and driving himself, slowly, some thirty-odd miles to Ely and a hospital. He was kept in bed for two days. None of this could be woven into one of his funny stories, the facts were too severe, too unalterable. But never did he lack material. On the wall of his office at the newspaper he put up the gaping, thin skull of a moose whose antlers were pale and brittle. It was one of his treasures. He put a green tennis ball in the hole that had been the mouth.

"It died a horrible death, that animal, it died of boredom," said Mr. Fitch, who sometimes would drop a cigarette butt in one of the Tiffany silver bowls on the mantle, prizes awarded long ago to the newspaper, beautifully engraved. A smoker, indifferent to his diet, an eater of red meat when some Princeton students thought of nicotine and beef as a small step up from cannibalism, he despised the obsession with health; joggers made him weary. On his desk was a cased machete, something he used as a brush axe in the woods. A friend loaned him a five-foot-long aluminum blowgun from the House of Weapons in Provo, Utah, which, despite some protests from others, Mr. Fitch put in use, aiming the quiver darts at a lampshade or the door. He was good at it. The moose, the machete, the blowgun were simply romantic exhibits, to remind you that he was not a child of pale Southampton beaches, of the Eastern shore, that his places were different, and of greater importance because they were coarser and more challenging. He asked someone to use the blowgun on him so he could report in his newspaper column, "Home on the Range," how it felt. A dart was fired from ten paces, lodging a good quarter of an inch into his back, Mr. Fitch wrote, causing a very unpleasant sensation, "something akin to being stabbed." He did not play with the blowgun after protests grew heated; a woman, with some reason, feared it might maim her if she walked into his office at the wrong time. He had grown tired of it anyway.

He beat up things with some regularity, on one occasion throwing all the light bulbs out the window from the second-floor poolroom of the Campus Club, one of the thirteen eating clubs for juniors and seniors, five of them selective—their members elected in a process called "bicker"—and the others with members chosen by lottery. (It was said that Cap and Gown, the most prestigious club admitting both sexes—as three clubs did not—elected him to be a member, but after getting in he wanted out, the whole thing a lark.) At Campus he was seen using the cues to whack the walls of the poolroom and, in the basement, shaking and kicking Force II, the pinball machine, which came to a premature death since others also assaulted it. The video games, made of stronger stuff, were unmolested. In his freshman year, the story now goes, Stona Fitch made a small, crude rocket, filled it with firecrackers, put a local mouse in the capsule and had a private launching. This caper was called the Mouse-tronaut. Elaborately rigged latex balloons, filled with water, were fired at members of the club next to Campus so that innocents on the grounds of Tower were often targets. No better bombardier than Fitch, a friend would say long after he was gone. The greatest risks he took required no audience at all: sometimes alone or with a friend late at night he would leap from one crenellation to the next on top of a building on campus, as a warrior might move in terrible, sure haste from one battlement to another. In New York, at a party given by a student whose family had a large Fifth Avenue apartment, he went outside on the terrace and walked back and forth on the narrow wall, sixteen floors up, his balance somewhat impaired by drink, his confidence not at all. A friend pretended, in pantomime, to push him off.

Without even planning it, Mr. Fitch became for some onlookers the James Dean of Princeton University, the brooding young actor who became the symbol of the restless, rebellious American males in the nineteen fifties. A few students who had never seen a James Dean movie thought Stona Fitch was carrying on with the chorus of an old American aria, but there was only one small resemblance between the two. James Dean was killed in a highway crash while driving his Porsche to Salinas to compete in a racing event. Mr. Fitch drove like a madman in a race no one ever called, sixty miles an hour in a town whose speed limit was twenty-five, braking at one hundred feet at Prospect and Washington in front of Campus, where he ate lunch and dinner when he ate at all.

If he asked for trouble it was only of a special kind. There were always the surprising surges of generosity and sweetness, unusual among the young, so that even men were touched. He liked giving flowers to women, suddenly appearing with a bunch of irises in winter when the price was still absurd, sometimes moving a stalk or two after they were arranged in the vase, as nicely as his mother might. It was she who taught him to love flowers and to learn the names; as a child he would go into the woods near his house to pick them and would bring them back to be put in water. And there were always the presents for friends when he felt like it: a white sweatshirt jacket for his last roommate, who played squash racquets—a sport that Stona Fitch spoofed—and later a small Indian box made of wood and covered with rushes, a lovely little thing.

Young women responded to him, one after another, because he was urgent not earnest, witty, extravagant in his stories, and often behaved, in that large Salvation Army overcoat, like a man on the run, the dogs not far behind. He liked large numbers of females, one by one, and then no longer did, backing off, then charming someone new within the week. His behavior was considered regressive; criticism came from classmates, from young men trying not to subjugate women while still keeping their attention. It was said how hurtful his treatment of women was, how fickle, how unfair, how chauvinistic, but little in comparison was said against him by the women left. Some classmates could give you a list of all the names of his girls, tell you how badly the rupture hit this one or that one, puzzled by why women in an age of enlightenment would even come near such a marked man. After all, women did not have to tolerate fickle or selfish men. They were making their own way very nicely. They had plans, they wanted careers. You had only to read class notes in the *Princeton Alumni Weekly* to learn, for example, how Jan Claire Viehman, '75, a project manager in one department of an electronics manufacturer, had for three years been working to implement a computer-based manufacturing and Material Requirements Planning (MRP) system. The system went up in 1982 and now, she wrote, "the company is running better than ever . . . Not bad for a religion major!"

The point is that some were jealous of Stona Fitch; this was the theory of a woman who felt she was a good friend of his. It was other men who could not understand his charm and did not see why women were so moved and held by his excesses, his moods, the terrible demands he made on his own nervous system, his rushing, and the faint hint of frailty behind his self-possession. A wild boy, one woman said, so it was the wild boy that won them over. Sometimes one of the women so taken with him, carrying a picture of Stona Fitch in Oklahoma in her wallet, would make the mistake of trying to plan what the two of them would do on her birthday or during the break between semesters or for Christmas. It drove him crazy, for he could not provide what he called The Planned Response. He did not want demands, his own were enough.

His reputation with women was so stunning that his last roommate, a conscientious and brilliant history major not given to exaggeration, said a group of sophomores formed a Stona Fitch Fan Club and invited him to their parties and wrote him notes. He could always make women laugh, and other young men, of course, did not always catch on how alluring this could be. A young woman could say of a man that he was hilarious or very funny as a high compliment, but men did not say the same about women. Females were not hilarious, they did not intend to make men laugh, they did not work at it.

His was not the fiercer, belligerent, self-protective masculinity of older American men in the earlier classes of an all-male Princeton, men raised to cover their feelings except for bouts of profound indignation, some of their attitudes summed up in a letter from an alumnus in November 1981. Charles Huber II, class of '51, was upset about the football team and wrote a letter to *The Prince*, blaming much on the university's president while proudly remembering a former football coach, Charlie Caldwell. Some people thought at first the letter was a joke or a parody written by a clever rascal among them, and were wrong.

"Why did we patronize Princeton football then and why do we so abhor it now?" wrote Mr. Huber. "First, Ivy (not Ivy League) football was good! In my day a twenty-two man traveling Yale squad beat nationally ranked Wisconsin at Madison, a so-so Cornell team beat Michigan at Ann Arbor, Princeton beat Navy and we were ranked number four by UPI at season's end." As a coach, Mr. Huber said, Charlie Caldwell made Vince Lombardi seem like a "pussycat."

"How did we recruit? The alumni recruited. Unable to promise booze and broads, they promised graduate school and preferential treatment when seeking jobs after graduation." Mr. Huber thought much had been diminished at the university.

"Why was football abandoned? Certainly the denigration of academic standards holds no water. Our athletes *were* the outstanding scholars . . . Success after graduation is a told tale. What happened?

"My suspicion is that football represents everything the current administration abhors. It was alumni-recruited—not created by the admissions office. It was elitist. It was rightist. Had a gay alliance held a dance in our day, Dean Godolfin would have called Charlie Caldwell to have the football squad clean house and knock heads. . . .

"Although the Princeton of today is larger in total numbers than it was in my day, when you subtract Bowen's smug diversity —minorities (with that abominable Third World Center), gays, pacifists, activists, anarchists, Dadaists—children with a mission or a talent, however bizarre, our Princeton was much larger.

"Thirty years ago Princeton was monolithic. We studied harder and played harder. We put in more hours in the classroom and wrote longer papers, more often. There were fewer high grades and many more low grades. We helped each other in the awful reality of the business world which came after. We were successful, and we gave. We gave because, however the world might change, Princeton remained the same and we could come back to Old Nassau and see winning football."

The response from students came in a wild rush. They were fun to write. Fred Frank, '85, wrote: "Heck, I'd trade my Heinrich Himmler decoder bracelet just to get a peek at Huber's application essay—'Advantages to Slave Society,' 'How I Whopped My First Faggot,' . . . It must have been something. . . . Three cheers for a first amendment that permits Charlie Huber to let us know what's happening on the underside of American life. Perhaps when he gets his white sheet and hood back from the dry cleaners he'll consider teaching a course at Princeton: The Dark Ages, A First-Hand View." A freshman, Chris Crenner, wrote about the squirrels at Princeton: "The imperious little brutes seem to have free run on the campus. Why, in the good old days every athlete with the mettle to call himself a Princetonian would have been out there stoning the immoral creatures. Just the other day I saw two of them right out in public. . . . And what's this with the black squirrels? No other Ivys have black squirrels. This is exactly the kind of diversity we don't need."

No one appeared to notice that he had called the reality of the business world "awful." Shortly after the publication of his lament, the Princeton football team, as if in response to such contempt, made history at their 104th match with Yale, 31–31. Triumphant graffiti appeared on the white-columned marble Whig Hall building; there was a huge bonfire on campus, under fire department supervision, to celebrate, but not all students who stood around the fire that night seemed certain how to celebrate, so they only stared at the flames. There was, however, deep pleasure and no man was more pleased with that weekend than Stona Fitch, who did not care at all about football. He and three others had written and printed several hundred phony editions of *The Yale Daily News* and distributed them in New Haven without being detected.

He did not boast when he told his survivor stories, the reminiscences of a commando who has just pulled through, elaborate as his Oklahoma grandfather might have made them in his younger days.

At Princeton his photographs of Minnesota were with him, and old snapshots of the grandfather in Wetumka wearing flashy ties and white Panama hats, a short but huge man smiling right at the camera, pleased by the diversion. There was an old photograph of his father too, in his immaculate sergeant's uniform, so crisp it looked as if he had just pressed it, posed in his parents' living room in front of a plaid armchair with doilies. He had taken the pose of all young men standing up and indulging others, hands low on his hips, leaning slightly on one leg. His very dark hair was combed in a pompadour. Waiting for the camera to do its work, he lifted his eyebrows but did not try for a pleasant face. It is a picture of a good-looking American, perhaps with a Cherokee ancestor somewhere in the past, clearly not a man even then with a frivolous disposition. He went to Korea with an infantry unit named the Thunderbirds, not to be an infantryman but to help take care of the wounded, in the same cold, the same terrain; doing administrative work for the mobile hospitals could not be called a cushy job.

Stona Fitch was not really clear about much else, which was probably what his father intended, putting him alongside so many

American children who are uninformed about the wars of their fathers. There are exceptions: the offspring of pilots, and the woman in New York who said her father had been at Guadalcanal and that, when she was growing up, his dreams sometimes made him send out noises from his bed so she knew that what had happened there was happening again. The fathers sometimes mentioned small things, whose meanings and symbols are hidden, scraps of stories given more often to their sons than to daughters.

Stona Fitch had some of these. Knowing even as a child that his father had been in the Korean War, although nothing much was ever said about it, he fixed on the souvenirs from Japan as proof: two inlaid jars, a small knife, some records—the old kind that feel so heavy now—in Japanese, including "Tokyo Boogie-Woogie." He remembered all of it, with his collector's eye, his peculiar attachment to things from the past, this child curator.

The dark-haired father, whom the son always described as strong and forceful, went to work in dark suits and white shirts, whitest of white because his company made soap, although he happened to be in paper products. The boy was resourceful, stubborn, out on his own soon enough.

He was obsessed with his stamp collection, which helped him ignore the strain between his parents. There were no arguments; he never heard yelling, a slammed door, complaints from one adult about the other. The father, so organized and efficient and serious, would sometimes leave notes for his wife on what should be cleaned in the house. She did not like it. Buying Christmas decorations with the children seemed to her a scheduled martial exercise, nothing left to impulse or chance because that would not be productive. The father had a stunning sense of order, of the correct procedure to get things done in the right way, and for all his exuberance, his son was like him in this respect. He did not like messes and was often neat and careful while pretending his life was chaos. He did not wish to be seen as tidy.

At home he knew the calm was reason for alarm. "It was all very quiet and it got progressively quieter," he said at the age of twenty. "I remember my father would come home from work wearing this kind of uniform—those very, very white shirts—and take off his jacket and tie and have dinner with us, talking about all sorts of things. After dinner my sister and I would go our separate ways and my mother and my father would be left at the table."

One year, his mother opened an office upstairs in their house where she ran a tour guide service for Cincinnati. She cared a lot for the history of Cincinnati.

The day the mother at last decided to leave, he was so deep in his albums he did not quite catch on when she came to his room to tell him. He had been avoiding her, letting the stamps, which were so neutral, keep him safe. "I cannot remember the whole scene. She was in and out for a while and then she was just gone," the son said.

She moved out, she came back for more belongings, she saw him often, she found a job in public relations in another state, doing very well, and then moved to California. He would, sooner or later, make a glancing reference to it, sometimes confusing his own age, believing he was younger—eleven, perhaps twelve—when the awful day took place. He understood when he was much older why his mother could not have taken him with her.

"I remember my father coming home from work that day very tired, his hair so neatly cut, that black hair and that very white shirt," Mr. Fitch said. "My father and I were alone a lot. We would go out and have dinner in town at a cafeteria or something. We were very close in lots of ways but the situation was pathetic."

The father did not know much about cooking, so the boy learned first and the two of them managed nicely doing hamburgers and steak outside on a grill, once in a while trying something more complicated. He became very good; his generation was allowed this. When his father traveled on business trips he was by himself in the house, which disturbed the parent much more than it did the boy. Being alone brought him forward in certain ways: he was never to dread it as so many do. Elected president of the student government of Indian Hill High School and the editor of *The Chieftain*, the newspaper, he learned—as many people have—that enormous amounts of work and deadlines distract from the hurt. As it happened he began going to the house of a friend whose own mother was divorced, and the woman, in time, grew so fond of this beguiling boy that she treated him as another child, expecting him to appear at dinner and to do certain chores. It became normal for the father, coming back from a trip, to go to her house to collect the boy. In this way the father grew to know and love another woman whom he later married; they were considered an appealing couple, an unusually good-looking and commendable pair.

Stona Fitch went on being the busiest boy of all. His mother too became attached to someone else, a man with an impressive business life behind him, who had become an artist of more than amateur rank. They always seemed to be in love and really were. Both his parents, it could be said, were now far better off, but, still they did not wish to speak to each other. That year he knew more about his father and what had been asked of him.

"It was very, very cold in Korea," the son said. "He told me about one Thanksgiving when the men were given special turkey and dressing, gravy and stuff, but when they left the mess it was so cold that the food froze on his plate before he could put a fork to it. He told about eyelashes freezing and toes and feet freezing and he made it very clear it was an extremely horrible experience."

Sergeant Fitch was attached to a medical unit, involved in setting up casualty clearing stations and keeping records; his son said that he seemed proud of having done a good job. "They even set records for getting up these tents. It was like a traveling circus, they set them up real fast and then took them down fast," he said. "I think they were mobile emergency units for surgery, or something."

When he was on his own in Minnesota, his father wrote often, always saying how much the son was missed, how proud of the son he was. They talked a bit about the Korean War after his eighteenth birthday, when he was required by law to register for selective service.

"My father said, 'You know, it was a horrible thing I had to do in Korea, but then again everything we do isn't pleasant and I learned a lot from it.' I think he learned from it more deeply than he'll admit. He's not so insensitive and gung ho that he'll say you must fight for your country. It's not that he doesn't love me enough so he wants me to go through the same kind of hell that he did, if I ever would, but he sees it as a kind of experience. I think he understands that it's not my duty to do it—I'd fight if somebody attacked Cleveland and I won't in El Salvador—but it's my duty not to run away from things. I don't want to run away from things."

Without knowing it, believing that he only wanted the money, Stona Fitch found the equivalent of joining the army the summer he turned twenty in July. The work was hard, dangerous, filthy, boring, and he performed it with people whose behavior was vexing and sometimes bizarre. He was all by himself in a town without resources or vitality; sometimes he would compare the different T-shirts in dime stores after work or on weekends sit smoking on a curb, looking out at nothing much, just moving cars.

He was working for an oil company in Nowata, in the north of Oklahoma next to Kansas, one of ten small outfits. There were only thirty-five people in Nowata, working in an area of about fifty square miles, renovating a series of wells that had drill blockage or other defects. Some had been drilled at the wrong levels. He was first hired to be a yard boy, driving around a huge fenced-in area picking up reels of wire with a winch, keeping it clear and clean, for six dollars an hour. After a week a man from a pulling unit said one of his hands in the field just quit, so Stona Fitch became a hand, working in a crew of three. Everyone who was not a boss was a hand. They called him a slips and elevator man, and, long after, he loved explaining the procedures even to people who did not know or care about the difference between power tongs and spin wrenches. Only white males worked in the field.

"You hook onto a piece of pipe in the hole, a piece that is thirty feet long, four and a half inches around. You do a lot of preliminary things until you grab this piece of pipe with a metal thing called an elevator, which is like a gripper, and hook a hook onto the top of this. It pulls the pipe out of the ground, and as thirty feet of slimy, cruddy old pipe emerges, you throw what are called a set of slips to anchor it. Then another guy uses wrenches to undo the pieces of pipe, which are threaded at each end. As the pieces are undone, my job was grab the end of the piece of pipe, get it out, unhook it, and stack it. I was to drag out the end of the pipe. You're dealing with heavy stuff; I'd hold a wrench under the power tongs as backup, to keep the pipe from spinning."

The danger came not only from the pipe, pulling and shaking, but from the things overhead running from the portable rig, hooks going up and down on cables that slipped out every so often. None of the crew would wear hard hats.

"They had a myth that if you wear a hard hat you will get hit on the head by the hook when it falls, and it will break your neck,"

Mr. Fitch said. "But if you don't wear a hat . . . " He did not; the others would have derided him.

Dave was small, obnoxious and driven; and he reveled in being a bully. He drove the portable rig and called Stona, who wisely told everyone his name was Steve, S-t-a-y-v-e. He would never drink water, even if it was 110 degrees, preferring very hot coffee, always placing the thermos in the same spot. Dave wanted to do a perfect job as fast as possible and annoyed other men so much that one tried to injure him once, but the distinction of being so disliked only seemed to make him nag more urgently. In the field most of the crews floated through the day, smoking cigarettes or dope, hard rock on AM radios. The bosses, who often had fingers missing, were old-timers, but did not try to whip the men. Only Dave, never still, never silent, wanted all of them tapped out.

"He had a little set of sayings he would repeat over and over," said Mr. Fitch. "Nobody could work with him. Being new I was put with him because no one else would tolerate him. He constantly yelled. He couldn't stand to get his hands oily. He would always wear white gloves, and he could not take it if they got spotted. He would say over and over 'I like to work people till they don't want to work more.' " Every morning, the three men in the crew would meet in Nowata, first buying something for lunch, although Mr. Fitch would only pick up a piece of fruit or candy bar because at 8 A.M. the thermometer was already eighty-five degrees and rising. Sandwiches could choke you. They bought a big bag of ice for a cooler and filled it with water from a hose. The white cotton gloves cost Dave a dollar every day. They were a moral imperative and if something soiled them, his face, always strained, would pucker as if the others were conspiring to upset him. Stona Fitch and the third hand would go through seven gallons of water a day, but Dave would not let a drop reach his lips.

"Different kinds of oil are a different color but mainly it's black and cold. When it comes out of the hole it is freezing," Mr. Fitch said. "What happened lots of times was that when we got to a well that was closed off we'd open it up and it would start to flow, blowing out barrel after barrel. Once you smell that smell you never forget it. It's vegetable matter, a kerosene smell, but as if something was rotting. Not pleasant. It's just weird to see it coming out of the ground."

At night, in his room at the Hotel Campbell, a boarding house, he would bathe and see how the water became oily and black as soon as he sat in it. It took three full tubs to make him clean. He would read all the time: *Ulysses* again, an anthology of every Faulkner short story, three Faulkner novels—*Absalom, Absalom!*, *Light in August*, and *As I Lay Dying*—Nabokov novels and *The Crying of Lot 49* by Thomas Pynchon. He read every issue of *Time* and *Newsweek*, every newspaper he could buy or find. The first room in the Hotel Campbell was small and almost without light; in a bigger second room there was a black smear on the wall where, for so many years, oil-field workers had touched the light switch. He thought that the man living in the next room stole television sets because the fellow always had a new one. There were very few tenants. In the lobby, with its sad shreds of grandeur that he noticed—remnants of a parquet floor, an old oak register—a cheap television set was always on, with no one watching. He didn't like television except for the news. After work he kept drinking fluids because he still felt dehydrated. If he did not get to Wetumka to see his grandparents on a weekend, he was alone, not speaking to anyone from Friday until Monday morning. He ate in the Bliss Cafe, or the Ideal Restaurant, but it did not count as a conversation when he gave his order to a waitress. There was no one to talk to and most of the time he rather liked that. It was the sort of punishment that suited him.

"It was a rough kind of town and the women there were just not to be reckoned with," Mr. Fitch said, meaning they were married or out of reach.

Dave's cousin, who was only sixteen, joined the crew to take a routine job. Dave stood in one place all day with a wrench in each hand, working them all the time; he reminded Stona Fitch of the Charlie Chaplin film, *Modern Times*. The cousin, Frank, lived with his father, known to be an unrelentingly violent man, and a step-mother who made sure the boy paid part of the rent. Frank found life harsh and confusing, its alphabet a mystery. One day Stona Fitch took Frank to the Bliss Cafe for lunch, but Frank did not know what to do. Oil men, unwashed, ate there all the time: three pieces of chicken, with potatoes, beans, iced tea, and dessert cost $2.50 that year.

"He confessed he had never been to a restaurant in his life. 'What do you do?' Frank asked. 'Do you just ask for all you want, do you pay for it now or do you eat it and then pay? Let's just leave without paying,' Frank said. I couldn't believe it; his first impulse was to try and rip them off."

It was rare that they ate in town. In the field Stona Fitch would have his fruit while Dave drank his coffee, but Frank would hide from the sun and try to be alone.

"He'd go dig out a dusty little place under the rig and get in there and curl up like a little animal," Mr. Fitch said. "When he came out he'd be all covered with dust. I found it so strange. He was incredibly stupid, the most stupid person I've ever met in my life. One time I watched him clean up. He took a bucket of diesel fuel, closed his eyes and poured it over his head. It's gasoline, right? He was just kind of rubbing the stuff in his skin. For about two weeks after that he was a funny splotchy color."

In an open, plowed field of awesome flatness, the crew would be the tallest objects for many miles; waves of heat, one after another, rose from the ground and wrapped them tightly. In the back of the rig was a company radio and a voice giving commands and making inquiries of the men in the different locations. They drove to and from each site at great speed, Dave at the wheel driving as if he were being filmed or chased.

"Dave liked us to bring two sets of clothes so that when we finished work we didn't get the truck dirty. You can't get oil on the seat, he would say, you can't get oil on the seat. But the truck was so beat-up, the windshield was busted, it hardly made a difference. We'd try to wash up in the field, sort of get some of the oil off, but he had us change clothes before he'd take us back. 'Frank, look what you did,' Dave would say, pointing at a little bit of grease on the steering wheel. He would never let Frank drive because Frank was unsafe."

He felt some pity for Frank but not that much; sixteen was not too young to be on your own and to have your wits about you. He knew the boy lacked what people called a "home life." He was not unkind, but he did not think there was much he could do for Frank.

"He's been through it, I tell you, that Frank. His father, who is known for having shoot-outs in Oklahoma, reminds me of a man soon to be in jail. Frank's on a bad track too. He was so slow the bosses couldn't joke with him. They don't like people like that."

Before long he began to like the work, once he felt agile and confident, to like the monotony and the meagerness of his life, the loneliness, the other men, even Dave. He understood why they loved being in the oil business, able to say they had brought in a thousand barrels that month. Dave, who lived in a trailer, invited him home to dinner just before he left and kept saying "drop us a line." His wife, a fleshy woman with hair the color of old lemons, cooked something, and as they ate they watched television, the cartoons that their child wished to see. "Drop us a line," Dave repeated.

On his last day, Frank was acting as peculiar as ever. Stona Fitch caught him taking off the top of a big diesel fuel tank that kept the rig running. Frank was trying to pour dirt into it. "You're going to be gone tomorrow. I'll make the rig so it stops," the boy said, as if he was honoring Stona Fitch by a final act of sabotage.

No one in Nowata guessed he was going to Princeton, that he read so much, or that he would always keep the photographs of Dave and Frank, posed at the wheel of the truck with his family pictures and the wilderness scenes. He made enough money to buy a yellow Volkswagen Rabbit and put some aside for bills. Later, when he talked about it, what interested some women was not the swinging and pushing of pipes but the isolation he had known. It was not the sort of summer that women often wanted. His father was not certain it was such a profitable summer; he thought his son would have done better to get an internship somewhere and to start concentrating on a career. Stona Fitch was not too clear on what his father's own job entailed; he only knew that this father was highly respected by employees at the plant because a friend of his had put in a summer there and told him so. He knew nothing about his father's office, the demands made, the problems at hand, if the parent was ever happy at work, or maybe thought men like himself did not need to be happy.

"Two things we don't talk about are Korea and job," he said. "I know that Korea is always back there in his mind."

Things happened. He worked during a summer for a newspaper in Anchorage, a city he later described as a "sleazy smear in the middle of the wilderness." There was a new photograph, unlike all others: Stona standing in the snow of Alaska, holding a rifle, without gloves, behind him an immense blue mountain with only haphazard patches of ice. He found nothing cheerful to say about Anchorage and its berserk disorder. "Balancing out the California, all natural granola-head crowd is one of the largest Moral Majority groups in the country," he wrote in a piece for *The Prince*, a free man now who could give his opinions. "Businessmen in three-piece suits step over drunk Eskimos on their way to work in the morning." It did not take long to do reconnaissance on Fourth Street if you stayed up late: there were the bars, the pornography shops, the rows of joints, the derelict natives all in one strip. Eski-mos sometimes tried to sell native carvings to buy drinks, and their bars, he noted, were called The Denali, The Montana Club, and The Scandinavian Club. He remembered the popular slogan in Alaska: Anchorage is what America was. That was not quite right, he said, Anchorage is what America is.

The white nights, the muddle of the place, the litter, the misery, and the clang of Anchorage made it so dreadful and so interesting that he had a good summer. Back at Princeton, where he kept complaining the place needed more metal, he called for a greater car culture in his column. "Each student, upon acceptance at Princeton, should be supplied with a beat-up but serviceable American car—a Nova, Impala, Dart, Galaxie 500 or Fairlane— and be responsible for keeping it running until after graduation," Mr. Fitch wrote. "No car, no diploma, it's as simple as that. We will take courses—Advanced Seminar in Creative Arc Welding, Seventeenth-Century Chinese Body Work, The Radiator in Amer-ican Literature."

Seniors grew visibly more perturbed, as they will every year, about finishing their theses, a requirement for graduation. None were exempt. They groaned and fussed and slept less, or more. They compared their degrees of despair. The subjects, depending on their major, were of their choosing. "Pluralism and Revolution: The Case of the Private Sector in Agriculture under the Gobierno de Reconstrucción Nacional of Nicaragua" was the thesis by An-drew Owens Moore for the Department of Politics. "The Unful-filled Promise: A Profile of Youth in the Eighties" by Craig Iver Forman was submitted to the Department of History.

Stona Fitch's thesis was ten short stories, called "Luxury You Can Afford," about people who wanted a way out of where they found themselves. He used Oklahoma and Alaska, not finding much difference between the people he knew in both places, none of them knowing how to live their lives.

Many students, suspecting that they would never again pro-duce such a coherent and careful work, tended to give lavish acknowledgments, much like writers at last finishing a first and troublesome book. So Bruce Reed, chosen to be a Rhodes scholar, who wrote "Our Mutual Friends: Dickens, Orwell and the Literature of Generous Anger," thanked his father, and his mother too, because she "tried to teach me to behave decently and who managed to convince me that honesty is the best policy even though she knew better." Bruce Reed also thanked the makers of Sugar Free Dr. Pepper and twelve others.

But not Stona Fitch.

He and three other seniors won a Francis LeMoyne Page Creative Writing Award, a very nice thing. At graduation—a ninety-minute ceremony held outdoors in front of Nassau Hall with its bronze tigers presented in 1911 by Woodrow Wilson's class—it was believed that Mr. Fitch and a friend skipped out to buy a beer on Nassau Street. When the ceremony was done, he was both dazed and pleased, much like a man suddenly informed of an armistice when he was not counting on being spared.

With his mother, the two of them so alike, he behaved with the authority and deference any woman might wish her son to show on a day to be remembered forever. All over the campus the air was rich with the love of mothers happy to chat with anyone the child had known in the last four years in the belief that, in this way, they would move closer to their sons or daughters. Fathers were no less proud but had duties to perform; it was up to them to see the child's belongings were properly packed and fitted into the trunk of the car, as if an inspection might be held and delay their departure. They bent over the trunks, arranging boxes and suitcases as if their lives depended on how tightly, how neatly every bit of it fit. So urgent was this task that they did not need to make conversation or pretend their inclinations were sociable.

That summer Stona Fitch happened to come back to Princeton with a young woman en route to somewhere else. He showed her his campus, *The Prince* office, the sweetness of his past. It was she who remembered how suddenly he had gone to tears, as if given a terrible chop in the chest. He said he did not know whether he would ever be as happy again as he had been here. It was not unusual: many of the graduates coming back behaved as if they could imagine for the first time their own deaths, seeing how easily their places had been taken at Princeton, the university so indifferent to their absence.

So Stona Fitch went out into the world intending a different life, wanting none of the things held dear to the class of 1983, intending to make his own leaps—the loner, his very own words, who didn't want to be lonely.

But when he came back to Princeton after that it was as someone different, a musician now in a group called Scruffy the Cat, his hair longer and an electric banjo, a Farfisa Deluxe, in his arms. The eating clubs hired such small bands to play on the nights new members were initiated or for parties. In February 1985 his black leather jacket had two new possessions on it: a small Shriner's pin and a large, oval metal badge that said: "Regulation chauffeur. Ohio, September 1939." Cab drivers once wore them, he said. There was his first tattoo, of dice, high on one arm.

In the little booklet handed out to promote Scruffy the Cat and its five players—its founder Stephen Fredette was described as born to wolves in Massachusetts—the writing seemed his. "We prefer to be known as a 'teen beat combo' but 'black jeans rock outfit' will do, thank you. It's fair to say, though, that we have been influenced by country western, the wide open prairies, and poor nutrition." He was composing some of their songs and music: "Some kinds of love never find you, And some kinds of love they only remind you, That some kinds of love are best put behind you."

In Boston he worked as a dishwasher and fry-cook in a restaurant-bar and was rather proud of the company he kept, saying he knew he would be doing menial work like this for the rest of his life to pay his bills and that was fine. "Ours is not to wonder why, ours is but to wash and dry," he wrote in a letter. When more bookings came in, Scruffy the Cat was often on the road, pushing hard to make shows in different states, and he liked getting them there in the van. Being in the band gave him an authenticity he needed, and he would say that all he was learning—it was a lot—would be of great use when his career as a writer really began. "Drive now, write later," Stona Fitch said. He bought an accordion in a pawnshop for the nights they only played in little bars where customers wanted the music to be more soothing.

In Colonial Club that night, the student members danced to Scruffy the Cat with elation, such wiggling and pounding, arms punching and jabbing the air, such spinning of hips and dipping of knees, that Stona Fitch appeared nearly solemn as he played. "It rinses all the poison out," said one twenty-year-old woman, worried about her thesis on the revolt against the Manchu dynasty but not when she danced. As always, a cluster of men stood in the back of the room to watch. The time when men eyed who was dancing so they could cut in was long over and it was impossible to get close enough to tap another man on the shoulder. Yet still there were small lumps of men in the back of the room watching. No women stood and watched, only men. It was thought they were shy, it was said there were not enough girls to go around at any party. They were simply the ones who gave the dancing too much importance and were uncertain of how others would see them if they moved to the floor. Women often asked men if they wanted to dance. Men could ask men but none did. There was enough freedom to do almost anything, even dance alone if you wished, but the pleasure came in performing with someone else. The band worked hard, all the power theirs—for when they stopped the dancers were stalled—and so the banjo player in the leather jacket seemed happy enough, sometimes even singing, at a distance now from the students, not paying too much notice to them.

WORK

*I*t was his bus, and the driver let you know it although he did nothing crucial except drive. There was the taking of tickets or money, stopping and starting, answering questions and making sure no one fell or tripped getting on and off, and an occasional greeting to the regulars. Carrying commuters from towns and suburbs in New Jersey to New York or those on shorter hops along Route 27, the driver would occasionally chat with passengers in the front seats, and this morning was saying that not just anyone could handle the job, it was not as easy as it looked. He spoke as if what was really needed was a moral mastery that could not be explained. By then women had long been driving buses for the company, but none worked this route. He went back and forth. They couldn't handle New Brunswick, the driver said. Could not deal with it. These were the two expressions used in the nation to indicate distress or apprehension; everyone spoke this way. He assumed you knew the stop at New Brunswick outside Blimpie's, and that the young men who often got on might be unruly—eating and drinking when that was forbidden on the bus, sometimes smoking, another sin—and were not the sort to take reprimands unless the driver impressed them as being able to enforce. You could not cuff passengers, of course, but you could tell them to get off. The driver was still young, so he rose swiftly, unbothered, when it came to lifting: passengers with babies, strollers, other children, passengers wobbling from the weight of shopping bags or bundles would be relieved of their burdens, which he tucked in the overhead rack, to their relief. The bus company feared passenger injuries and ensuing litigation, so he had orders to assist, but drew the line with the young bent over by backpacks who could barely maneuver down the narrow aisle with all that bulk. As the traffic thickened near Lincoln Tunnel, the driver said people did not stop to think he was in charge of thirty-five thousand pounds of steel. He did not see himself as having the same skill and stamina as a truck driver but rather the more intricate responses of a pilot often in bad weather.

"It's like flying a plane," the driver said. "The same. Maybe not so technical." He liked hearing himself say this, and plunged into the tunnel behind a convoy of other men driving other buses for the same pay.

"In our civilization, work is what man lives by. . . . It helps still the feelings of inferiority that unconsciously beset us; it gains us parity with our fellow and the acceptance of the community. It dignifies our daily life, no matter how humble. In it we may expend our aggressive impulses." These were the words of a psychiatrist named Sol W. Ginsburg, who wrote them forty-four years ago.

People Working read the signs which used to say Men at Work. More women are seen working as bartenders. They are meat packers and butchers because automatic machines now do the hoisting men were once needed to do. They put insurance claims on computers which used to require male inspectors or examiners to go out and look at the damage.

There are women now going to work for their own self-esteem, as well as women who badly need the wages, women with children to feed, and women who want power, as men do. Many work as hard as men and then even harder when they come home to their families. The successful ones, still considered an exception, are often interviewed, asked for the secret of their drive, asked how they manage to be so efficient, asked if there are small children in the family.

Poor women, whose mothers and grandmothers worked, are rarely interviewed on how they cope, their lives not considered an inspiration. The jobs they hold—cleaning houses, taking care of children of richer working women, working in factories and in places of grimness—do not make their lives admirable.

The difference between men and women is only that men are expected to work faithfully all their lives, without interruption or openly wishing otherwise. A job for a man may be a life sentence, ending only when he is considered too old, becoming smaller, frailer, and less curious. They may change jobs, but for men there can be no renunciation of work, having a job is not optional. For some men, work is a way of hiding without seeming to hide at all, work makes it possible to invent a different self, to create a more formidable personality, to have a chance to command.

Do or die. It is by this means they use their lives and are so judged.

Consider these four men, none alike, all with an aptitude for their chosen work, and in each one may be seen the traces of attitudes held by many other men, and not just those who intend to make their mark on the world through their jobs. There are plenty of men, after all, who do not like what they find themselves doing and, if they can, back out.

In this quartet, two men are consumed by their work—prefer to be—and do not doubt that they are on their way to grander goals. But the other two were not content in professions of considerable prestige, knew what the trouble was, and retreated.

Peter Godoff is a young salesman and entrepreneur, a man who has sold automobiles, musicians, and a sorbet which he created himself. He sells because he continually needs to see results, or rather to find out his effect on other people. Selling is how he addresses the world; it enables him to show love in visible form. Everything in this country is up for sale and he understands this. The space above skyscrapers is for sale, pity is for sale, the face of the winner of an Olympic Gold Medal, the voice and name of a serious actor who promotes a New York brokerage firm. Health, serenity, confidence, and war are being sold. The president was selling a new springtime in America. Mr. Godoff was selling his sorbet, which he considers something of his own self, not your ordinary low-calorie dessert.

Carey Winfrey was a foreign correspondent for *The New York Times*, an advancement for a gifted reporter on the metro staff who was looked upon with favor by those in the chain of command. Working abroad for the paper was essential to his career, and Africa, the only foreign assignment open at the time, always seems alluring and romantic to those who have never been there to work. He happened to hate it and could not understand why the life of a foreign correspondent was seen by other men as a wonderful, masculine way of life, a test, a calling. Because it is no longer required of a man that he be eaten by ambition—want to lead others, make a fortune, and exhaust himself—his departure from the *Times* was not seen as strange, only a pity. Other men also bolted. It was only when he was made editor of a food magazine published by CBS Magazines that he, who could not cook, was finally happy. He did not miss the *Times*, he loved the little magazine. At last here was something of his own.

Dustan Ball defended the property and goods of a merchant who sold food, and set ambushes for those who tried to filch or rob. What he had to prevent was thievery, as well as dishonesty among employees in a small chain of supermarkets. His job had a title: Director of Loss Prevention. This work required him to be a man on perpetual reconnaissance, to put in long hours, forever on the alert, suitably suspicious at all times. He did not make arrests or determine what punishment would be; he had only to expose the wrongdoers. He carried a beeper; it called him to trouble, to problems, a new crisis. It kept him under siege. And this he loved, for Dustan Ball preferred to feel pushed, not a minute to squander, the days never long enough.

Gilbert Hunn, a doctor who practiced medicine to pay his rent but not when he didn't want to, for some years decided not to have an important career as a physician. His lack of drive, a total absence of greed, his indifference to money were not remarkable where he lived in California, but were puzzling to his mother, sister, and a cousin in the East who all knew how brilliant he was and what might have been achieved. Once, when volunteer doctors were needed in Thailand to treat the Cambodians coming across the border after years in the forced labor camps of Pol Pot— people half mad, half dead, starved or diseased—he rallied, did not care about risks, and set forth. And that once, he later said, was the only time he felt he had saved lives and as a doctor done something crucial.

He wanted to wander and to have a home: the conflict, he

knew, was an old one. It was his belief that a staff job in a hospital, the dream of his mother, or having a private practice (he imagined patients with minor nervous disorders, low back pains, digestive problems, inflamed sinuses) would be the death of him. It happened another way—an accident, on a mountain.

"You'll never have to worry again," thirty-two-year-old Mr. Godoff, a bachelor in New York, said to his older sister, who was poorly paid in a good job. He spoke exactly six months after he had opened his own company, so small it had only two partners and no employees; it was the owners who hosed the kitchen and kept the books. A large company was not interested in marketing his product, a sorbet in twelve flavors made from his own private recipe, the unidentified ingredient his "mojo," a word used by jazz musicians to mean a secret charm, your very own juju.

It was as if he had been wanting to say such a thing for years, the exuberant assurance that an older generation of men in America might once have made to women who stayed home and felt diminished by five o'clock. There was a quaint ring to his promise, a bit of the silly sweetness of old-fashioned dialogue from a movie made long, long ago. His sister, however, although unrelentingly independent, was clearly moved. And a few of her friends, all working and intent on doing well in one way or another, thought it a lovely thing for a brother to pledge, much nicer than if spoken by a father or husband who might then treat a woman like a captive and expect a lifetime of gratitude or respect, in their usual beastly way.

Peter Godoff really meant what he said to her. At that moment he was close to making a huge sum, in the high six figures as they say. He always intended to triumph and has this one thing in common with other men who have made a fortune on their own. It is an abiding, almost startling, faith that they are meant for success and that the possibilities have only to be seized. Such men believe that human work is the one expenditure that counts, nothing else. That he believes making money is the only authentic goal for a man, the only possible clarification of a man's worth, is not unusual in this country. What sets him apart is his passion for what he sells, once the talent of a few musicians and now a good dessert. He sees himself as being immune to permanent defeat, at worst a man who could be balked only for a while. If the sorbet of American Glacé—his name, his product, his logo, his colors—did not bring him the world, something else would. Peter Godoff, a man of immense good nature and loyalty, could not see himself as a weed by the wall, he was the wall.

There are American women who want to succeed as well, no less ambitious or eager to make money, but it was not usual for them to believe their lives depended on it. The ones who succeed, of course, are considered exceptional or brilliant, but men who do are only seen as admirable. It is expected of them. Still, women were setting their sights high and recognizing the obstacles before them. A twenty-three-year-old sales representative for a Procter & Gamble division which markets toilet paper says to a reporter: "Toilet paper is a dying market. It only grows with the population." In four years, she thought she would start her own company.

Peter Godoff, however, had known power and chagrin by the time he was not much older than the Procter & Gamble woman who saw no future in toilet paper. At twenty-three, in Beverly Hills, he drove a sixteen-thousand-dollar 530I BMW, metallic silver with red leather seats, had his own secretary, was served drinks and food by a butler in a white coat, and thought how sweet the world was being to him until he set out on his own and within a year or so was flattened. Coming back East at the insistence of his family, who knew he was in dire straits and could arrange a job if he would come back to the fold, he appeared morose. He wanted to stay in California and open a wine bar, but with their entreaties and arguments the women in this family pulled him back, as the moon arranges the tide. The job was selling cars in Maine, an uncle owned the dealership, everything would be fine now. It was not. The trouble was, in his mind, that the family saw him as a problem—he was neither a lawyer nor a doctor, not a professional anything—but then he did what he most wanted.

He gave up cars and next plunged into food, first going to school in New York, then finding a job in a restaurant off Park Avenue and doing very nicely as a beginner with fish and desserts. Some of his relatives thought working in a kitchen, any kitchen, was no better than being a maid, and there was considerable talk about what Peter was doing with his life which their Peter did not appreciate.

Long afterwards he would say of his first days in the music business, "The Eagles were shipping platinum," as if when that era ended the industry was turning to ash; people in that world spoke with a certain extravagance when their own run ended.

His mother, once the children were of age, brought them Bloody Marys in bed on those mornings when they felt unthreaded by a late night. She believed in a life run on a certain bright, swift beat—a woman whose ideal day would mean shopping, lunch with friends, a good game of tennis, a dinner party at night, black tie. As it happened, she held a job and did the rest anyway. The deaths of two husbands, the end of those marriages, had not mauled her; she was now attached to a widower whom the children thought nice. She cornered her son, she shone when she spoke of him, she fed on his news, she thought him exceptional. So did his aunts, the Godoff women, and a Rosenstock grandmother, whose own family came to this country during the Russo-Japanese War and who, on her own, had supported herself in retailing and could even now, in her nineties, add any column of figures with the old fierce speed. That grandmother was a Queen Victoria, he says.

By twenty-seven he had been squashed, then willed his recovery, believing the race not at all over for him and that only the single-minded would survive. His sister long remembered what Peter told her once when she was feeling low: "If you get run out of town, run to the front of the crowd and make it look like you are leading a parade." Tired of working cruel hours in two New York restaurants for less money than he had once spent having lunch, Peter Godoff came back to life by inventing his American Glacé sorbet. His was not like the icy stuff sometimes served in fancy restaurants between courses to clear the palate, stuff which often punished the teeth. His sorbet tasted more like an ice cream but contained, of course, no dairy products, was low in fat, low in sodium, had no cholesterol, and a four-ounce serving was fewer than a hundred calories, Mr. Godoff said, dozens of times. He was crazy about his own stuff.

It was exactly the right time for his venture. So peculiar and persistent was the belief in the United States that no one with drive need settle for being sad, fat, odd, lonely, clumsy, dull, or for eating horrid meals, that bulk mail sent to ordinary people carried the cry of the lunatic. "Be a richer, thinner, fitter, better sport, traveler, gardener, gourmet, do-it-yourselfer, wit, raconteur, parent and person," it says on the yellow envelope promoting a chain of bookstores. People seemed in a delirium about calories, while consuming more and expecting to be better off in ways that remained unclear. They were not. Never had there been so much talk, such endless discussions, such fierce attention paid to all kinds of food and how to make it or where to buy it. The word *gourmet* lost all authenticity, no longer suggesting a superior quality or skill. People now wished to appear more cultured; cultured people did not moon for chili or Buffalo wings. What you preferred to eat was an indication of class in a country whose citizens thought it classless or pretended they did.

Peter Godoff, those fourteen knives so neatly hung in his tiny New York kitchen, did not think of himself as an accomplished chef, but all his life he had been delighted by food when other boys did not notice if the eggs were cold, the meat overcooked. As a child, before his father moved the family to California, he saw many more headwaiters humming around restaurants in New York than the average adult and knew a good *céleri rémoulade* from a bad imitation. In Beverly Hills his mother hired a Japanese cook, so the children knew about sushi when their playmates were still fussing about cereals. Now his time had come. Food steadied people into thinking they were not really subordinate: even the bagel, that hard glazed roll once claimed by the Jews of Eastern Europe, had been changed. Sold nationally it was flavored with cheese, herbs, garlic, or nuts, honey, and raisins. A pretender to the croissant was easier to buy than a stamp. Special sections appeared in newspapers on how other people, always richer, eat, live, dress, and entertain. Recipes grew slightly more complicated. There were columns on wine advising us what to think, to be aware that the sauvignon blanc is the most underrated white wine grape in the country. In *The New York Times*, where the fever burned highest, recipes ran with prominent titles as if they were excerpts from very good novels: "Leslie Newman's Bombay Chicken Wings," for example, or "Kate Tremper's Tomato and Green Chili Sauce to Go with Salmon." In some cases the credit for a recipe was given more modestly, as it might be for the translator of a foreign work, so on the day readers were given a recipe for Brazilian stuffed flank steak, *matambre,* there was only a modest acknowledgment which read, "as by Philippe Henry de Tessan."

Men who once would have consented to little more than grilling a steak or hamburgers—men always do the barbecue, perhaps on the grounds it involves slightly more risk and more theater than meat loaf made in the kitchen—now were braising endives and making lasagna. No one so precisely described the times as a women from Ohio making small talk in the Miami airport about her trip to Ecuador and her family at home. "My husband was in steel, but my son is going into cookies," she said.

Middle-class children were encouraged to be choosy and venture far beyond hamburgers and pizza. When a ten-year-old girl in New Paltz, New York, was asked what she would choose for A Last Meal, the child selected pickled baby corn, fried fillets of fresh sunfish, fried mashed potato cakes, wild asparagus tips with lemon butter, cucumber salad, a Brie cheese and pastel petits fours. Her mother wrote this to Craig Claiborne, the eminent food writer and cook, who heard from quite a few readers after he published his own menu for "one last great meal on earth," with recipes. He was not envisioning an atomic blast, the idea was just a caprice. He chose fresh caviar, striped bass with champagne sauce, and stuffed squabs Derby. After a salad and a cheese, three wines and Dom Perignon champagne, Mr. Claiborne preferred grapefruit sherbet, to which one might add crème de cassis or vodka.

Mr. Godoff saw and always remembered the choice of a grapefruit sherbet. Years later he sent a quart of his own American Glacé grapefruit sorbet to Mr. Claiborne, a sort of salute, a homage, and besides, he really wanted to know the reaction of the maestro.

He drove to Southampton to deliver Mr. Claiborne's sorbet, directed by a friend to leave it at the house of Joan Whitman, bringing sorbet for her as well. A gallon of grapefruit and a gallon of raspberry were in the car when he was hit by a brown Mercedes, which suffered a probable eight thousand dollars worth of damages. The rain kept on. Resuming the voyage, he found the house, but Mrs. Whitman was out. He was greeted by her mother, who showed him that the crowded freezer was too small for his tubs. There was nothing to do but empty it, arrange the contents more methodically to make room for his sorbet, thank the admiring mother, and drive back in the rain for another three hours. He had a persistence that almost never failed him. A letter came back, Mr. Claiborne liked his sorbet very much. It was a document to be framed.

When a Texas corporation, not in food but seeking to diversify, took an option to buy and distribute his sorbet, Mr. Godoff knew joy. The Texas men, a father and son, were straightforward and agreeable, hardly the slime he imagined all businessmen to be when he was growing up in the sixties—his hair long, his feet in clogs, needing music the way other people required a minimum number of calories. Even now in the mornings he will not get up and dress without hearing Early Dylan—always Dylan, although he has 4,500 record albums and 150 tapes. Early Dylan to him meant *Highway 61 Revisited*, 1965. In the early, eventful days of American Glacé, he still took time to change the music on his telephone answering machine message so that it was worth calling him just to see what was playing. One week there might be a bit of jazz played on the guitar by Michael Franks, the next a sax solo from *Avalon* by Roxy Music, then "The Ghost in You" by the Psychedelic Furs.

He carried a purple Leica bag everywhere, but when it was time to fly to Texas for meetings, when it was time to think of papers and figures and the gain of millions of dollars, the bag seemed wrong, not sufficiently serious. His sister said he needed a fine leather attaché case and paid for it herself in the shop after he picked out the one he wanted, her present. (Once, having no money at Christmas, she sent him as a present a short story on one page of paper. It hung on his wall, framed.) He was always comfortable in stores, conditioned by his mother, who obliged him to meet her after school at Saks Fifth Avenue in New York until some parts of the store seemed as familiar to him as their apartment on Central Park West. He was thirty-two when for the first time he bought his own underwear; his mother had always done it. When he read that women bought underwear for ninety percent of the men in the country, it did not surprise him.

A physician in New York brought American Glacé and the Texas men together, and stood to make a nice little profit if the deal clicked. "You couldn't be in bed with better people," the doctor said, an old hand at arranging such liaisons. He was an acquaintance of Peter Godoff's partner, Bruce Gordon. The two young men had known each other all their lives; their own fathers had long been partners in a company that designed and printed record jackets. Peter Godoff was not born to hardship and could not come across with the much-loved American story, the refrain dearest to us, of how a poor boy had made it out of a mill town or a village in Arkansas where people used to get malaria from the mosquitoes. Those stories were becoming scarcer in the East among his generation. His own childhood seemed to possess a perfection for him, his father a cultured, energetic, intelligent man, a jazz musician who had once studied the piano for some time with a stern Russian teacher of considerable reputation. In Beverly Hills the family often went out to dinner, the children composed and pleased to be able to order for themselves, so that, long after, Peter Godoff remembered going to the great restaurant called Scandia and how, when he was no more than nine, he preferred to begin with cold prawns in a mustard dill sauce. He would proceed to chicken cooked in a heavy cream and a rich strawberry dessert. It would always make him slightly sick and very happy. He did not suffer from pudginess.

American Glacé was born as gluttony and abstinence, greed and denial collided and caused confusion. Ethiopian restaurants, where the food must be eaten with the fingers, became a craze in Washington, D.C. Small boys were taught to bake by enlightened mothers (who saw that they already cared for nothing as much as cars and dump trucks). Magazines for men put recipes in their stories on food, the instructions so wonderfully clear a youngster could attempt to cook. "Mushrooms and the Man," one men's magazine said, "Soup to Make You Weep." In the cities, depending on the seasons, people were dressing up to look like Japanese field workers, World War II bombardiers, tournament tennis players, chorus girls from another era, mercenaries, fixated runners, ballet dancers, ranchers, prairie women, and photographers off to the front.

After his father died, the family—the Godoffs and the large number of Rosenstocks—expected fine things of him and were watching. American families who had recently emigrated still expected that every child would do better than his parents and should, to reward the family for its existence in America. In both families, there were not a lot of men—they died first—but the Rosenstock women, who gave the commands, were tireless. The Godoffs, in his eyes, were more artistic, intellectual, cultured, and detached, holding themselves to a higher level of comportment. He always remembered his father's older sister telling him, when he was ten and had a cold, to refrain from coughing. Stop it, the aunt kept saying, it's not good for you, as he struggled to comply but could not. The Rosenstocks monitored relatives with military vigilance, picked up noises and tones of voice with the instincts of great sentries. If anyone makes the first small noise of approaching indigestion, Peter Godoff says, the Rosenstocks are on the telephone to each other. Without the telephone the women would have withered. He became accustomed to issuing his own daily communiqués.

As a child he had gone up and down Rodeo Drive on his skateboard and thought of the Polo Lounge as the nice neighborhood place. Although their own house had a pool, on the day of his bar mitzvah he was sent to swim at the pool of the Beverly Hills Hotel when the ceremony was over but the party had not yet started. On Tower Road where the Godoffs lived, Jack Lemmon was across the street and the director George Stevens and the actor James Coburn were their neighbors; Spencer Tracy was up the road, so he saw Katharine Hepburn driving by in her station wagon when the actor was so sick. In seventh grade one of his friends, the son of the actor Richard Conte, would bring him home after school to shoot pool; the two boys were not surprised when Fred Astaire dropped in one afternoon and joined them. Neither child was distracted or made shy by such a presence.

His father liked having his children sit at breakfast with him. His father liked having jazz musicians come to the house to jam, and would be at the piano. The father liked seeing his son perform in school, and the two often went to the movies together. On a Saturday morning when he was thirteen, he was with his father in the music room of their Beverly Hills house, watching a ball game on television. All the servants were downstairs, his mother out, his sister somewhere else. The two of them were going to pick up a new Continental convertible that day in October 1965. (It was the year, he will tell you, when the Beatles film *Help* came out; he and his father saw it together.) All that happened was that the older man suddenly slumped in his chair, no time to say a word or cry out. They went back East after that. He thought the entire family had been balanced on his father and then began to tilt.

In every house his father had his music room, and supervised Peter's piano lessons, being so critical of the teachers that one by one they were released until, finally, the boy gave up and pledged himself to the guitar. He owned four guitars. He went to Wood-stock the week before starting college. So did 450,000 other people, listening for three days and nights to music and behaving beautifully when it was thought such an unconventional crowd would certainly not. "I don't think we'll ever see it again," he said. Almost nobody does. At the University of Hartford, a free man—everything possible, Dylan by his side, long of hair and scornful of shoes needing laces, a supporter of Senator George McGovern in 1972—he had a fine four years. Then it was time to go out in the world to understand commerce and how to make money. It was intended that he start in the dealership of a relative, not a pretty business but one which had made a male relative very rich. His own beloved father had once sold Studebakers. On his first day at work the fifteen salesmen in the showroom hated the sight of him, saw him as an intruder, a family spy, a creep, and just the kind of kid who made them sick to their stomachs—not that their stomachs ever knew a serene day.

"I went from Woodstock to Oldsmobiles," he said. It was 1973. He was a nicely raised young man with good manners; he stood up when older people entered the room.

"I cut my hair but I kept my wooden clogs and wore them in the Bronx. They hated that," he said. "It was a circus there. One of the world's biggest dealers, and there was yelling, screaming, fistfights on the floor." He needed to make money and in this dreadful place saw what had to be done, the way some men suddenly perceived how they might survive in the army when resistance was futile and a certain collaboration would be of profit. Mr. Godoff was not allowed to sell cars, he was to observe, unless he brought in the customer. It galled him.

"It was a very slow Saturday. I had been there a month," Mr. Godoff said. "In the automobile business you work on the 'up' system, which is a rotation. The customer coming in goes to the first salesman in line. But you learn to 'skate,' which means to steal the customer away. On this Saturday there was bumper-to-bumper traffic on Fordham Road, all the salesmen were sitting around, not selling anything. I walked out in front of the dealership, which was all glass, and began to walk along the cars, talking to people stuck in traffic. 'You look as if you could use a new car,' I'd say. 'Pull it up there on the sidewalk, pull it up right here, and let's talk.' The men were furious, they called me the spear-chucker, they said I was spearing people. I sold four cars that day." The manager agreed he could be a salesman.

He began to steal the "up," pretending to know the customers by name, greeting strangers warmly, asking about their children, the absurdity acting on him like a strange amphetamine. This is not what he set out to be: a disciple of Dylan, early worshipper of the Beatles (his father, prescient, understood why very early on), a disc jockey in the college years, loving the Rolling Stones and the Grateful Dead. Loving the Byrds, Steely Dan, Asleep at the Wheel, the Buffalo Springfield, the Jefferson Airplane, and Cream, the British group who gave the first concert he ever saw, loving Pink Floyd's *Ummagumma*. These are some of the names carved on his heart, no matter that most of the groups had long perished because of, as the phrase goes, "internal dissension" which led to their "disbandment." He would have taken them into protective custody if such a thing were ever possible, knowing how much could go wrong for them and did. Now in the far reaches of the Bronx, in a world of men who did not want to know those names or that music, he was catching on, he was becoming a guerrilla, face darkened, the knife between his teeth. He invented ways to "skate."

The manager of the showroom was a veteran of World War II, who had been in Burma, he said, still alive after setting off a land mine and losing parts of both legs. Ever since, he had needed two canes to move about. "He walked in pieces," said the sister of Mr. Godoff. This man, small with powerful shoulders, would often hit his own legs with the canes, so people quite naturally assumed both limbs must be artificial. Noise is what this fellow feasted on: harsh, sudden, wrenching noise, the more disturbing to humans the better. The manager rang a bell, activated his electric alarms, set off a siren on the grounds that all this, nothing else, would "get the place hoppin.' " His voice was not used to inspire or soothe; rather he yelled, screamed, and roared, but assumed cold anger for his role in the little skits he and Mr. Godoff put on to bewitch a gullible customer. Their performances were masterful and deepened the bond between the conspirators who, alone, knew how very good they were. The manager liked young Godoff and was bringing him along.

"I would come in with a couple, saying 'I have to check this price out with the manager to see if it's okay. I really want to sell you this car, but I'm new here,' " Mr. Godoff explained. "The manager would then pretend to be upset by the price and call out so the customers would hear: 'Peter, this is the last time. I told you we won't accept deals this cheap, you're giving away every car you sell. This is the last. You're fired.' Then the manager would throw down the papers for the sale and tell him to clear out his desk. The customers would usually be aghast and say, 'Oh, what a nice boy, don't do this to him and where do we sign?' " The difference between the cost to the dealer and the list price on a car, depending on its make, used to range from two thousand to twenty-five hundred dollars, Mr. Godoff added.

"I was twenty-one years old. I hated it, I couldn't handle it anymore, it was so awful. I couldn't do it," said Mr. Godoff. "Yes, my conscience. The money didn't mean a thing, I felt it was like stolen money. I didn't want to cheat the customer, but all American cars are badly made, there isn't any American car that is any good. Anyway it taught me how to sell, how to deal with people on all levels. I could sell bankers or I could sell pimps."

It was part of an American temperament to insist that he had come out of it a better man, strengthened in some way. But it was a madhouse, of course: if people asked to drive a car before purchase, the salesmen knew how to discourage the very idea, to react as if some monstrous privilege were being demanded. The more time a salesman was off the floor, the less money he made. People were told the car wasn't there, the car would be delivered later, and just sign here. He could tell you about some cars that broke down a few blocks from the dealer, cars sold to those having neither jobs nor their own addresses and who would never be able to meet the payments and all the time knew it.

Ethics were not thought of as admirable. The manager wrote a promissory note for a couple from Connecticut who had purchased a new car and come to take possession but forgot to bring their new license plates. Not wishing complications—the car was not credited as a sale until it left the showroom—the manager assured them that his written word would prevent any problems with the police anywhere. The piece of paper he triumphantly provided, so they could drive away, said nothing more than: "OK

Buzz." Only the Chinese doctors from the hospitals in the area were considered impossible; blandishments and buffoonery and hardball salesmanship did not move them.

He was twenty-three when he went to work in Beverly Hills for the Cherry Lane Publishing Company, hired by a man named Milt Okun. His boss was a partner of Jerry Weintraub of Management III, a large and powerful concern handling complicated, fickle assets—musicians, songwriters, and music publishers. Management III also produced movies, television specials, and handled actors. The company needed an entire floor for its offices, places of such calculated splendor that even his sister was stunned when she saw them. Persian rugs lined the hall like handkerchiefs. In his office, with a collection of Mayan figures on custom-built shelves—they belonged to the office—he sat behind a large, wood Parsons desk. The stereo equipment cost more than ten thousand dollars; one window looked out on Wilshire Boulevard. He started a small collection of American Indian art. Given a car, a space in a garage, a whopping salary, a huge expense account, and the constant attention of the butler whose purpose was to see that no one perished from thirst or hunger, Peter Godoff knew happiness.

"I didn't even know what I was supposed to do," said Mr. Godoff. "I was in music publishing, that was part of it. On my first day around four o'clock my mother called, and as I was talking to her on the telephone there was a little knock at the door. The butler poked his head in and said, 'I have some fresh fruit that I just dipped in chocolate, would you like some?' And then, 'It's almost cocktail time. Would you like a margarita or shall we open some wine?' On Fridays we could, if we wished, drink very cold Dom Perignon, served before everyone drove home.

"I had tremendous freedom to do what I wanted," said Mr. Godoff. "Management III was in everything. We had Bob Dylan, Neil Diamond, John Denver, and Elvis Presley. I was there the day Elvis died and we were ordered not to say a word. Not a word. John Denver was very big, a nice man but I couldn't stand his music. Kenny Rogers had his first single coming out."

Management III did not want its men to be bored. "We had a playroom with video cameras in it. It had pinball machines," he added. "We had a real kitchen." His sister remembered how every receptionist at Management III was blonde, possessing a certain vacant but good-natured beauty which had not yet taken them very far.

He put more than ten large cacti in his office on the little tables near chairs and bestowed personalities on them. Not a bully, he would still, when feeling playful, say to someone, "Watch out. The cactus on the right of you is okay, but don't let your arm hit the cactus on the left because it will come off in your hand and it is dangerous as hell." It made some people quite wary. In those days you could "credit card anything," he would say, and the power he had, or lacked, or hoped to acquire, kept him bewitched. But he did not see the first faint twitches of something new coming closer that would put him in peril. He did not imagine that a film called *Saturday Night Fever* could upset his life, that disco music would wash everything else away.

"When I found something I believed in, I went crazy for it," said Mr. Godoff, not overstating his tendency. What made him crazy in California was a couple named Keller and Webb whom he wanted to manage and take to the top despite what he called their "self-destructive act." Keller was the songwriter and Webb the singer and his wife. Leaving his job, the office, the view, the playroom, and the butler, he formed Peter Godoff Management, expecting to produce and manage this gifted, stubborn pair who had not even hit the charts. He took on a country western singer as well.

"I spent two years of my life living and breathing Keller and Webb," Mr. Godoff said, who still sees them every day because an old poster he had made is on his wall. He believed that Keller and Webb would be taken on by Bob Dylan, who allegedly was making a deal with CBS Records to start his own recording company, called Accomplice. But, as it is said in the industry, the deal was not happening.

"Dylan went Christian," said Mr. Godoff, giving his version of the terrible events. "It fell through. For two years I worked with Keller and Webb. Gave them my heart and soul. Baby-sat, nurse-maided, let them cry on my shoulder. They were one of the most remarkable talents I ever heard; her voice was—ah, if you could hear it. The record companies wanted her, not him."

The funds he had been promised for his own company never came, so he spent his own savings. Keller and Webb were lured away by someone he was sure was a fraud, and no record company wanted his cowboy singer named Dan McCorrison, another client. The record business has no class, Mr. Godoff tells you, it's like the automobile business, without honor. He had been trusting about the money, which was withheld, and the loyalty, which was not there. And the timing was wrong for Dan McCorrison, who had only done one album.

"Finally after we faded into the sunset, Dan and I, about six months later, country western was the thing that hit. At the time Kenny Rogers hadn't hit yet, Willie Nelson hadn't hit yet. It wasn't until after *Saturday Night Fever* that people got bored with that disco shit. Ah, I hated disco. Well, timing is everything. Dan may be punching cows now. He was a cowboy from Colorado, a good songwriter, a manly voice. One of his songs, 'I Carry Your Smile,' went 'I carry your smile every mile, your light on every dark night, and something, something . . .' "

Keller and Webb were the ones who wounded him when they dismissed him. His sister, who saw things more coolly, thought of Fleetwood Mac when she heard Keller and Webb but nothing more, and assumed her brother's genuine devotion was not unrelated to the fact that Webb was adorable to him and unheralded. Her brother was always partial to California blondes or women with European accents. When the family moved from New York to Beverly Hills, it was he who immediately loved this new terrain; she, dark and worldly for her age, felt shock that the natives all looked alike, and she could not as easily get the swing of things.

"They had a nice little house in Hollywood, they were very clean people. They were not your typical musicians with beer cans all over the floor," Mr. Godoff said. "She would make little sandwiches and play the piano and sing to me. She'd wrap me around her little finger. I trusted my taste musically. The last time I talked to them was harsh. I said, 'You've really hurt yourselves, you've always done it to yourselves. I am the one person in this town who really believes in you, who gives you absolutely one hundred percent and trusts you.' She thought I wasn't powerful enough; they were selling me out for somebody else who had promised a bill of goods and who they thought had more power. I said, 'It's not the power that counts, it is someone like me who will give everything.' "

He thought when Peter Godoff Management came to an end that he had been horribly hit but was not a man who would die out. Back East he went to work in Portland, Maine—another dealership owned by a relative—this time not letting it be known he was a nephew. Here he was called Foreign Car Director and to his relief, sold only BMWs, Peugeots, and DeLoreans; the other men had the Cadillacs and the Oldsmobiles. These salesmen, so different, did not raise their voices, attack each other, steal customers, scheme, or flatter; people were not deceived or overwhelmed. Transactions were carried out in great calm and without the fierce and compulsive chatter he had made and heard back in the Bronx, where silence meant defeat. The salesmen in Maine were almost as somber and self-assured as physicians during office hours. In this new place he did well enough—even creating and producing his own television commercials for his cars—but knew something was irredeemably wrong and could not be corrected. Thinking of himself as a man who took some pride in being nicely dressed, it surprised him when the other salesmen signaled disapproval. "Peter, we don't wear red socks here," one of them said softly. On another day, when he wore expensive corduroy pants, a salesman quietly said, "Peter, we don't wear colored pants here." He loved eating the shrimp and lobster of Maine, a nice young woman liked him, sales were good, and he now knew it was true there were parts of his own country where he was slightly suspect. "It was lonely and strange for a New York Jew," Mr. Godoff said.

His mother's second husband was dying when he came back, and he did not keep himself apart from it by making excuses or leaving it to the women to root themselves by the hospital bed. His mother had been married for fifteen years and Norman was loved. When the older man could not walk, and no longer cared, it was his Peter who carried him to the bathroom. When his stepfather could not tolerate food, it was the stepson who would find strawberries and hold up a small, perfect one and plead, "Eat this for me." Sometimes Norman would even try. The young man had already been through the death of his Rosenstock grandfather, navigating through that illness with self-possession and unusual tenderness. He knew what was required when there would be no reprieve, how men looked when they had no life left. So much had been learned that October day when his father was sitting in that chair, a burnt orange wool, and no longer took a breath.

"After my father I had no problem with death," Mr. Godoff said. "I have a viewpoint which some people think is very cold."

When he enrolled in a restaurant school, serious about this new métier, he thought of nothing but preparing and serving food. Completing the course, he found his own job, one of junior rank, in the restaurant Le Périgord Park. Asked to bone a trout, he did and was hired. He took home $160 a week—once what he had paid for lunch in Beverly Hills, or a dinner at Mr. Chow's. He learned to put ice and lemon juice on his hands when he burned them in the ovens for the soufflés that were stacked and low. It hurt but the others always did it. He did some pastry. He was the garde-manger, which meant his station was the cold appetizers like fish mousses, vegetable terrines, and salads. He kept learning; soufflés became small triumphs. He did desserts of his own creation.

"It was so hard but it was wonderful," he said. A woman having dinner gave the maître d'hôtel ten dollars for him after eating one of his soufflés. Peter Godoff was deeply touched. He loved the chef, André Guillard, the master in the kitchen who would cry *vas-y, vas-y,* wanting them to go faster, and it was André who made it bearable to be in a kitchen, working six days a week from 1:45 until 11:30 P.M. for such meager wages. It was André Guillard who taught him how to make La Pomme Glacée Gatinaise and allowed him to make this dessert for the annual dinner of the Lucullus Circle, forty-five of whose members gathered in the main dining room taken over for the occasion. The menu would have crushed an average person, there were ten wines, a cognac and a marc. Afterwards, when some of the diners seemed close to snoozing, everyone from the kitchen, each one wearing a clean white toque and apron, gathered in the room to hear the president of the Lucullus Society comment on each course, each detail of the dinner. A hush fell for, after all, it was as if a conductor were discussing the performance of each musician in a symphony orchestra. His dessert was titled on the menu *l'Apothéose, La Pomme Glacée Gatinaise.* The apples removed from the skin were cooked with calvados, sugar, and butter, the skins baked then caramelized, the fruit mixed with fresh whipped cream and put back in the skins, all of it then covered with spun sugar and served with strawberry *coulis.* The dessert was favorably mentioned, indeed in a jovial tone. Feeling humble in that room, so grateful to be present when only twenty-eight, such praise pierced his heart. His burned hands did not matter, the odd hours that ate up his life, the strain, were forgotten.

Hugging and shaking hands, he left Le Périgord Park to cook in the kitchen of an Italian restaurant that was just opening, but it was not to his liking. His employer was a sour man who did not want Peter emerging from the kitchen to greet friends who had come in at his recommendation; there was even disapproval of his coming out to welcome his own mother. Now was the time to go out on his own, he could no longer loiter. Women in the family called, analyzed, fussed, consulted, inquired, hoped. There were small, steady portions of news: his banana sorbet went on the menu in the dining room of the Museum of Modern Art, in the cafeteria a machine served his grapefruit sorbet.

What he wanted was something of his own to captivate the world—if not a place, then a commodity which might be a gauge of the best of him. At nineteen he had been seized by a vision of what his life should be and it had not entirely disappeared, as a pulse will fluctuate but not stop. Since he had seen the film *Casablanca* twenty-five, perhaps thirty times—there was a point at which he stopped counting—he wanted to be Rick in a white dinner jacket, running Rick's Café, the gin joint, his face the thin and gloomy face of Bogart. He wanted to be able to say to the croupier, "Let that woman over there win on twenty-two." He dreamed, maybe still does, of opening a diner with booths on a fancy block off Fifth Avenue called Pete's Eats, the cutlery and china to be very good, the food excellent, the waitresses looking like women once did in the movies, chewing gum perhaps, their hair in pompadours. People would queue, applaud, come back, praise.

Let that woman over there win on twenty-two.

His grandfather Harry Godoff, named Hershel at birth, was born in a village in Russia and set forth on the perilous journey to America at the age of thirteen. His own mother had died, his father remarried, and children of that Russia had no childhood left at such an age. Remembering wisps of stories heard as a child, old refrains, laments for those dead, Peter Godoff says that Harry, the undefeated child, came, survived, rose, and then sent for the entire village from Russia. Details were not at hand. What mattered was the soul of the immigrant who would do that, bring a village to America.

Harry Godoff, forty-six years after his death, was still mourned by his daughters. In this country he had made his way by manufacturing cotton zip-up dresses in flower patterns that housewives wore during the day and called housecoats. He owned real estate in Brooklyn. He took his daughters to the opera and to concerts so that for themselves they saw the hands and violins of Jascha Heifetz and Mischa Elman and knew rapture as the parent did.

The facts were that Harry Godoff was from the village of Zelenitsa, near the town of Zhitomir, and in New York did raise with his own three the two children of a dead brother who had arrived here earlier. He brought over a sister, her husband, and their children. There was an attempt, too, to get out more relatives, but the transaction failed when their ranks swelled, when those who were not Harry's own relatives joined the group and the number grew alarming. All would come or no one, the word from Russia came back. It was beyond his means.

Peter Godoff loved this grandfather and kept the happy version of the story. That is what men in the Godoff family did: they sent for villages, they took children under their wings, they said, "Don't worry and it will be all right," and made money so that those of their own blood would be safe for a certain time and know, in this way, how they were loved.

Years and years after people quit *The New York Times* and were no longer reporters or foreign correspondents, they tended to remain peculiarly possessive about the newspaper and how it was being written and run, as if they had not left at all and their opinions were still of consequence. In the right company, the former foreign correspondents would sometimes give way to urgent reminiscences, rarely pleasant, emphasizing the injustices and stupidity they had suffered, often at the hands of editors who would query, chop, or weaken their stories. And yet the departure for nearly everyone was a shock. A cultural reporter even confessed he was so startled by the loss of this affiliation that he felt compelled to tell a man fixing his typewriter, at home, that he had written for the *Times*. Another man—for years soaked in the Third World, considering it his first world when he was now long out of it— dreamed from time to time of messages, tersely worded as always, the command clear: "Proceed to . . . *soonest.*" What had never changed was the covenant: the correspondent did not disobey. He proceeded soonest—to Katanga, to Lagos, to Saigon, to Nicosia, to Beirut, to Belfast, to San Salvador. The names blurred.

The principal players on the newspaper, having the most freedom and the most prestige, were still the foreign correspondents, although the Washington bureau would place itself first. In 1970 a woman was sent to the *Times* bureau in Vietnam, but it was still a regiment of males who provided the news from overseas. This changed but not too much: of thirty-five correspondents abroad in 1984, four of them were women. One had covered El Salvador by herself for two years, another was stationed in Cairo reporting on Arab countries. It was not a newspaper any longer of stern and watchful fathers, the hierarchy permanent, editors directing their own troops, bureau chiefs carrying out orders, men on the desk in New York assessing the work. Some women ran things too and were not more lenient. It was always presumed that those working abroad would be people of a certain exaggerated metabolism, nourished by crisis and more by chaos, forever willing to dance in and out of disaster and make the story sing, as they once said. It was not unlike joining the army, to be sure; the rank was decent, but one never knew what the final cost would be.

In Africa, Carey Winfrey was covering war and peace and wondering why. He did not like being a foreign correspondent at thirty-seven and hoped he would not disgrace himself with *The New York Times* by making his misery clear while still doing his duty. Years later, long gone from the newspaper, he would say he had simply been too old for it, although there were men his age and older doing a good job and caring deeply about whatever story they were hooked to. Much like ballet dancers and models, the Americans feared growing old and doing the same work; a man then in Cairo said he had nightmares at the thought of having to cover an OPEC meeting when he was sixty. A colleague was doing it. This worry ran through all of them: filing at fifty when your legs and your wind were gone unless you were in Paris or London, Bonn or Buenos Aires, Rome or Rio, where things turned up but not with such constant nastiness.

Carey Winfrey had prepared himself as best he could. He read books on Africa, he was briefed, he went through the old clips written by men he was never to meet and whose names now meant little. He shopped. He bought new shirts in case there was no one to do the wash. He even took with him his own bed sheets. He felt himself ready, if not eager, and was mistaken. He might have refused, but no reporter was going to do well at the *Times* unless he had been abroad, and that year there were no openings in the cushier spots.

There was, of course, a war for him when, late in the summer of 1979, he went to the prettiest city in Africa, Salisbury. The fighting in Zimbabwe was in its seventh year. The country's name was now African, but it had long been called Rhodesia in honor of Cecil Rhodes, who himself had seen to it that the territories astride the Zambesi River were taken by Britain, whose agents secured concessions and treaties from the principal African kings of the region. Many whites kept calling it Rhodesia and did not choose to observe the change. That month there was no hard, running story pushing the foreign press corps in Zimbabwe so that they had to forsake dinner or file when they needed sleep. Mr. Winfrey was not as roughened or nearly as reckless as some of his colleagues, who had been abroad much longer and worked other wars, at least one, sometimes three or four. Peace talks, to begin in London that September, had for them weakened the story in Zimbabwe even more, the war had gone on too long, like Vietnam or Northern Ireland. It was always a better assignment for the British: Rhodesia was their former colony whose rebellious declaration of independence from Britain in 1965 had led to fourteen years of crisis and eight major efforts to bring peace.

It was not, in any case, a story that seized the heart of Mr. Winfrey, who by now just knew degrees of depression, not release from it. But he went to work. In fact he went to the funeral of a man he never knew, to ask the mourners how they felt. When Holgar Jensen of *Newsweek* heard about it, he thought it peculiar, that going to a funeral was somehow unwholesome. He did not go to funerals *himself.* It was clear Mr. Jensen thought it a sly, not quite manly, thing to do.

It was not an auspicious time for a newcomer. At this point the press was distracted by the story shifting to London, predicting among themselves with some repetition that the peace talks would surely break off. The peace talks did not. Needing story ideas, Mr. Winfrey, diligent if downhearted, found out about the dead man by reading the local morning newspaper, *The Herald,* whose death notices and readers' letters were always of interest. The others, except for the UPI man who kept extensive notes and records, were in a slump at this point, behaving like journalists whose lives required something larger and perhaps more terrible, not just this endless struggle between black liberation forces and white colonials. Or, as a deeply bored English writer put it, what came down to five men with rifles looking for five other men with rifles.

Each month a thousand whites were leaving, only able to take out the equivalent of a thousand dollars, so their houses were easy to rent or to buy. No one spoke of a family trying to escape; there was a language for their leaving, an expression that sounded strangely triumphant but was not. It was "taking the gap," a rugby term for a player with the ball plunging through a hole in the opposition's line. There was always a good story on people "taking the gap" but an even better one, with its darker chords of heroics and death and ruin, on the whites who would not go. Interviews with Africans were trickier to do and not as likely to turn out well. It was not thought by some correspondents that people wanted to read about them anyway.

That August morning, however, with no real plans for the day, Mr. Winfrey noticed nine entries under *Deaths* for Field Reservist Donald Arthur Baker, a fifty-eight-year-old farmer in the Virginia district who like most white males—including those even older— did periods of military duty. He had been killed when his car struck a land mine on a dirt road near his farm about forty miles southeast of Salisbury. Mr. Winfrey, who wore a jacket and a necktie, rode in a taxi to the Anglican church in Marandellas, misjudged the distance and arrived at the end of the funeral. A shy, correct, and appealing man, he did not mind having to ask questions of the dead man's friends or relatives because it was for *The New York Times*. The name of the paper had the power of a rich, stable government, even there. He always said that gave him the courage to do things that might be awkward or embarrassing. The funeral for Mr. Baker, born in Rhodesia, who enlisted in the Air Force during World War II, was shot down, captured, reported dead, and held four years as a prisoner of war by the Germans, was not meager or rushed. A good many whites came, experts by now at putting on stoic funeral faces, the younger men holding rifles, and after the church service, everyone moving on to a tea at the district commissioner's house. It was an imposing place with a fine lawn and garden and brilliant marmalade bushes. "Mr. Baker's mourners drank tea, ate cakes, and crumpets, and wondered who among them would be the next to die," Mr. Winfrey wrote later. He circulated easily, a proper and respectful American with a neat little brown beard, asking questions in a low voice, never pushing, his face so attentive and patient that even the widow did not mind talking to him. She did not, for a second, give way, but spoke urgently of how she was "sticking," of how she would not go to South Africa, she would run their place herself. There was a eulogy by a friend—a man who had long ago left England and been happy in his new country; the friend came close to breaking down and did not permit it to happen. He said that all of us would meet someday in heaven and that the young men there would have to look Don Baker straight in the eye, as Mr. Baker had always looked people in the eye, and tell him they had done their best, that Rhodesia was just the same as when he left it. Some women could not manage to hear all this; a few leaned against their young husbands as if dread had suddenly jellied their legs. The men permitted themselves some response: an arm around a woman's shoulder, a slight pressure of the hand, a word or two, but no more.

Mr. Winfrey, who had made a name for himself as a charming and inventive writer on the metro desk in New York, had very little trouble with such a story, which ran two days later. It was, at that point, one of his better weeks in Africa, although he remained suspicious. The weather was perfect, sweaters needed at night. The Hotel Meickles was splendid, with elderly white housekeepers, some with Scottish accents, supervising each floor. The rooms did not smell of disinfectant or insect spray. Laundry came back. The lights did not go out. The hotel restaurant had an excellent menu, educated or wealthy Africans were also at ease eating there, the service was very good. Salisbury was not a dying city where restaurants closed for several days because there was no food. He knew the jacaranda trees were beautiful, the city haunting—the rest of us said so often enough.

But his life had been so disturbing, he still showed strain. And I, who had met him in New York in his debonair days, thought a small tic was at work in his face but was mistaken. He seemed jumpy and tired, a man serving his sentence and no longer curious about its effect. Meeting him in the hall of the hotel one morning, I asked him how he felt. Working on a magazine article, I was feeling tip-top, relieved not to be in the Federal Palace in Lagos, the Ambassador in Accra. He gave a wan smile: "Oh, just the usual assortment of fears, hopes, dreams, anxieties, insecurities—different kind but of the same weight and shape." He knew that I had once needed and loved such a life with the *Times*, but he was certain now that he was not suited to it, that nothing about it would ever be endearing, no matter what I said. The sound of the telephone in his hotel room, for example, made him fearful it was the foreign desk in New York calling, that he would suddenly be ordered to Nigeria again, or Chad, or the Central African Empire, that a coup in some small country would be looming up, some disaster that required coverage, and, thus, his immediate presence despite all obstacles. That month, there were only two correspondents for the *Times* in all of Africa—Mr. Winfrey and John Burns in Johannesburg. It chilled his blood. He said he had forty-five countries to watch when Mr. Burns went to Europe.

He was a changed man now, not deeply resembling the cheerful Winfrey in New York who had just come back from covering the Jonestown massacre in Guyana with several other *New York Times* reporters, an assignment he considered *overseas under duress*. The Jonestown assignment gave him great confidence; he saw himself now as a man ready to write the hard news, a man rising, his ascent now clear. It was his first try at reporting abroad on what he thought was a foreign story. When he was invited to join the foreign staff, it seemed a glorious idea and sent him to stores, long lists in hand. He was to be based in Nairobi, covering the sub-Sahara north of the Zambesi River. That day in New York at lunch, he did not seem to grasp what lay ahead, what abominable forces can work against you. He left for Africa with two trunks of sheets and towels, notebooks of the kind he preferred, and enough trousers to last several years.

"I arrived in February asking, What have I done, everyone I care about is somewhere else, but thinking that would pass," Mr. Winfrey said, glad at last to be spreading out his pain. "I spent two weeks in Nairobi, opening bank accounts and things like that, then to Nigeria for three weeks. One of my first shocks when I had been there a week was an assignment to do a piece for the Business Day section on the Nigerian oil industry and its future. I had spent my whole professional life avoiding such pieces." It was inconceivable to cable New York that he could not or would not do the piece. He was scarcely a meek man, but neither was he a trouble-maker willing to inflame editors and get off to a bad start. The story was tiresome, the interviews were hard to get, solid information scarce, the idea tedious. On the third unproductive day he returned exhausted to his room at the Federal Palace in Lagos, where the air-conditioning and the lights often went off, wanting to lie down. He needed a nap but instead slept until 3 A.M. On waking he saw that the door, which he had forgotten to double-lock, was open and that he no longer possessed a Rolex watch from the Marine Corps Okinawa PX—"the good one, before they started putting dates on them," he said later—about two hundred dollars in Nigerian currency, all his credit cards, and a tape recorder. The theft turned him into a man devoid of will and purpose. He sat for some time in the bathtub, hearing strange noises of loss and of grieving coming from his own abdomen, noises he had never imagined he could make. He was still sitting in water when the hotel security guard knocked.

"The security man comes in. I hastily throw a towel around me and try to mop my red eyes. The security man says, 'I'm standing outside the door and hear sounds.' Then he begins to imitate me, he moans over and over. I keep saying, 'I know, I know, that was me. My watch is gone, my Rolex which I've had since 1965.' The security man continues to moan. Well, I spent the whole day reporting the robbery to the police in a police station. It required about five different forms to be signed and going to the head of a line that had forty people on it, paying the bribe, and facing their jeers when I came out. But at that point I was willing to take any shortcuts due to privilege, skin, gender, money in the pocket—whatever."

He did not think of himself as a sheltered, self-indulgent man, but that day in Lagos convinced him that he had made a *grievous* mistake, that the whole thing was a catastrophe and that his life—which had always seemed, by luck and by chance, to be interesting and productive—had taken an alarming turn. He was astonished at how long it took—sometimes six, seven, or eight hours—to get a story to New York that had taken two hours to write. That year foreign correspondents did not have portable computers, which might have made a difference to him; he had always loved using the computer terminal in New York.

There was no one around, especially another American, whom Mr. Winfrey could admire or emulate except his colleague, John Burns, but Mr. Burns had grown up in South Africa and then gone to Canada with his family after Sharpeville. The British often had a certain wildness, a calculated lunacy, that was new to Mr. Winfrey. "Hacks" they would often call themselves, with some glee. Very often the press corps covered the same story in a great fretful lump, driving out to the countryside to hear the Bish—the nickname for the Methodist Bishop Abel Muzorewa, who was black and headed a new government still managed by whites—or other official speakers who did not know when to cut it off. After such a day, a Brit would call it a "hack horror show." The Americans, who commuted to Salisbury from Nairobi or Johannesburg, bringing in wine and cigarettes, did not make fun of their profession, were not disposed to call themselves hacks. The idea was horrifying. It was not their kind of wit; they preferred irony, or the soft, mocking lament of Jack Foisie of *The Los Angeles Times*, who was sixty that summer. A lean, white-haired man with a small smile of considerable sweetness, he was often taken to be the perfect specimen of a true-blue, nicely aged American country boy. This was hardly the case, although it was a useful camouflage at times.

"Yahoo, another one for the memory book," Mr. Foisie would say in his nice, low voice, with the permanent curl to his mouth. You said it in airports where the flights, late taking off and late landing, took you places where you did not want to go; in hotel rooms where the phones did not work or were of no use even if they did; driving down no-name roads, probably mined, to find out not much at military briefings whose purpose is to conceal, not inform; on any day so futile and frustrating your life looked like an excerpt from *Looney Tunes*.

One more for the memory book. In his room at the Hotel Meickles —where all the transient correspondents stayed, advising each other to have laundry done by Lameck, the room boy on the sixth floor—Mr. Foisie was watching television before it was time to eat. He liked the Meickles, and the other correspondents had given him a birthday party in its rather grand restaurant when he reached sixty. He had five years to go before he could return to the United States and retire on a farm near Seattle which he had helped one of his children buy. He and his wife, Mickey, had not much liked living in Cairo, but they were happy in Johannesburg and wanted to stay. He was not sure when this tour was up if he would be kept on in Africa. He hoped so.

"It all depends on how I do," Foisie said. He did not seem to think this a strange or self-deprecating thing to say. It was simply the truth. It did not count that he had covered three generations of American men in three very different wars. He understood the perishability, the immediate obsolescence, of yesterday's dispatch. None of it counted. And if he knew the sepsis that can afflict a foreign correspondent, the peril of doing it too long, he did not speak of it to us. This was not a man to splash sorrow around. One night at dinner in the large house of the UPI man, whose meticulous files we all consulted, Mr. Foisie listened as Carey Winfrey kept explaining why he was quitting the foreign staff, how awful he thought his life in Africa had been, and how he was longing to get back to work in New York—his voice rising, even though everyone knew exactly what he was saying. I tried to catch his eye or kick him under the table. What Mr. Winfrey was also saying— it came close to being insulting—was that he could not fathom why other men stuck it out.

"We hadn't planned to spend our lives this way," Mr. Foisie said. "We're just passing through." He could always raise a laugh. Mr. Winfrey was able to elaborate the next day when he was calmer.

"I don't want to develop those parts of myself which would make me 'better,' " he said. "I don't want to get better at bribing the telex operator. I don't want to develop the talents of a foreign correspondent. I want to be a better writer and understand people better, not learn how to get Pan Am to put me on a plane that's already booked. The time spent out here is all wrong for me— sixty percent on logistics, twenty-five percent reporting, five percent writing."

The loss of what he had given up in New York, where he had been a reporter for two years, kept jolting him like a series of electric shocks. He had a marvelous apartment, a splendid ex-wife who, despite the divorce, remained a good friend, a job where you had two days off and went home at 7 P.M., movies, good food, bookstores, and an enchanting young French girlfriend who also worked at the *Times*. He felt all his energy was being seized from him in airport waiting rooms, in hassles with immigration people.

His loneliness was huge, unrelenting. He did not get a house in Nairobi because he was rarely there. He had once believed and acted on the principle that it was almost a duty to make the most of your potential. Sign me up for everything. If tapped, don't say no. He had never suspected he would loathe being a foreign correspondent, and one way of calming himself was to keep a record of the wretchedness, although he tended to keep records of everything that happened to him anyway. He was, as his former wife once said, a man who firmly believed an undocumented life is a life not worth living. So he kept a list of the fifty-one flights he had made since late February 1979 through August. It read like a dirge: Nairobi–Lagos–Kano–Lagos–Cotonou–Lomé–Abidjan–Accra–Dar es Salaam–Kampala–Nairobi–London–Dakar–Monrovia–Accra–Douala–N'Djamena–Douala–Nairobi. There was a wonderful break when he went to New York to tell them he didn't want to be on the foreign staff anymore, was forgiven and told he could come home in November when a replacement went out. And then, back to the old beat: Monrovia–Accra–Khartoum–Nairobi–Lusaka–Salisbury–Nairobi–Salisbury–Johannesburg–Kinshasa . . . , the list of the different flights he had made in less than eight months grew longer and more onerous. In Lagos he knew exactly what story was the 250th that he had written for *The New York Times*.

He missed—horribly—the third floor of the *Times*, the huge newsroom with its maniacal energy, its rivalries and tribalism that always fascinated him. Most foreign correspondents dreaded and feared the place, not wishing to sit among 140 reporters, under the eye of A. M. Rosenthal, the managing editors, and the men in his cabinet.

Mr. Winfrey was different: he understood how to do well in institutions, how they work and what is required from you. As a boy he had been sent by his well-known father, Bill Winfrey, the trainer of Native Dancer and other horses in the stables of Alfred G. Vanderbilt, to a military school outside of Baltimore. He spent summers in Saratoga during the racing season until he was seventeen. He went to Columbia; spent three years in the Marine Corps, one of them on Okinawa, another in California as an adjutant in an infantry training regiment where he processed men who had begun to show unacceptable behavior disorders; went to the Columbia School of Journalism, where he won a Pulitzer Traveling Fellowship; worked in Hong Kong; decided not to write about the Vietnam War; and landed his first job at *Time* magazine reporting, and later writing the press section. He was good. He loved it. Mr. Winfrey bloomed and was noticed. He left to become executive producer of "Behind the Lines," a television program on the press for the PBS station in New York, until the funds for it expired. He and his wife, Laurie, went around the world for five months, and he thought for the first time it might be interesting, certainly challenging, to one day be a foreign correspondent. His memoirs, *Starts and Finishes* (a justification to be sure for documenting his life so thoroughly) was published in 1975—a coming of age in the fifties (as the book jacket pointed out), its author reaching manhood during the decade that ended with the death of President John F. Kennedy. What made the book of interest was his famous father, and *his* father, also a horse trainer, but what was most unusual about it was Mr. Winfrey's attention to detail. Pearl Harbor was attacked not when he was an infant of four months, but an infant of four months and *one week*. His parents met in Miami Beach, his father had gone to Florida to race his horses. She was pretty, tiny, animated, often silly, working in a branch of Best & Company as a model. They were married in 1939. When World War II came, his father joined the marines. Few details of their lives seemed unknown to their son.

Their first few years together were dazzling. The young up-and-coming trainer with his pretty wife was much in demand. They went to parties; they got the best tables at restaurants and nightclubs in Miami, New Orleans, New York, and Saratoga. They took fishing trips to Havana and had ringside tickets to the fights at Madison Square Garden. For my mother there were sequined dresses, new cars, a mink coat, and a house in Miami.

Parris Island came as an enormous shock to her. She was unprepared for the tiny, dirty room with the toilet down the hall that the United States Marine Corps deemed appropriate for the wives and children of privates first class. She took it personally that she was not allowed in the officers' club. She found the enlisted men's club loud and rowdy. After two days

she returned to New York to await word from my
father that he had found suitable accommodations.

So pampered was the boy by his mother that many years later,
visiting him in New York, Mrs. Winfrey, recalling the gaiety of the
war years in Miami, remembered the time she was wearing an
ermine jacket and Carey was eating an ice-cream cone. She picked
him up, the white fur was smeared with blobs of chocolate; she
didn't care at all, and kissed the child. He was two when his father
left and four when he came back. The peaceful years were over.
Mr. Winfrey wrote,

> My mother's idea of child raising was based on
> the pleasure principle. Make me happy. Keep me
> smiling. Straighten my room. Buy me toys. If I
> wanted it, serve me French toast every morning with
> Vermont Maid syrup. And if I did not like plain,
> white cow's milk, let me have chocolate milk.
> "Chocolate milk!" My father, who had lived on
> C rations for weeks at a time and was proud of it, was
> aghast. Tell him I was out stealing hubcaps. Tell him
> I had played doctor with the little girl across the
> street. Tell him I had driven his car into a palm tree.
> But don't tell him I wanted chocolate milk. Not at
> breakfast.
> The more outraged at my pampered behavior my
> father got, the more my mother sought to make life
> easier for me. The more she softened my path, the
> more he sought to toughen it. (The pattern, thus
> established, was to last for more than a decade. In
> years to come he contrived summer jobs for me away
> from what he considered the protective atmosphere
> created by my mother. He sent me to a military
> boarding school, the deprivations of which so of-
> fended my mother that on vacations she spoiled me
> to extravagance, creating a kind of geographically in-
> duced schizophrenia.)
> My mother became more openly affectionate; my
> father increasingly hid his love behind a stern facade.
> He fervently believed that I needed toughness more

than anything else and that if he didn't provide it, no
one would.

The divorce came when he was at McDonogh, a military
school outside of Baltimore where he learned to be so fantastically
tidy that for the rest of his life he could not tolerate any disorder:
an unwashed dish, a gray bathtub, unaligned hangers in a closet,
unfiled papers were offensive. It was at his father's insistence that
he was taken from his mother in Miami and sent there at the age
of ten. The boy's parting from her provided his first unmanageable
sorrow. The school was only a few miles down the road from Alfred
Vanderbilt's Sagamore Farms, where the stable's brood mares, stal-
lions, and yearlings were kept. It meant that his father would be
able to see him. At any rate, it was explained that the move was
necessary. "In short it would make me a man," Mr. Winfrey wrote.
"When he put it that way I found it difficult to argue. Naturally I
wanted to be made a man of."

As a child, going to the stables with his father, he had learned
to ride as few children ever do, high in the saddle, wanting the
stirrups as short as possible, even later, when full grown, remembering Eric Guerin, who rode Native Dancer, and Eddie Arcaro,
considered the best jockey in the world. The French woman once
complained wistfully that it was not pretty to see him on a horse,
all bunched up like that with his bottom sticking in the air, but
she did not know much about exercise boys or jockeys. Family life
was ruled by racing schedules: it was every spring, summer, and
fall in New York at Aqueduct, Belmont, Jamaica, and Saratoga.
November through March meant Florida: Hialeah, Gulfstream,
and Tropical Park.

His life at *The New York Times* began after he met A. M. Rosen-
thal, the managing editor, on assignment to write a profile for Clay
Felker, who was then running his own magazine, *New York*. Mr.
Rosenthal consented to an interview, but the finished story, too
unwieldy, never ran, although the two became friendly. It was not
Mr. Winfrey's wish to make enemies or write psychiatric case his-
tories, and he was flattered that the older man clearly liked him.
"When are you going to come here to make an honest living?" Mr.

Rosenthal asked Carey Winfrey, not an invitation that could be nonchalantly turned down. He joined the *Times* in March 1977, writing features, which was what he most wanted to do, not hard news or investigative pieces. Attentive readers of the paper began to know his name, which seemed to him a gauge of this very good new life.

In Africa, there was little praise except for a message sometimes from the foreign desk on a nice piece, such messages being called "herograms" and always a source of strength to the recipients. Friendships sprang up fast with other journalists he met in his travels based on "incredible, desperate mutual need," Mr. Winfrey said. Once in Lagos, coming back from the airport despondent—he had gone there to catch a flight which no longer existed, whose only reality was on a worthless schedule—he saw a large crowd assembling on Bar Beach with five stakes rising from a newly built, high platform on the sand. It was for an execution. He behaved as he thought a good reporter should, rushing there to interview the doomed men, and was able to speak to two of them. One man, with less than an hour to live, said in English he thought capital punishment for armed robbery should be continued. He watched the men die from a terrace in an expensive apartment house overlooking the beach. He had noticed signs of a large, fancy party going on in the building and politely asked if he could join. The host was delighted. The guests, in their London suits and expensive dresses, were in a playful mood, reminding him of New Yorkers at a Tall Ships party. But this was to watch an execution. All of the doomed men, including two Ghanaians, had committed armed robbery.

"What horrified me is how long it took," he said. "There was a squad of men but they didn't all fire at once. There were forty or maybe fifty shots. The bodies jerked back but they all stayed up. In the beginning they hit a number of them and then went from left to right. At the party people stopped to look and then went on talking. There was no horror expressed. Any questions I might ever have had about the deterrence of capital punishment were once and for all finally eliminated." When his story on crime in Lagos, the leading topic in the city, was published, it was the first piece of his he had seen in two months. In Abidjan, the capital of Ivory Coast, a Pan Am stewardess happened to have a copy of *The*

New York Times, and he was so stunned he blurted out "I wrote that story." But he felt, and quite correctly, that he was not doing his best work. He was beginning to write in cablese, he said.

After being on the road for six weeks he planned on meeting the young French woman in Paris, when a cable came which said, "Idi Amin falling advise fly Dar es Salaam for transport into Uganda soonest." *Soonest,* that word pierced him, an order to overcome all obstacles and go. Mr. Winfrey, who immediately slid into yet another depression, spent a week in Dar es Salaam trying to get into Uganda, reading and rereading about three books a day when the international press corps arrived. Nothing was the same.

"What a difference it made, instead of *them* against *me,* it was now *us* against *them,*" Winfrey said. "Suddenly there was someone to have breakfast with, lunch with, dinner with, and to bemoan the inefficiency and lack of that respect which we all thought we deserved," he said. The Tanzanian authorities drew up lists of journalists who wished to go to Uganda. Then a fresh set of lists was compiled, giving rise to vicious rumors that so-and-so's name had been left off. Finally the press was promised it would be flown into Entebbe and told to be ready at 5 A.M. in the lobby of the Kilimanjaro Hotel. With cameras, knapsacks, typewriters, and suitcases, the press was ready to go. Nothing happened. Every face, every ashtray, showed the effects of such a tiresome wait. At 3 P.M. they were moved out, put on a plane, flown to a military base, and told that Entebbe was locked in. There was a messy scene when the reporters were informed they had a choice of going back to Dar or on to Arusha; such an option divided them into two hostile groups and began a fierce, impolite debate.

"Grown men screaming and yelling, with leaders emerging in the two camps," Mr. Winfrey said. "You were suddenly back in the fifth grade deciding where to take the class trip." It was somehow determined that all of them would go to Arusha. So they did. He remembers the British reporters as being rowdier and yet sometimes more reasoned. In the bus a major fistfight seemed about to start between a BBC cameraman—a former heavyweight champion in Sierra Leone—and a British television correspondent who had the elocution and poise of an old boy from a good public school. Others kept them apart. A conspiracy theory took hold that the journalists were being deliberately kept out of Uganda.

"Through all of this a growing sense that I had gotten myself into something similar to the Marine Corps, which at the time had seemed worth enduring to make a point," Winfrey said. "But at age thirty-seven the idea of doing something to make the same point had lost its appeal."

It came as something of a shock that the Mt. Meru Hotel in Arusha was so gloriously efficient, handling the band of ill-tempered and suspicious reporters as if such visitors were an everyday occurrence. In five minutes everyone had keys, rooms, hot baths, showers, drinks, and courteous attention. The next day they did indeed reach Kampala, which had been "liberated" by Tanzanian troops only two days before and was a city of joy, flowers, ringing voices, and tears of thankfulness. People threw flowers at the bus, so the reporters began to behave like real people, smiling and waving back and feeling buoyant themselves. It was thrilling, Mr. Winfrey had never known anything like it, it was life at its richest. He was reminded of what he had read about the liberation of Paris, and he realized he might be happy at last. Everyone was. Nothing went wrong. The journalists went to Parliament to see the new president, Yusufe Lule, sworn into office. *"Oyee, oyee Lule,"* people shouted. Hurray for Lule. Mr. Winfrey, with a fat, full notebook and high spirits, did not know where to send his story out, for the single switchboard at the hotel, not working, was ringed by desperate journalists who assumed they would be accommodated. A police officer saw Mr. Winfrey was wandering about, inquired if he might help, and then led Mr. Winfrey to the Central Telegraph office, where the reporter saw "wonderful, happy young Ugandan men running switchboards, doing miraculous things," and knew he was saved. An American television correspondent for ABC-TV was on the line to his office in New York and, somehow, had someone call and connect him to Joe Lelyveld, then the assistant foreign editor of the *Times.* So Mr. Winfrey was able to hear a voice from his own newspaper saying congratulations, you have a good story. He wrote it in the post office. He got through to New York in ten minutes and began dictating to a man in the recording room named Charlie Kline, whom, he said, most foreign correspondents have never met but feel is their closest friend. There was never another day abroad when he so reveled in what he was doing.

But the next day was the other side of it. By 3 P.M. all communications out of Uganda to the rest of the world were cut off, and only the wire services had moved their stories out in time. The paper led with a Reuters story, and the one Mr. Winfrey had done was wasted.

A week later, Mr. Winfrey and the others went to Jinja, the second largest city in Uganda, where Field Marshal Idi Amin was expected to make a last stand. The Sudanese ambassador in Kampala gave a British television correspondent his own Mercedes in exchange for an airplane ticket out of the country. Mr. Winfrey was in a minibus which broke down, when Mohammed Amin, a Nairobi-based film cameraman–photographer, considered by all as brillant on logistics in Africa, stopped on the road in a full jeep.

"I dashed for the jeep, remembering how Peter Arnett had run for a helicopter in Guyana," Winfrey said. "Four of us got on, four were left behind. Another example of the kind of talent I don't wish to develop."

Everyone, sooner or later, who worked in Vietnam seemed to have a memory of Peter Arnett of the Associated Press, and there were many men who wanted to be like him. An admirer once said he looked like the French actor Belmondo, with that nose and that smile. He was a legend among American journalists, not just because he often had the news first but because he wrote so well. He worked in Vietnam from 1962 until 1970 for AP, then each year until 1975 he would come back for a few months, a historian of the war whose own life was so deeply hammered in that history. He saw generations of young soldiers arrive and leave—their tour in Vietnam was only a year—and he was not much like the silly *Time* correspondent who said: "It was the thrilling Hemingway life at last: danger, excitement, and mud." There was a huge American press corps in Vietnam, sometimes numbering five hundred, but it wasn't a foreign story at all. For most of them, who simply tracked the American troops, it was a local story. Mr. Arnett did not see the Vietnamese as shadows, as nuisances, as ingrates; he married a Vietnamese woman, whose own family knew sorrow and were silent about it. He was the reporter who during the 1968 Tet Offensive heard an American major, explaining why the town of Ben Het had been demolished, say: "We had to destroy it in order to save it." The remark was widely quoted for some years in the United States. Other reporters heard the major too, but perhaps they had a protective deafness by then. The sentence of a major didn't mean much during Tet.

In April 1975, when the war was ending at last and each day brought fresh infusions of panic among the Americans, the press corps was shrinking as people left, believing that to wait was to invite capture or death. Mr. Arnett had no intention of joining the final American evacuation on April 29; it seemed astonishing to him that any journalist would pull out when he was about to have the best story of his life. And he thought the Vietnamese would take over in an orderly way, which they did. One bus, full of American reporters, was held up not untypically for five hours in Saigon before it reached Tan Son Nhut. Mr. Arnett, passing the bus bulging with his old colleagues, was stopped in the street by two officers in the South Vietnamese army. Each man was with a child of his own. The men wanted to get out and pleaded with Mr. Arnett for help. He kept saying there was nothing he could do, which was true. The Vietnamese officers began to beg and he could not bear it. Finally Mr. Arnett had the driver open the bus door and quickly pushed the Vietnamese inside, almost tossing the men in before the driver could interfere. The passengers, his American friends and colleagues, didn't want any Vietnamese with them and started shouting, "No, no, no!" Mr. Arnett held the bus door shut so the Vietnamese and their children could not be pushed out. The bus left with them.

The next day there were only a few American journalists in Saigon and many more foreign reporters. Nearly one hundred and fifty American journalists had left. In the afternoon Mr. Arnett wrote—as he had done thousands of times before—the dateline "Saigon, South Vietnam," never to be used again, in his final dispatch of that war, describing the first pith-helmeted, green-uniformed Viet Cong soldiers to spill into Saigon around noon on April 30. It was a long story—about two thousand words—and he did not have that much time, but nothing he ever wrote was better: "Then as awestruck residents watched, heavily armed infantrymen weaved their way past the last flimsy barricades of oil drums and sandbags, and Saigon was theirs."

In Guyana in 1978, the press had been flown to the nearest airstrip outside of Jonestown, and informed that helicopters would take them there in shuttles if they would assemble themselves in groups of ten. Mr. Winfrey was told *The New York Times* would be on the second shuttle and saw no reason to fuss or to conspire. Mr. Arnett, never one to rely on official arrangements, realized the weather could turn bad and that he had better get on that first flight. He ran for it, others began to race behind him. On that day Mr. Winfrey thought it a shaming spectacle: the press couldn't follow instructions and carried on like animals,

"I was being quite supercilious and quite ashamed of our colleagues," he said later, in Africa. "I learned. You never wait. It's a question of what might be there, of compiling a certain bag of tricks. I admire those who do." He always remembered how Peter Arnett suddenly started sprinting.

In Jinja, the reporters went right in, side by side, with a brigade of Tanzanian soldiers, who were sometimes firing their rifles and often being lovingly touched by ecstatic civilians pitching bougainvillea blossoms, *oyee, oyee*. Males were rounded up and made to stip to the waist to see if they had any marks on their shoulders from rifle slings or packs that would identify them as soldiers. Some civilians fought over the towels, blankets, and calico print cotton as they looted a textile factory. *Oyee, oyee*.

Africa blessed Carey Winfrey that day in Jinja. When he moved with the troops, he knew love. It made it much uglier when, after ten weeks, he went back to Uganda. President Lule had resigned his office and was succeeded by a fifty-nine-year-old British-trained lawyer. What was promised and did not happen in Uganda made him very sad and hardened what he felt: nothing good was going to happen in these countries and he did not want a historical analysis that contradicted such an opnion. He did not need any more proof.

But his affliction had more to do with himself than with the poverty and disorder he so constantly saw. There was his own fear of what he could become in time if he stayed abroad and ended up like the other men, not much minding it anymore. He was in Zimbabwe when he brought all this up, in a war zone with soldiers everywhere, and white men in their sixties going into the reserves to do their bit, and the seductive warriors in the special units like the Selous Scouts. The unit was named for Frederick Courtney Selous, an Englishman who became the most celebrated elephant hunter on the continent and whose great admirers quite naturally included President Theodore Roosevelt, who wrote of him, "He led a singularly adventurous and fascinating life." The Selous Scouts were considered very tough indeed, and did not always appreciate being compared to the American Green Berets, whom they thought of as amateurs, it was said. On trips Mr. Winfrey did not seem as fascinated by a war zone as did some of the others.

"The interesting thing about Guyana was half the reporters were wearing clothes they had had made in Saigon—oh, safari suits and pajama outfits with epaulets. Always khaki. The affinity between the foreign correspondent and the military is amazing, and it's reflected in what we wear. The parallels between the military and the longtime foreign correspondent—the roughing it, the manhood, the endurance, the stoicism.

"If you're not careful, after three or four months you're going to have an evening's worth of war-stories-or-hardship-or-funny-stories-of-adversity-overcome with the other guys around the bar, and you start finding out you really are enjoying it," he said. "If you take being a foreign correspondent to the limit, then you become a Selous Scout."

Before his birthday he asked if he might come home and New York said yes. A. M. Rosenthal greeted him warmly when he appeared, indeed it was noted by some that he even hugged Carey Winfrey. That November he was in New York again, cheerful and confident, not at all the same man I had known and felt so sorry for in the Nairobi airport when we arrived together late one night on a flight from Johannesburg. That night Mr. Winfrey's suitcase had not come out with the other baggage. He accepted it almost passively as a predictable blow, realized he might never see it again, knew exactly what shirts were now gone, and went straight to the *Times* office in the middle of the night prepared to write off yet another loss and open the mail.

Back on general assignment in New York, the second story he wrote was about the balmy weather in New York on Thanksgiving weekend. "I know I should feel I am too old, I am too serious to be doing a weather story," Winfrey said. "But I liked it, it was fun."

But no longer that much fun, so in time, without making a fuss, he left. Unlike so many others who resigned, he had no real grievances. He was not quitting because of an unforgivable transgression, a great story butchered, cruel messages, unreasonable editors, or any suspicion on their part that he was getting out of hand. Before, he had always left jobs assuming it was for the best and that something just as fine would come along. His was a life without narrow squeaks. He did not think it worked against him, switching so often. It seemed as if he wanted something work would not provide and was restless, holding no convictions about exactly what work he should be doing. He wrote a screenplay and began a novel, not unusual ambitions for a journalist but ones that rarely yielded the expected. He was lonely, the apartment shone, never to be so maniacally neat again. The French woman suddenly seemed too young for him, he thought. At night she wanted to go to parties, to discos, delighted by noise and crowds when he wanted to sleep. They parted but remained dear friends; he never provoked anger in women when they ceased being lovers, not a man this affectionate and reasonable.

After his marriage to Jane Keeney, a painter, their Christmas card carried a colored photograph of their faces; two nicer faces you could not hope to see in your mail. In March 1983 Jane Keeney and Carey Winfrey—who did not call themselves Mr. and Mrs. or anything—announced the birth of their twin sons, Graham William and Wells Millar, and he lost no time in beginning their scrapbooks. When only a few months old, the infants were held up to see Native Dancer in an old film on television. Mr. Winfrey no longer walked through rooms with a can of Ajax and a sponge looking for dirt. Dirt did not matter so much, he no longer fussed. He became an American husband in a new age of reform, helping with babies, the meals for all of them, the logistics, for his wife worked too. He shirked nothing and reasoned that he probably did forty-eight percent of what was called home management, better than most married men. He loved his job as he had always loved all his jobs in New York: this time it was being the editor of a CBS magazine called *Cuisine*, which he improved.

Explaining himself, he would recall one of the last interviews he wrote for *The New York Times*, going to Connecticut to visit the poet Robert Penn Warren. The poet told him: "A young man's ambition to get along in the world and make a place for himself— half your life goes that way. Then if you're lucky, you make terms with life, you get released."

He had been lucky, Mr. Winfrey said. In Africa he had never

imagined that what he wanted was children; such an idea was so remote. But now the two babies made him feel that to have only one child at a time was deprivation, not nearly enough. He knew tenderness he had not known himself or thought about. He talked about his sons.

The old life became very distant; he did not think about the sorrow or excitement of it. Journalists he had known in Africa would come through the city and be certain of a welcome, but then fewer of them came. There were new countries calling them. Reading *The New York Times*, he was saddened to see what the men who came after him in Africa had to report. An editorial denounced Prime Minister Robert Mugabe for his campaigns against the Ndebele minority. Alan Cowell wrote from Zimbabwe that Joshua Nkomo, an early leader of Zimbabwe's independence movement, the rival of Prime Minister Mugabe, who was now considered powerless, said, "If this is a democracy we fought for, then we did not understand each other." When the Winfrey twins were eighteen months old, *The New York Times* correspondent Clifford May filed from Uganda that the State Department estimated that as many as one hundred thousand fatalities—by slaying and starvation—had resulted from the Ugandan army's actions to eliminate guerrillas opposed to the president. The president, Milton Obote, complained that terrible things were being said and that if people compared the present government with the reign of Idi Amin, they were dreaming. "They have not tasted suffering," he said. Others knew him to be wrong.

In New York, Carey Winfrey and his wife tried to be in bed by eleven, ten was better. The old dreams of messages, of calls from the foreign desk, did not rot his sleep. Africa made no claims. He planned to tell the children. He would speak of the day in Kampala when people had thrown flowers in the streets in their rapture and hailed everyone who passed before them, and how he had stopped taking notes to wave and smile back.

In the office of *Cuisine*, Mr. Winfrey was talking to a Vietnamese writer in California, Tran Tuong Nhu, assigning her to write about her mother. This extraordinary woman always refused to cook until she was taking a triple degree at Oxford University and began to long for the food of her own country, the daughter said. In a rented room, the mother, with only her memories of tastes and no recipes, began cooking on a hot plate. The assignment pleased him for, as Mr. Winfrey felt, he was hired to find good writers, not because he knew the difference between *blanquette de veau* and *navarin de veau*. But he was learning that.

"This is more fun than writing about Nigerian oil," Mr. Winfrey said to a friend who had known him in Africa.

Men of a certain standing, usually with substantial salaries, like saying their jobs are "fun." The Secretary of the Navy, who must persuade Congress to embrace his weapons budgets and strategic theories, said his job was the best in Washington and "the most fun." A broker says he has had fun trading on the market. Women do not often use the word *fun* to describe their work, even if they like it immensely. Men who said it meant they had the upper hand, the game was going their way, they were in no danger of losing control.

Mr. Winfrey, however, really did mean fun: the November issue included pieces on mail-order hams, chocolates for cooking, a Thanksgiving dinner for two, an essay translated from Russian on the joys of eating *chebureki*, and a short essay, "Laying Up for Winter," by Henry David Thoreau. So when *Cuisine* was suddenly and secretly sold to another publisher for a very good profit, he felt strangely bereaved. Even when he was made editorial director of all CBS Magazines, he thought it possible that he had held, then lost, a job he had enjoyed as much as any in his entire life.

A number of people called or wrote the magazine saying how much they would miss *Cuisine*, which helped him in those first days of shock. He and his wife were at a party in New York where he was one of three men whose publications had been shot out from under them, casualties of the times. His only consolation was that *Cuisine* had done so well when he presided that another publishing empire wanted it, seeing his handsome magazine as a dangerous competition to one of their own. That was his theory and it certainly was of some comfort, a tribute you might say.

Stealing, often known as shoplifting, is now such a problem that consumers are under constant surveillance, but consumers sometimes forget this. A man who was eating grapes in a supermarket was confronted by a security guard and then, enraged at being considered a shoplifter, he sued for thirty thousand dollars in damages. A circuit judge in Louisville ruled in favor of the security company that employed the guard. People know they must not nibble at the fruit in open bins but often forget. Grapes are the most tempting, no one starts on an apple.

Precautions against stealing were installed across the United States, in department stores and in shopping malls, in supermarkets and small groceries. Theft was rampant; women walked the streets of American cities with handbags close to their bodies, and men have been told not to keep their wallets in their back pockets where they can be easily plucked out, but do so anyway. Nice people stole too, from their offices—staplers, stamps, tape, message pads, pens—but did not consider this in the same zone as putting a sirloin under your coat. There was acceptable thievery and the other kind.

Dustan Ball knew all about it. In his job he was on perpetual lookout, paid to be suspicious and inquisitive. He did not fuss about little grapes either, when bigger things were going on.

He was director of loss prevention for six supermarkets and a restaurant in central New Jersey, serving very different classes of people, as he points out. It used to exasperate him when people tended to assume that he was a store detective. Once at a party, when a man asked what the difference was between his job and a security guard in a bank, Mr. Ball said, "About thirty-five thousand dollars." People did not seem really willing to hear about the complexities of a management job in loss prevention, even at a time when an estimated $52 billion a year was dripping out of industry, hotels, retail stores, and small and large grocery stores and supermarkets because of stealing. Never had there been such a persistent and successful epidemic of employee theft, of shoplifting, of pilfering, of snitching, done not just by the deprived or the desperate but by people who either did not think about it or did it as a lark. Or because it made them feel, however briefly, slightly triumphant.

It was Mr. Ball's business to prevent and detect all forms of theft, particularly by customers or employees, as well as any violation of the company's policy by its workers. As he saw it, it was his job to create a first line of defense, to do scrupulous and never-ending reconnaissance, to confront the suspect—he was armed in case it became a nasty business and the person resisted—and to call the police or recommend dismissal after he had questioned the suspect. One week there was a forty-seven-year-old woman, a cashier, who for six months had been giving groceries to a friend and her daughter by reducing the prices of food items; on one occasion she charged her daughter $2.33 when she bought $119.20 worth of food. Another woman on line saw this and telephoned the store to complain of the discounts being given. The cashier was questioned, fired, arrested, charged, convicted, and required to pay a fine totaling sixty-five dollars—including a fifteen-dollar court fee—by a lower court, to the disgust of Mr. Ball. In the restaurant he discovered a busboy taking an unauthorized one-hour break so he could smoke a marijuana cigarette, which led to his dismissal.

Sometimes, although not often, Mr. Ball was sympathetic, as in the case of an elderly woman living on a small fixed income, probably Social Security, who was caught stealing M & M's candies and Polident, a powder to clean false teeth, and let off. But he showed no pity at all for the man who had thirty dollars in his wallet and turned ugly when caught with a $1.39 package of bologna he did not intend to pay for. There was a warrant out for him. Another man, who tried to conceal thirty dollars' worth of things, including a little night lamp used in children's rooms, was discovered to be on parole. Mr. Ball was not moved when he was insulted, when people wept, threatened retribution, or began to plead.

Even in small stores there are mirrors or video cameras to record who is putting hamburger into their pocket, who has put a jar of Nescafe inside their coat, stuffed cheese inside boots and bread inside their handbag. In one of his supermarkets, where the customers are all well-off—the kind of people who want the best olive oil, ginger and dill, scallions and different kinds of lettuce besides iceberg—there is a tiny catwalk above the meat compartment, often manned by one of Mr. Ball's men on the lookout for people stealing filet. He did not consider it his duty to determine need, Mr. Ball said, although in the case of the old woman who wanted sweets and to brighten her teeth, that much was certainly clear. He was always polite and rather formal when the moment came to move in, although he was too important to take care of each random offense.

Loss Prevention devoured much of his life. Sometimes he wrote articles on the subject, emphasizing the importance of store managers' checking the percentages of store business by department, the totals of each cashier, or the average cost of an item recorded by the cashier. Cashier percentages and time of day were major points with Dustan Ball. "In a 24-hour store, the morning cashiers at 9 A.M. will be doing 23 percent of their sales in meats, by 4:30 P.M. the cashier will be ringing approximately 2 to 23 percent in meat, by midnight down to 10 to 12 percent of sales will be in meat. These percentages are available by looking at cashier reports generated on ECR equipment, or they could be done manually," Mr. Ball wrote in the magazine *Professional Protection.* "Percentages and average cost per item can be used by departments and compared to overall store figures as an indicator; then surveillance, monitoring by video or ECR or other forms of investigation can be explored."

He favored the average cost per item method. By dividing the total dollar sales for the store by the total items sold, you develop an average cost per item sold in any store. If the average cost of an item sold in a store is $1.19, then a cashier who falls below $1.00 should be the focus of attention, he wrote. In the magazine *Security Industry and Product News,* Mr. Ball noted that of the two hundred areas of enforcement handled by the FBI, their third highest priority was white-collar crime and that "theft may have its roots in the less serious and more prevalent forms of workplace deviance."

So constant and pernicious was the jargon used that at times he could laugh at it. But Dustan Ball no longer saw the humor in the phrase "workplace deviance." But he could always make himself clear. "Cashiers who seem to always wait on the same customers should be closely observed. Phone calls asking if a particular cashier is working should be scrutinized as well," Mr. Ball wrote. "Don't ignore the cashier who is frequently late, the unloading crew that haphazardly handles products, or the employee thefts at the so-called lesser end of the scale, such as eating cookies, or drinking a can of soda without payment in advance." He often used the language preferred by those in Loss Prevention. "When the employee sees management's reaction to punctuality, dress code and store policy violations as being tolerated or ignored they may conclude that management's attitude in a theft situation will be similarly lax," Mr. Ball wrote in *Security Industry and Product News.* The publication spelled his name incorrectly, as many people do. His name was inspired by the actor Dustin Farmer, whose first success was in Cecil B. DeMille's *The Squaw Man* in 1914. His father, who liked the actor, changed the spelling to make it a "little different."

Mr. Ball did not lash out at cashiers, or handcuff them when wrongdoing was certain, nor did he advise store managers, not skilled in such things, to take over. The correct procedures are delicate and complex; if they are not observed a dishonest employee could be exonerated in a civil proceeding because of a sloppy or amateur investigation in the store. When there were discrepancies in the receipts of cashiers, Mr. Ball wrote a notice to the union stating that the employee has violated store policy by not properly controlling cash. Dismissal comes soon enough. In cases of collusion—a cashier charging a friend less than the price —he always urged that the loss prevention supervisor be brought to take separate statements, to interrogate without giving the accomplices a chance to collaborate on their account of what happened and so forth. It was his responsibility, too, to prescreen job applications that go to the personnel department, now known in many companies as "human resource development." Mr. Ball also purchased equipment for the supermarkets and restaurant—front-end scales for produce, registers, supplies for maintenance for all the stores. And more: there were salesmen, vendors, drivers, all with different receipts, claims, forms, and various papers to be checked if he was to be successful in building the first line of defense.

None of the work made Dustan Ball an unusually suspicious man, or a moralizer, or a man much interested in general injustices, destructive human tendencies, psychiatric theories about stealing or why a man on parole would steal, among other things, a child's night lamp unless somewhere there was a child afraid of the dark. An offer to pay for the amount of goods stolen by a suspect if the matter would be dropped had to be refused. The "theft factor," as people in his line of work put it, was the point, not human flaws or the impulse that made people suddenly want a free can of tuna fish.

His company had 450 employees. It did a business, with all the supermarkets and the restaurant, of well over $5 million a year. It spent more than one hundred thousand dollars for equipment and salaries of personnel in loss prevention. Mr. Ball was not about to say what the "shrink" percentage—the money lost because of stealing—was; the figure was more intimate probably than his own bank balance. His wife handled all their money anyway. She was an accountant, very level-headed, now at home raising their ten-year-old son and two-year-old daughter. He gave all his salary checks to her, keeping not more than forty dollars a week for himself. He rarely ate lunch. He was too busy to spend money anyway—the beeper saw to that—driving back and forth, coping with workplace deviance and the theft factor and all the reports he had to read and to write.

He was required to be suspicious and rather enjoyed being so. Driving through East Orange, he did not fail to notice a sign saying pallets were for sale. The pallets, which cost his own company four dollars apiece, are heavy crates, very useful, for shipping food. It took only a few seconds for him to realize the pallets being offered for such a reasonable price belonged to his employer.

He was not a vengeful man, he did not punish people for the joy of it. And without coyness he would explain how he attended a food marketing seminar for executives in which they were asked to grade themselves on their characters. His faults, said Dustan Ball, are that he is disorganized and inclined to be lazy. He worked to obliterate such defects. Mr. Ball did not talk about fulfillment, but he knew the job richly provided him with what he most needed: adversity and the strenuous life. He had no theories about why he might need this. He felt uneasy when he was not hard-pressed, working weekends, moving from one store to the other, never surprised by human behavior, and glad of his little beeper—its voice as nasty as a smoke detector—which became a sort of monitor. He was not interested in leisure, health, nutrition, sports, movies, books, international news, the economy, music, nuclear arms, politics, or food. What held him was his job and whether someone was swiping the expensive cuts of meat.

On nice days, driving his nine-hundred-pound Honda with its special Ford engine, Mr. Ball did not pass as a mild figure. He was over six feet tall, at least two hundred pounds, and although his Vandyke beard and mustache were neatly trimmed, he did not have the shiny, clipped, shaved look of men in big cities who are stockbrokers or lawyers. There was too much hair, and it gave him away—a former police officer, a deputy sheriff, and a detective second grade. He went into the food industry in New Jersey because his wife's father had been in that business for forty years. He worked late two nights a week, and on Saturdays too, but every night he would come home with problems on his mind. He knew he was sometimes cantankerous, not an easy husband or a cozy companion. Sometimes there were spats.

"I'm involved with decisions—the new store—I have spent the day spending thirty-five thousand dollars for check stands, a hundred and forty thousand dollars for register equipment, deciding on an eight-thousand-dollar baler or a six-thousand-dollar baler —they bale and recycle cardboard," said Mr. Ball. "I'm involved with decisions about the water company or how to hook up. . . . Then I go home and hear, what color should we paint the bathroom? Who the fuck cares? Paint it any color you want, I don't care. This is not a command decision. But instead of being like *that*, you say, gee, I don't care, what color do you want? Then you go to this: Do you think we should go out with the Joneses or the Smiths on Friday? I don't really care. Well, do you want to go out? Sure, I want to go. What do you want to do? I don't care. What do you mean you don't care? I don't care, we'll do anything you want to do."

He thought his wife, a bookkeeper, would go back to work after their two-year-old daughter was older. Mr. Ball was also busy with the New Jersey Food Council, he was chairman that year for the Loss Prevention Committee, he was a former vice-president of the Metropolitan Security Council of New York, chairman of the Legislative Affairs Committee for the Society for Industrial Security. It wasn't money that pushed him, although he liked to be rewarded, and if he thought of his future, what he wanted was to have his own business, in loss prevention of course, making a hundred thousand dollars a year. But for now, all his attention went to the six stores and the restaurant owned by others.

"We have people from all walks of life stealing. We have caught exchange students from the university or the colleges who stood to lose their scholarships—they don't really look hungry. See, if you get somebody who steals a package of cupcakes and they look starved, you can say, *eh*. But when they steal nine pairs of socks, they're not going to wear those nine pairs, they're going to sell them. Or they'll steal a filet of beef when the refrigerator in their dorm holds three packages of cold cuts," he said.

He wasn't involved in apprehending all the shoplifters, he had store detectives to do that. He didn't lose his temper or threaten when he snatched someone in the act, pulling off something big.

"It's business," said Mr. Ball. He was saying that men like him did not take it personally. You were tested of course, often the air was a little thin; it was to be expected, even wished for.

"It's the adversity that you run into throughout life that makes it interesting. Oh, when things are nicely screwed up I'm the happiest at work. When I look down the road and figure if I work twenty-four hours a day for the next ten years and there is no way I can catch up, I'm thrilled to death. When things start running smoothly and I don't have a project going or a store going up, I'm not real happy there. It gets boring."

Growing up deep in the countryside—where until he was five he thought the dog was a real relative, Mr. Ball liked to say—he lived with his family in a large house eight miles from Factoryville in Pennsylvania. There were four bedrooms upstairs, a living room sixty by twenty-six feet, a piano and lessons for ten years, an organ, and what he calls a formal dining room, meaning the room was used for only that. He knew the size of the living room because when he was fourteen he helped his father lay the carpet. A successful self-employed manufacturer's representative who sold cast-iron pump casings, a man who detested his name Byron and traveled a lot, the father would do things that would take your breath away. This is exactly how his son still put it. Once the father needed to fix the lawn mower and did, not outside, but spreading it all over the kitchen table, not minding where the grease went, spraying the familiar obscenities around the room, the language that, on any day, so suited him. When the child was small, the father would not be harsh if the boy hurt himself and cried, but whining was something else, he would set at the boy to stop this second. Men don't whine. The father drank in bars, not at home, and waited to be offended. He had been a boxing instructor in the army, and in the National Guard. And it did not amuse him to be called Bud or By, to hear people say, "Hi, By."

"He'd fight in a wink. You could hurt his feelings in a second. The problem was, with his background in boxing and a background in jujitsu, when his feelings got hurt he tended to drop somebody," said Mr. Ball. "He'd be sitting at a bar, somebody would say something that, pardon the expression, pissed him off, and rather than sit there and argue about it, he'd punch him in the mouth. That solved the problem. He was involved in bar fights until the age of forty-eight." He never thought it disgraceful. His father let his drinking hurt him, but after his heart faltered he stopped once and for all. When his mother, a gentle and quiet sort, tried to stop Dustan from doing this or doing that, the father would accuse her of fussing too much.

" 'Leave the kid alone,' he'd say. Oh, she paid her dues, I'll tell you. My father was a piece of work," Mr. Ball said.

In the years before the father decided to retire when only in his forties, the parent did much of his work at home. He often had to wait to make a call if the party line telephone was busy, which irritated him so profoundly he grew unreasonable. When he asked the telephone company for his own telephone, the request was denied on the grounds that it would mean having to run a wire three miles, too much work at great cost. The father could not abide the party line chatter and one day, when the line again sang with conversations he thought trivial or worse, there was nothing to do but shoot his own telephone. He did, with a .22 pistol. Of course people were talking on the line when he aimed and fired. Dustan Ball thought his father had been arrested for destroying the property of the telephone company, but he eventually had his way. His own telephone was installed, the cost three hundred dollars, a shocking expense, but the father was a man who had done very well. Money was not at all his problem. The son heard all this when he grew big enough to be amused.

The older man never did help with the housework. There was no talk then between men and women of who would change the sheets, no doing the dishes on alternate nights, no little treaties like that. He made the money and did the heavy work around the house; he came and went as he pleased. He wanted the child to push for himself but he was not unreasonable, not given to doling out punishments if Dustan's grades were not very good. The boy had a friend who was mercilessly pushed by his parents and, when he did not come up to snuff, was refused permission to take the test for his driver's license, a profound humiliation since driving cars was what the sixteen-year-old males thought was the purpose of their lives. Around that time, when his friend was shriveling from his own father's disapproval, Dustan came home with a terrible report card. His father gave him a dollar, saying, "This is for having the balls to bring this home, okay?" Sometimes Dustan's lack of motivation caused problems. His father would be riled up when he gave away a Ping-Pong game. Dustan was crazy about Ping-Pong and good at it all through high school and college. But if he saw that opponents wanted to win "so desperately that they were thoroughly upset with themselves," Dustan Ball would give the games away. This was not how his father saw life. But he had a practical side, for he didn't want Dustan to play football at a time when, because of his size, it appealed to him.

"He said this: If you want to get into a sport where you're going to get your legs broken, if you're going to get into a sport where your head is handed to you, do a sport that gives you recognition," Mr. Ball said. "His attitude was that if you wanted to do something that, later on, is going to bring you arthritis, twisted legs, bad ligaments, all the things that are associated with sports, don't be part of a team, take a sport that gives you personal attention." He liked baseball, he liked basketball, but Ping-Pong most of all. His father taught him a little jujitsu.

The father was a man of immense violence but he didn't hit the child. He tapped his wife only once, because she smacked him first, as far as their son can remember. He didn't kick his German shepherd dog, or the other German shepherd that was his wife's pet, and he doted on the pig, Mary Beth. The pig was allowed inside their house and often tugged on his mother's skirt when it wanted to be fed or noticed. It was a much-babied pig.

"There was a picnic grove across the street. Mary Beth went to a picnic, and she tugged on a woman's skirt, as she used to do with my mother, so that you'd feed her, but the woman panicked and jumped. The skirt got half ripped off and the neighbors said, the pig's got to go, you can't have a pig walking around pulling people's skirts off." The father minded a lot, but they gave in and killed Mary Beth and shortly afterwards the family ate her.

The father was the sort of man who still believed the best blood is that which has the most iron in it. When Dustan Ball spoke of his father—who was sent to work in the coal mines in Scranton by his own father, then employed by the railroads—he spoke not only of his fists and the frequent flares of temper but of the things they loved together—guns and cars. There are names he can recite in a hymn of love: the Ainsley Fox set of matched double-barreled E-grade shotguns, a twelve-gauge and a sixteen-gauge for hunting rabbits and birds; the gun that his father particularly prized, an Ithaca Trap twelve-gauge, a sporting, not hunting, gun; a Remington .35 automatic rifle, which he liked for deer hunting; and a .30/06 caliber Springfield rifle with a scope, also for deer.

"I had my own guns from the time I was eight, nine years old," Mr. Ball said. "Now, in my house when I was a kid walking up, there were always guns in the corner in the gun closet. Guns were a way of life, it was a big thing, a big sport for men. The first thing my father taught me was how to make sure a gun is not loaded—open the bolt on a rifle, or on a handgun check the revolver cylinders." What he could not describe so easily is the great happiness he knew with the man. They went to Florida in the winter where Byron Ball had a little house in Jacksonville—just the two of them, because the mother did not like going places, she wanted to stay home with her garden and the flowers, watching the dogs.

The man doted on the boy, saying: "You will do what is right until you screw up." It was fine with him that Dustan lied about his age a few months before his sixteenth birthday and got his driver's license. Other boys would have to be home by ten o'clock during the week, maybe by midnight on weekends, but Dustan was not held to such hours. It was: Until you stay out late and get into trouble, you're fine, okay? His father bought him a 1954 Chevy because he didn't want the boy to touch either of his Cadillacs, a red and white Sedan de Ville—Coupe de Ville—and a 1957 airport limousine with jump seats in the back. Four days after he was given the Chevy, he wrecked the car, driving forty miles an hour on ice and snow.

"I piled it up," Mr. Ball said. "I called up my father and said I wrecked the car. He said, Well, you made it to the phone, I assume you're all right. I'm all right, I said. He said, It could have been my Cadillac. I said yes, it could have been. He said, I told you so."

Later Dustan blew up the Cadillac airport limousine drag racing. "I was losing—losing was a very bad thing when I was driving —so I downshifted at about eighty miles an hour and flames came out from under the hood. I ruined the engine and the transmission." There were other cars, some so cheap you could have called them junkers, but often he ruined or wrecked them. Then the better ones, not so fine as the '58 Corvette, a two-passenger convertible with a custom-built transmission made by a friend of his who was a mechanic (a Borg-Warner aluminum transmission with a Hurst selector), and the car he took to Arizona, a '72 Silver Hawk Gran Turismo. To this day he will tell you that Studebaker was probably twenty years ahead of their time in design but that model never took off.

He thought he began getting a little wild his fifteenth year, drinking and too quick to fight with no reason at all and going through cars. His very long hair was an issue, it caused disturbances. He was big for his age, nearly his full height, and he ran with boys who were older.

"Driving like a maniac, you know, a hundred, a hundred and twenty miles an hour, going through radar traps and outrunning the local law. That was fun. Getting in fights, the police breaking up the fights. I never got locked up but I got smacked in the mouth once by a cop. It was my own fault, I mouthed off to him. And when your friends are there, well, it can't hurt. I stood there and looked at him. Actually, it hurt like hell. But on the outside I was cool, you know, hey, don't feel anything.

"I am probably not as good a father as my own was. I don't have my son with me as much, don't do as much with him. I probably push him away because when I get home I am tired and aggravated—I've been busy, busy, busy. But I openly tell him that I love him, he doesn't have to be a little soldier, you know."

But he saw clearly that in the country, when he was growing up, when the roads were closed in the winter, he had been more self-reliant and inventive than his boy. "One of the problems is that when you take my son away from his friends, his structured activities, his school, his etcetera, etcetera, and etcetera, and put him in a room and say 'enjoy yourself,' it takes him twenty minutes to recover from the shock that he has nothing planned." It did not occur to Mr. Ball that the child was so like him, hating dull little lapses in his life.

He though it was the natural order of things for male adolescents to like violence. "With young boys I don't think that will ever change," he added. "It is genetic. I think that the aggression young boys go through is almost inbred, something in their genes. There is an aggression at the fifteen- sixteen-, seventeen-year-old level of rebellion, of independence, of asserting yourself. And needing risks. With the driving, well, people wouldn't ride with me, only a couple of friends of mine. But I drove sane with the girls." He did not think much about it, such abstractions, even when he was with his boy, whom he described as a ten-year-old going on sixteen, a child he doted on as his father had doted on him.

In the year Dustan Ball became seventeen, his father died, not from his heart but from cancer in December when he was only fifty-four. His mother, that quiet woman so fond of trees and flowers she thought of them as her religion, died of cancer, just as slowly, a year and a half later. He was eighteen and was left very little money, a college student in La Plume, Pennsylvania.

"The details of sitting with my mother, as she breathed her last breath and died, do not bother me. I built a stone wall. I realize that part of the reason is that when my dad died I had to be, quote unquote, the man of the house, on my mother's terms. I had to be strong. I couldn't cry at the wake, the funeral, because my mother was depending on my strengths. Whether this was true or not, it was the impression I had. It was the impression I had as a young boy.

"I can talk about all these things, all this death—father's death and mother's death—as being facts, occurrences. And I see that in my later life, my married life, in my relationships with others, if my feelings get hurt, if I am upset, then I find it very difficult to talk about it.

"What happened is that when something was bothersome to me, then I couldn't share my feelings with anyone, not with my wife, not with anyone. I held it in. When I was single and had a girlfriend who annoyed me it was, as the Jews say, you sit *shivah*. It's like the girlfriend died, you might have killed her. Not that you act as if you didn't like them anymore—you visit them, hello, how are you—but cold, no feelings." What little Yiddish he knew came from his wife, and he took those expressions as his own, often changing their meaning to suit himself.

Even after he was married for more than a decade, he could not open up very easily. After his father's death, his mother inherited the house and everything else, but when she died without a will he was still a minor. The family house went for $19,500, a fraction of what it was worth, its true value he thought being closer to $35,000 or $40,000.

All that was left for him was a small sum of money from what is now, as Dustan Ball was quick to point out, a piece of property certainly worth $150,000. He had to sell his father's guns for cash. He did this, and other painful things as well, in the tidying up of the lives of the dead couple. Then he was on his own, a scholarship student with student loans so he could attend two colleges.

Because his mother was sick a year and a half before she too died, he found out that by constant motion he could dispel any depressive relapses. At Keystone Junior College he kept his grades up, he said he was on the student council, president of the sopho-more class, president of the drama fraternity, chairman of the library committee, vice-president of his dormitory, and was selected to be listed in the *Who's Who of American Junior Colleges*, considered by some as a mark of distinction. He won a small scholarship for outstanding performance in technical theater.

On his campus, the antiwar mood made the students intent on peacefulness. Compared to other places, it was rather quiet; the students did not try to kill off the war in Vietnam with protests or disorder. The draft didn't alarm him. He just didn't want to be taken by an army. "I didn't want to join anything I couldn't quit," said Mr. Ball, who was saved by his number 294B in the national lottery. He was poor now, fifteen dollars seemed a lot, and one of his part-time jobs was selling vacuum cleaners in New Jersey, often door to door. It was going well enough until he made a sale to an elderly woman living in a small two-room apartment in Trenton. Perhaps the woman was lonely, glad of a little visit, but she was not sensible, so he sold one to her easily enough and then felt disgraced.

"I took her check and went home and said to myself, 'It ain't worth this.' I was ashamed to be earning money this way because she could have used that two hundred and sixty dollars to do a lot of things besides her rugs," Mr. Ball said. The particular vacuum cleaner he sold struck him as ridiculous unless you owned a restaurant, it did too much. It came with a variety of motor attachments, tools, and a lathe. You could spray paint rooms, you could carve wood. The woman in Trenton only needed a Hoover.

In a year when people were accustomed to the loss of hundreds of young men every week in the war overseas, his cousin Richard, who had lived near him in Pennsylvania, was killed in an automobile crash in California after making it through a year in Vietnam. The funeral was in Tucson, where the mother lived, and Mr. Ball came back from it just in time to take, and pass, all his exams at Ryder College except for sociology, which he hated. The sorrow, which he thought would lift in time if he didn't touch it too much, then hardened, and all he can tell you is he didn't do so well in college after that.

He was working for a fine arts degree. His major was lighting and set design, a field he thought was not too crowded, knowing very little about the profession since he had not been to New York or ever seen a Broadway play. It did not seem to matter; he had a fine instructor in his technical theater courses, and began working on actual productions, often enough plays by Bertolt Brecht. In *The Death and Life of Sneaky Fitch* he played the part of a sheriff who is killed midway through a scene, which left Mr. Ball free to run upstairs and finish the light cues after he was dragged offstage. The college often put on plays out of town. He filled in when the lighting technician at the Bucks County Playhouse had an appendicitis attack on opening night for a student production of *Threepenny Opera* and, without cue cards, he managed well enough, only forgetting to kill one spotlight at the end of a blackout, which no one noticed.

"I enjoyed it," said Mr. Ball. "But I found it to be repetitious, which began to bother me." Even after he left Ryder College, without his degree, planning to be married in April and to move to Arizona where there would be work and sun, he kept on doing the lighting for college plays until his departure. There were concerts by Vanilla Fudge, Big Brother and the Holding Company with Janis Joplin, the Fifth Dimension, and the Modern Jazz Quartet. Then he and his wife went south, not suspecting there were no jobs for him at all. He was competing with retired military willing to work part-time for not much, with Mexicans willing to work for substandard wages while they tried to get a *mica*, an alien's green card. To his surprise Mr. Ball was not needed anyplace and the new scaffolding of his life seemed to wobble.

They had been married for only two months when they embarked. He drove too fast for her taste; it used to frighten her. "Did you ever see a Jewish girl cross herself?" said Mr. Ball. Like many other young men at the time, his face was shadowed and made secretive by all his hair; he wore it shoulder length, his mustache wending down into a beard was about three and a half inches long and slightly unkempt. An ad in a Tucson newspaper said the county sheriff's office needed deputy sheriffs. He appeared, took the Wunderlich personality test, sailed through it, was told he had done very well, was asked to come back that afternoon to take a written exam, learned that the department was interviewing for the police academy, took the test, waited while it was corrected, was told he did it in record time, and was then recommended by a personnel officer who said he had done "real well" and to come back to take the physical test the following day. He did, it was a cinch—all those push-ups and sit-ups and chin-ups nothing much for a twenty-one-year-old—and so was an oral test with a psychologist in attendance, all of them pleased by him.

He was offered a job, which meant starting immediately for the sixteen weeks at the Southern Arizona Law Enforcement Academy in Pima County and then, on graduating, being assigned to a substation at Ajo, 140 miles southwest of Tucson, with a starting salary of $626 a month. The name of the town was garlic in Spanish because of the small, brilliant flowers that bloomed in the valley and smelled faintly of that bulb. One of the oldest mining towns in the state—copper is the reason—Ajo was near a huge Papago Indian reservation created by an executive act of 1874 and close to the Organ-Pipe Cactus National Monument, an area of more than five hundred square miles where the immense saguaro cactus grew, a plant that often waited a century before showing a new branch. The organ-pipe, with its twenty-foot stems that rose from a common root, had pink-petaled flowers that bloomed at night from May to June. Ajo was eleven miles from Why, where there was the Coyote Howls Trailer Park and a Western Auto store that sold almost everything, and forty-nine miles from Gila Bend (named for the river cutting across southern Arizona to Colorado), where people coming from California would usually exit for a vacation. Phelps Dodge owned the Ajo copper mine and much of the town, because the company provided housing and a hospital for its employees, nearly always men. It was difficult to find a decent place to live: he finally bought a trailer, sold it, and then bought, for eight thousand dollars, a house which took too much of his time because it needed work. At first, being a policeman was tricky, although he credited himself with being a man who could adjust to nearly anything. It was 1970.

"In the early sixties when I was growing up it was perfectly acceptable to be a young kid, go out, party with the guys, fight, cause trouble, make hell," said Mr. Ball. "In the last part of the sixties all that was uncool in colleges, everybody was going 'peace brother, let's not think of the violence and war, let's think of being peaceful.' So I said okay, sounds good to me, I'll do that for a while, I will get my head on straight. And then, suddenly, in the police department you try and approach a man acting up on the street with 'Hey bro, this is crazy, you can't be doing this,' and he throws a punch at you and it's right back to the 1950s where you have to fight your way out of a situation." Here, in the new job, he saw the culture as thin and erratic, not the foundation for a useful code of behavior, so he avoided any more thoughts about it.

The deputy sheriffs in Ajo were kept busy; there were problems with the narcotics smuggling and the sale of marijuana across the border, which was only twenty-nine miles from them—a ridiculous thing he thought, that border, because it was as easy to penetrate as it was to slit a tea bag. No one could guard it effectively. He used to catch the same illegal aliens—mostly thin men, not yet old or crazy—feed them, send them home, and shortly see them again when the Border Patrol was called to take them home.

"They loved us, we were the decent folk, they didn't care for the Border Patrol that much," Mr. Ball said, believing it. "And it wasn't really by design if we did treat them poorly. You might catch twenty at a time, you would only have two cars and couldn't get another, it would be all hot and nasty, you stuffed them into one car, they would smell horribly and they made each other sick. That was nasty. But when we got them to our office, we fed them, got them clean."

Not a vicious man, he knew what the aliens had been through to get that far—the heat, the desert, the lack of water, the furtive march—and something of the desperation that kept them trying it, but he always kept an eye on them because they carried razor blades in the collars of their shirts for shaving. They could not afford razors and they used the blades over and over. Still, the dullest blade could be used to cut the skin of some other man, so he always watched.

Bar fights in Ajo were more interesting; they were exuberant, and rarely causes of grief or what he considered bad injuries. They were sudden spasms of theater for him, he knew what had to be done and in doing it felt a bizarre joy as if allowed on stage in a role whose lines he always knew. Once, working the midnight to 6 A.M. shift—the hot shift he called it—by himself, for the other man working as dispatcher was also the jailer, he got a call about a fight in progress. He went to a bar called The Hot, its formal name being Mocambo, to find an Indian boy beating two cowboys, really thumping on them, Mr. Ball said. He was a young Papago, a man of such fury and so without ordinary human caution that he was punching and pummeling the two larger men as if his life depended on their defeat. Mr. Ball moved in, fast, to the relief of the two white men, for a second remembering the jujitsu his father had taught him although he didn't have quite the time or the composure to do it properly. He did what he always did: grabbed the Indian boy by the hair and flung him against the car. Handcuffs were at last put on those wrists, the boy shoved in the back seat, and only then did Mr. Ball pause, trying to get his breath because he couldn't even talk on the radio, by now quite filthy and sore. The Indian's name was Billy, if he had a Papago name it was not known.

"He did a nice job. Fought like hell. I could hear people standing around saying, 'Kick ass, hey, the cop's going to get his ass kicked.' They were thrilled," Mr. Ball said. "Ah, it was great, great fun." Billy said nothing. His face was bleeding, discolored, swollen, and mashed in places. His arms were behind his back; if you handcuffed a prisoner with his arms in front he could still inflict injuries. Billy bled. Because of Billy's terrible condition, Mr. Ball could not book him straight off, first he had to go to the hospital. In the emergency room, a doctor, older and perhaps a man of refinement or some adherence to ideals, seemed upset. "I am not going to work on him while he is chained like an animal, please take the handcuffs off"—this is what Mr. Ball recalled the doctor saying, and he didn't care for the man's tone one bit. Mr. Ball spoke his piece—he was not intimidated by doctors after all—then obeyed, so the boy was now free to begin his ballet all over, lashing out first at the doctor, then going for the policeman. Mr. Ball dragged Billy down to the floor by his long hair, jumped on top of him, and put the cuffs back on, expertly.

"By this time I am thoroughly beyond myself, I am pleased,"

he said, not blaming Billy, only furious with the doctor who thought the Indian boy deserved decency in that room. He didn't know what Billy's problem was, alcoholism or unemployment or wretchedness—the afflictions of the Papagos were not his business, nor did they interest him. "I am not a social worker," Mr. Ball said. Billy was often arrested, and they had one more terrible battle together. Once again Mr. Ball managed to overpower the Papago, whom he pushed over the hood of the car, the dark head almost down on the metal, while pulling one arm high behind his back, nearly up to the neck. But Billy made no noise at all, not the slightest sound, and he never asked Dustan Ball, who was about to break his arm, to ease up.

" 'Billy, give me the other hand, I want to handcuff you,' I said. 'I will not,' he says. 'Billy, give me the other hand.' He only says, 'I don't care, man, you can kill me, I ain't going to give it to you.' I pushed his hand up behind the back of his head and it had to hurt whole bunches, and he shot that other hand straight out across the hood, just refusing all the time, so I dragged him off the car, we did the whole thing again, roll around in the dirt. I finally got him handcuffed. I could have broken his arm and he would not have given me the other arm. Very tough and strong-minded. I didn't admire him particularly, but he was a good old boy, you know? You could respect him for the fact he was courageous, no doubt about it. But the point is it gets to being stupid, when it comes to a point where somebody's going to break your arm, there's a time to concede because it's going to happen, you're going to jail. But Billy, he would not have done anything to prevent it, by giving in."

But he didn't hate Billy or want to make trouble; what had happened between them was fair, he says. He never felt vindictive afterwards toward any of the men he took on.

"I didn't dislike them personally, and I've carried this attitude over to this life, my work, whatever I'm doing. Some of them that were locked up I liked a lot. I couldn't tolerate their behavior, it was in violation of the statutes, the law, but just because they were burglars or causing trouble didn't mean they weren't a lot of fun, all right?"

His wife was not grateful to be living in Ajo, which outsiders saw as a dinky place where the heat was intense. They didn't go out often because Ajo was so small and, Mr. Ball said, everybody knew who he was and there were always people coming up to him running off at the mouth about a traffic ticket or the locking up of an innocent man, an outrageous incarceration, or some major injustice done to them or people they knew. It made him uncomfortable, he just wanted to relax and be unnoticed. Dustan Ball did leave when he felt that Dustan Ball, then acting detective, was not appreciated, the raises and promotions too small. But there were fine times for him in that place; he was never to have such fun again.

There was the night of the fund-raising party, a dance and buffet for the sheriff of Ajo, who was running for reelection. His deputies, although not men of stunning social perceptions, understood their presence was expected and paid for tickets. Men and women were supposed to wear jeans and Western shirts. The wives were looking forward to it, a little evening out with nice food and music you could dance to, husbands by their sides. The fight started outside in the gravel driveway when Mr. and Mrs. Ball and a dozen of the other deputies with their wives were settling in for a cozy time. He thought the brawl involved the pregnancy of a young white woman who had come to the dance. Her father, who was nearing fifty, and a young Indian, thought to be the lover of the daughter, were going at each other with unusual vigor, even for Ajo, where there were fights all the time of the utmost nastiness. The nineteen-year-old son of the white man went to help and, in no time at all, the brawl became a major disturbance that was ruining the little party for the sheriff, his well-wishers, and the women. Others joined in when Mr. Ball and his colleagues went out to stop it. A patrol car with officers came. The yelling, the pushing, the smashing increased. Some men did try to separate the Indian and the girl's father, but these two did not want to be parted, they wanted to be even closer, in each other's arms, face to face, chest to chest, for the killing. There were only four sets of handcuffs when the on-duty police came. Dustan Ball took on the man with the expectant daughter, but once in the back seat of the car, his arms behind him, the prisoner tried to reach for the .38 in his boot, which required Mr. Ball's old routine of yanking the man out, pinning him down, getting his boot off, then putting on handcuffs.

"I wasn't into hitting. I'm an arm-twister, the judo and jujitsu type of thing, and I like fixed objects, automobiles and buildings," said Mr. Ball, who meant if you threw people against them, it had an instant effect. The Indian, the father, and the son were only charged with disorderly conduct, liable to a small fine, not confronted with the more serious charge of assaulting police officers. Mr. Ball's pants and shirt he wore for the dance were a mess. He knew the older man and the son too, liking both of them. The father had been to his house, they had gone shooting together, they were friends.

"The son says, 'Somebody almost broke my arm,' and I looked at him and I said, 'It was me, you were fighting and struggling, what can I tell you?' He said, 'Yeah, all right, fine,' " said Mr. Ball. "So the fight was broken up. No hard feelings. Everything went back to normal."

But, of course, that wasn't the case when Mrs. Ball had a chance to address her husband at home. She was agitated. She spoke of the evening in less than loving terms.

" 'It's bad enough that you were fighting,' she says to me, 'it's bad enough that people were getting hurt, but *all of you enjoyed it!*' " said Mr. Ball. "And she was right. It was not ordinary. You got to raise all kinds of hell and you got paid to do it." That was all there was to it. It made him feel skillful, feverish in a healthy way, keyed up, the way some people do playing tennis. He could tell you what he felt it was not: *not* cruel, *not* brutal, *not* pointless. There was no meanness to it, no one was badly hurt, no deep feuds arose. And if, by chance, you asked him why the Indians and the whites seemed to be constantly attacking each other, he only said they didn't, the fights were just natural, they happened when somebody got in another man's way. They made him happy. Long afterwards, he seemed wistful about these battles—the desperate embraces, the pushing, the twisting of arms, the click of handcuffs. He found a purity in all of it, and knew that it had been three and a half years exactly since he had been in a scuffle in New Jersey, this too in the line of duty.

The sight of a man's bleeding or battered face upsets no one unless an eyeball hangs loose or the skull splits. Every night on television children may observe men being beaten, kicked, choked, knocked out, deformed, or killed. In old World War II movies the noble armies and the wicked ones perish in great pain from machine guns or mortars, they are bayoneted or burned or drowned on torpedoed ships. On the evening news wounded and dead marines are pulled out of rubble and lifted on litters; only the faces of the living are shown. Men grimacing in pain are playing games that give us pleasure: the football player who can no longer walk is cheered as he is taken off the field, there is talk about his knee, a shoulder, surgery, and when he will come back. The boxers harming each other know great applause.

So persistent is the belief that men must inflict and endure that an American child by the age of six will know what may be his lot; if he is poor, the men in his own family roughened, the neighborhood hard, school puzzling. Men with expensive faces and fine jobs will not have to touch each other; harm can be done in different ways. Dustan Ball had not thought about this; the subject was so familiar and any discussion would bore or irritate him. But his old friend, the Papago known as Billy, perhaps understood better what men will do when there are no other assertions to make.

Sometimes men are moved to make threats, to promise a terrible commotion will take place, a regrettable scene, when they do not wish to fight at all or are unable. To be peaceful, in unbearable circumstances, is a concession too dangerous to make. Others are watching. Even if such assertions are only for themselves, even when it is a woman they believe must be protected, the effort can be strangely touching if futile. Eight years later I can still summon up the face of a man named Willis who lived in a small town in South Carolina, a face overlaid with fury because his wife had been so ill-treated by their employers. Both of them worked in a plant that made fiberglass cloth and screen, a factory that was so dangerous and a place of such humiliation that its workers, as one man said, were treated like "little dogs." The wife had been hurt doing a "pick count" in the weave room, a method of measuring how fast the looms are working; she did not notice the large holes in the concrete floor because a group of machines had been moved from the area. She fell, her right knee hitting a steel pipe. The first aid room was kept locked and it was not certain who had the key. There was never a nurse on the premises or anyone trained to treat injuries. Employees were sent to a doctor some distance away. That day a supervisor went home to get ice cubes for her knee which he brought back in the plastic bag used for a loaf of bread. The overseer in the weave room came, looked at the leg, patted her shoulder, and said, "I'm sorry, I can't stay here longer, my son's got a ball game." Someone gave her an aspirin. She was left alone for nearly an hour, weeping, until an elderly black janitor passed, asked what was wrong, saw for himself, and fetched her husband, Willis. For a year the leg gave her trouble. The bosses at the factory, as everyone called them, said she was only permitted to see the company doctor, who was considered too old and useless by many of his conscripted patients. Her salary was stopped and workmen's compensation payments, when finally obtained, did not exceed more than sixty dollars a week. Returning to work she could not easily stand and a foot turned black and swelled.

She went to a laywer, she made trouble, she refused to be pacified. Listening to her story in the mobile home where the couple live on a few acres of their own land, Willis waited his turn. A huge man who suffered a light heart attack in the last few years and was a diabetic, he worked in the preparations room of the plant running a slasher machine. It was here where ovens coated the fiberglass yarn. The heat sickened even the strongest among them and the only respite was in the bathrooms, which were air-conditioned. But if you stayed in there too long, Willis said, a supervisor would bang on the door and call, "Come out or go home." That meant having your pay docked.

In the preparations room a boiling liquid called sizing would often splash on the floor and coat it like a thick glass, making the workers lurch or fall. Willis had suffered a hernia, hurt his back, and dislocated a leg in various falls, a predictable occurrence although it was safer now since some improvements had been made to prevent the liquid spills. For years he and his wife wanted to be members of the Amalgamated Clothing and Textile Workers Union. There was a union organizer in town who held meetings for the dozen employees brave enough to attend. Many others in the factory, which employed six hundred, feared losing their jobs if they made known their disgust.

Reciting the disabilities and strain inflicted on Willis and others she knew, his wife spoke sharply but was calm. "He has to hang on anyway," the woman said. "If he don't do it somebody else will."

After she explained the allergies she had also suffered, a reaction to a chemical used on the yarn, and the hassle over who would pay the bill of the doctor who treated her, Willis spoke. He wanted it known that he had not taken his wife's suffering and abuse with equanimity and once more repeated the lines he said he had bellowed at his superiors in the fiberglass factory.

"You'll walk on me before you aggravate her again, I told 'em, you're not making her cry," he said, as if these were words that might command some justice. His wife stopped crocheting for a second and, in appreciation, reached out to pat his hand lightly.

When asked why they had not long ago gotten out, the couple were quiet, as if they lacked any belief that life would be easier elsewhere. They liked the town, its population slightly over six thousand, not far from the dark and marshy woods where Confederate troops once dug in and died to slow down Sherman and never did. Then she spoke, making it clear why moving on had never seemed much of a solution.

"I'm related to everyone on the road here," she said. "The Smoaks, the Prines, the Padgetts, and the Linders."

There were children who had never seen automobiles or who could not remember them, so a ten-year-old boy, seeing a jeep come closer, asked his father, "What is that thing with eyes?" As each vehicle passed, the dust rose and covered the Cambodians like nets. There was not enough water in the camp to waste a cupful. The Cambodians went on coughing and paid little attention to the noises coming from throats and chests. The Khmer cough, some foreign volunteers called it. There was a ward for the children who were alone, their parents or relatives missing or dead, and bright yellow T-shirts had been put on them just that morning. The child whose number was 348, named Mook Eark, was the size of a five-year-old although he thought himself to be nine. The children, after a nap, were each given two crackers, but he seemed uncertain whether they were his to eat, or to be saved, or only to hold. He no longer knew how to make these decisions. The Cambodians who spoke to Mook Eark wished to be kind, but he did not move or look in their faces when they touched him. He obeyed if you told him what to do. When asked what happened to his parents, his relatives, among the desperate bands of Cambodians who had reached the border of Thailand, the child simply gave the word "die" and more details were not needed, the explanation ordinary by now. It was a common story; all of them by this time had been deformed by years of fear, terror, starvation, disease, and abuse that not even the poorest among them could have ever once imagined. A woman who had learned English on a home economics scholarship in Ames, Iowa, tried to write a letter to an American visitor because she could not speak without weeping. She was afraid that normal people would not believe her, that a woman wearing my blue jeans and shirt with such a protected skin would think she was lying, but she was afraid too, of seeing your face if she told it all. "Three days in the forest, in the jungles and some times we jumped over the swollen dead bodies caused by mines . . . It was a journey to the death," she wrote. "Forgive me please if this letter disturb you." A forty-year-old man who had once taught mathematics in a provincial high school supervised children in the afternoons and sometimes would read aloud from *Essential English for Foreign Students* and of the wondrous life of a character named Mr. Priestley. "This is Mr. Priestley's cat Sally," he read. "She often sits there at his desk when he is writing." But at first his little audience was not certain what a cat is and had to be shown the picture. He explained what a book is. Mr. Priestley went to bed at 1 A.M., the mathematics teacher said, admiring a man who did so much work with a nice animal by his side. He gave a little squeak to the new words of English he spoke. The teacher did not himself know the state he was in, how difficult he found it to stop talking or moving.

In their thin clothes many Cambodians had skin that looked like bark. The educated ones spoke of a Third Country, a magical place that would want them, where they might find a healing.

In Inverness, California, a quiet, thirty-eight-year-old physician named Gilbert Stanley Hunn was learning all this and more. On the public broadcasting station of his radio he heard reports in 1979 after the Vietnamese forces had expelled Pol Pot and freed the Cambodians from the slave labor camps of the Khmer Rouge. Hundreds of thousands of them had walked, or crawled, to the border of Thailand, where they imagined they might be safe. They fled Cambodia and in the fleeing often died or were pushed back to die. *The New York Times* reported that by June, forty-five thousand Cambodians had been forced at gunpoint by armed Thai soldiers to go down a steep cliff to a heavily mined, unpopulated area without food. The cadavers were seen as a threat, a problem, intruders in a poor country that could not receive them. Walking to the border, families lost track of each other and were afraid to call out in the dark. Some lived long enough to reach Thailand but could bear no more and gave up.

Driving to Point Reyes one day in late summer to help with the banding of migratory birds there, Dr. Hunn and a friend heard on the radio a BBC report about the Cambodians who had reached Thailand, the description so clear that it startled them, for until then they knew little about Cambodia or its people.

The newspapers and magazines ran stories and pictures. An Associated Press photographer stood near the head of a five-year-old girl lying on a mat, a French doctor bending over her with two aides as they struggled to find a vein for a blood transfusion. The doctor searched her arms, her groin, her neck, but the child was shrunken from malnutrition and could not even lift her head or speak the name of her mother. Thirty minutes after the photograph was taken the child died; the doctor and the photographer did not stop working. That was October.

In the one-room library of Inverness, Dr. Hunn was paying attention, reading newspapers and magazines, and made up his mind he must go. He saw nothing on television, as neither he nor his friends owned a set. Going to the library several times a week, even when he had no books to return, was a ritual, one of the calls he made during the day, being a man at leisure who usually worked only weekends. He even advised the librarians on what books to order. Everyone in Inverness knew him and people would sometimes ask him about a rash, an ache, or symptoms of an allergy, because he was patient and did not make them feel foolish.

He was tall and the beard grew thick and fluffy. A passenger on a flight east once asked him who his swami was, so meager were his possessions and so old were his clothes. Gilbert Hunn thought it very funny; no one took him for a physician and that was fine by him. He mumbled, he giggled and was very calm, a calm so deep that a friend thought his thyroid was out of whack, which was not the case. Some Americans found it disturbing to meet a man who would not push.

In the community, people took careful notice of their health and most considered cities cesspools. Few touched meat and he, too, was a strict vegetarian. Here it was considered pitiful to be fat, to be out of breath when hiking unless asthmatic, and not to know the names of trees, flowers, berries, and fruits. Some women learned how to weave and were skillful. He learned how to hike and climb and overcame a certain clumsiness; he was very tall and liked being told his legs were nice. Foxgloves and forget-me-nots and mint grew wild near the house he rented, a house in a glen where you could see a small stream. There were wild blackberries and red elderberry shrubs, large sword and lady ferns, redwood trees, alders, bay laurel, oak and Douglas fir. He lived with a much younger woman of some beauty, who had grown up in the country, knew the names of everything. It was she who put in the huge red geraniums in the planters on the deck. She knew how to do all sorts of things that were wonderful to him. He liked to cook but was a messy man, the only doctor in the country who did not care if his nails were not quite clean. The garbage sometimes piled up when he was by himself. He read and hiked and saw friends and sometimes went to Big Sur for weekends. He worried about neither money nor time nor his career. The young woman he adored was more energetic and eager than he, bolder in some ways. Friends and family fussed, then forgave him on sight, speaking of his sweetness and brilliance before, once again, asking the question that unsettled them: What was he doing in California, a man who once showed so much promise? His passivity alarmed them, as if in this country it was subversive to be a doctor and do nothing, not even make money. Once Gilbert Hunn hoped to be a physicist, but his parents expected him to study medicine, and medicine, as he put it, was easier to do. He did not like the responses required of a doctor, the way patients became so dependent, elevating the doctor to a great height because they knew nothing.

"In most cases people look to you for the ultimate decisions; you are the guiding force behind all decisions," he said. "It's astounding that all these people can't function without the doctor saying 'do this' or 'do that.' "

Of all his friends, no one saw the dilemma so clearly, or understood so well why Inverness was lovable, as Matthew Naythons, his dear friend. He was a doctor too, a bit younger, who had suspended his career in medicine to take photographs for *Time* and the stills for an occasional movie whose director he liked. Dr. Naythons had also been raised in Philadelphia, felt the high hopes of his family, moved to California, and for a while supported himself by working shifts in hospital emergency rooms.

"Gil fell very easily into the California experience; it's so easy out here if you want a rural life-style, very beguiling. You live in

Inverness and there is not a real drive to earn money, not a lot of stimulation. It became, for him, very comfortable just to hang out; a lot of people in rural Marin do just that," he said.

"Thailand was so different, in a way he wanted the drama of it, he needed to break from the mundaneness of practicing medicine as he did," Dr. Naythons added. "Working emergency rooms in certain rural hospitals is a rather easy branch of medicine. It allows you to practice but lead a different life the rest of the time. People come in and go out, it's attractive to some young doctors. You make $960 for a thirty-six-hour shift and afterwards there is all that free time. Gil was bored by that routine, but he liked helping people. The bad side of it is the loss of the tremendous stimulation you get from practicing, from monitoring—the gains from watching people get *better*. So you lose touch with what you hoped for when you started medicine. All of that was happening to Gil."

The two men met in Thailand, both working as physicians and glad to be. Later Dr. Naythons, who had for some time been fascinated by his new career as photographer, went on careening from one chaotic or inflamed country to another, dancing in and out of war zones, such a life often suiting him. It made Dr. Hunn slightly wistful, his own existence so placid and predictable by comparison; he was always pulled toward journalists, imagining them to be original and uninhibited, much cleverer than he.

The Cambodians came into his life slowly, until it was impossible to turn them away, so persistent was their presence. He volunteered to go to Thailand, to the camps near the border to treat the survivors and, to his surprise, was not immediately dispatched. Weeks passed, to his irritation. His application floated. The voluntary agencies he applied to did not respond but, at last, the International Rescue Committee in New York sent him on his way.

Before his departure, people in Inverness came up to him in the street or public places to say how they admired him for going, good luck and take care, they sang. This was something very new for him, the praise of decent people who saw his voyage as a noble one. He had detested the war in Vietnam and kept himself out of it. So much had been done to punish the people of Indochina by his own country, Gilbert Hunn now wished to be an American who helped to save some of them. This is not what he said to anyone at the time; he spoke without flourishes and did not command immediate attention.

It was as if all those years he had been waiting to be summoned and now heard himself called.

When in December 1979 he finally reached his destination, the worst was over, but even on a day considered normal there was no normalcy at all. In Thailand the Cambodians were not refugees, for refugees have certain rights under international law, so the camps, under the jurisdiction of the International Committee of the Red Cross, were called holding centers to pacify the Thais. The first, opened that October, was called Sakeo, about forty miles from the Cambodian border, and eight thousand Cambodians arrived on the first day when the bulldozers were still at work. There was heavy rain. A volunteer nurse from Dublin remembered how thirty to forty Cambodians died on the buses taking them from the border to Sakeo. A few dozen Cambodians were put into a tent, but the tent was not properly raised and the volunteers had to crouch, she said, as they moved about trying to treat people lying on mats on the ground. The tent filled with rain. The IVs had to be tied to a bulldozer and she wore a miner's lamp on her head so she could work. The volunteers were not allowed to spend the night there, and the Irish nurse had no choice but to obey. She was twenty-six and had once wished to go to Africa with a medical mission. There was no one there to watch the Cambodians during the night. Their mats began sinking. In the morning when she came back, many were dead. They had drowned in the dark rainwater, unable to struggle, and now lay almost concealed in the mud. And the rest of it the woman could only whisper: in the morning sun she saw that the living were beginning to bake as if in a slow and methodical oven, their lips starting to turn black. By herself the nurse could not pull them from the thick slime heating and hugging their bodies.

Gilbert Hunn was assigned to Khao I Dang, the second center opened in November, its population believed to be 111,000 if not more, making it one of the world's largest Cambodian cities although it was mostly bamboo and thatch. Only Phnom Penh now had a larger number of Cambodians. Fifteen miles from the border, it rose from a scrubland which yielded no water, so daily rations were brought in by truck. The medical wards were the simplest structures, partial bamboo walls lined with blue plastic. There were no screens or shutters, so the flies knew no obstacles and went everywhere. It was typical of Gilbert Hunn that on entering his ward, so unlike anything he had ever seen before, he approached a nurse and said, "Hi. I'm Gil, what can I do to help?" He began.

His children lay on slats of plywood put over the springs of cots, for the Cambodians found mattresses too hot and puffy. There were forty to seventy-five patients; an adult in each family brought the sick children food and stayed with them, not complaining. The prevalent diseases were pneumonia, otitis media or severe ear infection, viral upper-respiratory infection, gastroenteritis predominantly viral, neonatal malnutrition, and measles, he said. The silence of the children in pain was at first startling to him, and soon he stopped noticing the stench. You could not guess the age of any child, all were too small and every child under five that he saw showed signs of malnutrition. In that December there was a death every day, no matter how hard the foreigners fought to save the sickest child. He was the replacement for another American doctor from California; the two overlapped for a few days. Dr. Hunn remembered this man's agitation and how he wept, cried out, and excoriated himself. It made him uncomfortable and impatient. The three nurses were Americans.

"He would get really carried away, crying, saying, 'Oh, I did that horribly,' " Dr. Hunn recalled. "People would tend to look at him as if he were an idiot. They thought it was histrionics. When you see so much that is bad, you cannot give way. If you are welling up in tears taking care of someone, it might affect the decision you have to make." It was what nearly all doctors would say; he had become one of them again for the last time. But there were the deaths of children that took pieces from his heart, so, when possible, he would step outside just for a second to be alone. The International Rescue Committee sent another American doctor from Vermont, who became his friend. These two worked well together, quiet men so beautifully trained and now on their own without labs. At night the five Americans in the ward would leave Khao I Dang and be driven to a house rented for them in Watna, fifty-five kilometers away, where they were comfortable and given their meals. It made him uneasy and slightly sad to be so taken care of; at night he slept on the floor of his room on a mattress. It was cooler and made him feel less pampered. Although no one, of course, profited from such gestures, as he well knew.

In that ward, at Khao I Dang, without running water or toilets for the sick, he sometimes felt pride. "It was the first time that I actually felt I was saving lives," Dr. Hunn said later. And there were small signs of triumph all around him in this vast place: children began to play again, making toys of empty sardine cans pulled on strings. The more prized toys were the little wagons made of empty IV bottles set on homemade wheels. Everywhere something was being organized—charts kept, orders given, problems under consideration, committees conferring. Nothing kept down the dust or stopped the coughing, yet no one felt hunger or fell sick without being helped. Many adults were wrapped in shock or sorrow so deep their faces were still those of people in danger. A woman, speaking French, remembered how well she had once done in school in Phnom Penh and then said, knowing you would not guess it, "And I was pretty once." Under Pol Pot she had pretended to be an idiot, dim-witted, her speech senseless, to save herself and two children, for the educated were killed first. Sometimes she forgot that her face did not need to twitch now; the little spasms were an old habit. One day in the new year, an audience of as many as one thousand Cambodians at Khao I Dang sat on the ground before a stage to watch a performance by dancers who, so long ago, had studied with the Royal Ballet in Phnom Penh. Costumes had been made, so people saw brilliant colors again and remembered what gold and red meant. The faces of the dancers were changed by thick makeup and assumed a holiness, their mouths and eyes large and brilliant. Some women wept and lifted up children, even infants, to better see the dancers, as if the youngest would now understand what Cambodia had once been.

People had malaria and worms; the Americans learned that the Khmer word for worms sounded like "prune." People needed eyeglasses and children needed vaccinations; both were soon to come. Families lived in small structures where the crowding was inevitable but no one minded. Many adults did not know how to master the horror of what had happened and could not even attempt an explanation. The reasons why they had suffered were beyond them, beyond anyone. The savagery of Pol Pot's followers against people of their own race defied all reasoning. "For us, how can we explain this to ourselves?" a Cambodian woman said in

French. "Think of the questions we hold and will never succeed to answer." Many of their tormentors were at Sakeo, where most of the Cambodians were from the countryside. "The Sakeo stare," the foreigners called it to describe how the Khmer Rouge men would look at you, their black hearts and black looks scaring all people, as a woman said.

On the border hundreds of thousands of Cambodians lived in settlements; political allegiances broke them into groups, made them silly or dangerous, led some men to pretend to be in armies, some men to practice with firearms. Doctors with some voluntary agencies treated the Cambodians living there, a more dangerous business because there was fighting, skirmishes, intimidations, threats, and quarrels. At Khao I Dang, which was more peaceful, no one could leave without permission, impossible to get. There were guards, rules, warnings, and possible danger for the disobedient.

At Christmas some foreign volunteers had small parties, but a thirty-five-year-old pediatrician from Berlin, working with a German group on the border, quietly told his colleagues that too many children had died for him to be able to go to a party. His group of German doctors in *Soforthilfe*, or Direct Help, arrived with their own equipment, set up their own hospital, and asked for nothing. Others believed this upset the International Red Cross Committee, which did not exactly approve of such autonomy and efficiency. Once seeing a group of journalists nearby, the German pediatrician said to them: "You come, you bring nothing, you take your pictures and go away. Next time you come, bring food for these people." No answer came back.

Gilbert Hunn had a more complacent nature and was not able to speak with such clarity or bitterness, since he expected almost nothing, or very little, from people and had not the inclination to say so. But he liked journalists on the whole, and their rapid habits of work and metabolism, their tendency to rush about, were a source of fascination and, sometimes, very gentle amusement. He took pictures—an accomplishment most of the world could claim —so their cameras interested him. He could never move as quickly as they did and did not delude himself about that.

Deaths dropped, sick children stabilized, fewer were coming in. He grew attached to some of the children, but none won him over as much as a child of unusual spirit and caprice who called him, in his own tongue, Grandfather. Together they played and knew no sudden divination of their own deaths.

There is a photograph, cherished now, of Gilbert Hunn at Khao I Dang with the tiny boy sitting on his shoulders holding onto the man's thick curly hair, something the younger Cambodian children found strange and wonderful. The child is pleased to be in such a lofty perch, looking at the world from above as he had never seen it before. Arms and legs are too thin, but the small face is alert and slightly flattened up, it may even be swollen. The boy's age was marked down as four, hard as it was to believe, and it was thought he suffered from a vague viral illness, inexplicable. In pain he cried, sometimes he hollered. The doctors worried. Long after, Gilbert Hunn could not remember whether at that point there was no X-ray machine or whether what was missing was a technician. It was thought the boy might have tuberculosis, but there were not yet drugs on hand for the treatment and the more serious problem was that any treatment in order to be successful would have to be sustained for a year. No one knew where the boy might be in a year.

He was called Theng. After a large wart was removed from one foot, he could not walk for a time. The nicest days for Gilbert Hunn were when he made rounds with the child on his shoulders, a highly impractical arrangement which delighted them both for two weeks. The boy held on by holding the American's hair and amused himself, when possible, by tugging the doctor's beard, such a mysterious, quite wonderful thing. A thin woman, no thinner or more silent or more stricken than thousands of others in this place, stayed by the child all day and every night. No one there was sure who she was, a grandmother perhaps; most of the Cambodian women had lost their real ages and even the young did not feel lucky. An interpreter, who had once been an archaeologist, was too busy to inquire, and so were the four other Cambodians obliged to leap between the languages. *Fever? pain? where? blood? stools? diarrhea?* were their words. When Theng showed edema, or swelling, it was thought he might have nephritic syndrome. Dr. Hunn was gone when treatment for this condition was started.

The child did not respond and then was taken out of Khao I Dang, away from the devoted thin woman and the volunteers who did not want to see him go. When word finally reached Gilbert Hunn—long after and by chance—of this death, he began to weep in Inverness, and not even the meadows or the trees could calm him. He thought the treatment may have killed his boy, the bird-child on his shoulders who had laughed, pulling his beard, and made the doctor smile too. He had heard that X-rays showed the child suffered from renal tuberculosis. "The thing that is so appalling is that the treatment for nephritic syndrome is a cortisone derivative, the worst thing to give to someone with tuberculosis," Dr. Hunn said. He could not be certain, of course, but the suspicion sickened him.

There were successes; they steadied the doctors and nurses who watched the children die and who knew what could have been done in the hospitals of Europe and America. It was useless to think of this.

"Look here," I began as we rested on a bench in the Metropolitan Museum. "It was I who, after all, must have chosen that disease, a disease which usually takes out children or young adults; I must have wanted some burning out of the brain. And if you make a living writing about the dispossessed and dying, then there is a certain rough justice if you come down with one of their diseases."

All this I told him, on and on, as the reason I had been stricken with meningococcal meningitis in Thailand while writing about the Cambodians. He was happy to be in the great museum, in New York on his way to see his family in Philadelphia. By then my recovery was complete, no signs of permanent impairment had been detected although I had a secret or two about the brain, which was still sulking. A sympathetic man, Gilbert Hunn did not take kindly to my theory any more than if I had said the Tarot cards warned of such a sickness, but he heard me out. He did not often listen to such emotional extravagance inspired by a nasty disease, although he supposed that women who grew up in New York might be disposed to talk as I talked. He was not going to humor me and made clear it was not a question of my choosing, at Khao I Dang, between meningitis and pneumonia, tuberculosis or dysentery and thus, in the end, believing I had my own way. He went over it all again, the lesson I knew so well I could recite it: the pathogenic organisms in the nasopharynx, the acute inflammatory reaction of the membranes covering the brain, the extreme stiffness in the neck, the headaches so violent and bursting, the high fever, the patient often in a maniacal state—all this a result of the intracranial catastrophe. It was a protean disease, sometimes difficult to diagnose; doctors could be easily deceived and meningitis progressed most rapidly. It made me sleepy to hear it again.

He could not see the rough justice I was speaking of, only interested in recalling the assault on the brain and finally the defeat, not difficult, of the meningococci organisms. In the Bangkok hospital the staff doctors had not understood what the matter was, gave up, and ordered me tied to the bed for my own good. Days later the eldest doctor, a European who said long ago he had seen the terrible meningitis epidemics in China, explained I had not spotted, as if the absence of a rash had deprived him of the crucial clue and such an admission, therefore, rendered him blameless.

The trouble began slowly: a bit of bronchitis, which was not too expensive a price to pay for a notebook filled with the stories of Khao I Dang, so many notes on suffering that I had used the old private shorthand for death and disaster, the Pitman of Vietnam. The weary and pinched babies who lay too still in the cardboard boxes, the French nurse needing blood donors so urgently one morning, the Cambodian child I had leaned over to more carefully note his rough, hoarse breathing and the chills that made him tremble. The dead and the stricken, fewer in numbers by then, were still carried inside lengths of cloth strung over poles on the shoulders of Cambodian men, and all you could see was the feet of another corpse, the feet of the dying. On that New Year's Eve it had been eight years since I had left the war in Indochina and had wanted, as of that night, to forget all I had seen, heard, to become a partial amnesiac, willing to relinquish even the better memories: the smell of gardenia bushes one evening on a street in Phnom Penh, the pink cathedral of Saigon at dawn.

In the Bangkok hotel room, the fever woke me, made the bed dip and slide, the walls start to slant, straighten, then move again. The room swelled and shrank, as did I. Was it the Cambodian boy, my face so close to his, whose fever had now moved to me, my breathing so much like his?

Matthew Naythons, who had met me in the Hotel Trocadero, where the journalists stayed, heard I was sick, perhaps with the flu, and came to the hospital to visit. He entered the room, did not recognize the woman who lay in the bed, left, and walking down the hall suddenly realized who she was. He asked Gilbert Hunn, in Bangkok for a few days, to come with him to the hospital, so the pair of them with their grave and amiable medical manners, careful not to offend the staff doctors by their assurance, began the treatment, starting the spinal tap and then the penicillin. Once, in the coma, I knew it was he sitting by the bed, patting my hand, although a doctor might dispute the possibility of such a vision when you are unconscious. There were tiny yellow flowers in his beard and hair; he appeared as a large, friendly sort of bear who was worrisome only because half a dozen children were hiding, although whispering and coughing, under my bed, and had to be protected. It was the fever, of course, the inflamed lining of the brain, but he was comforting and the children finally came out to stroke his fur.

"You kept trying to get out, so I had to restrain you," Dr. Hunn said in another city when all of it was past. "You were very strong." None of this was known to me and I was glad he was so tall and heavier than I, for it would have been disgraceful to have attacked a woman doctor. One did not need to worry about punching or kicking men.

Many women spoke of his sweetness and how he reminded them of a teddy bear, a compliment, but one he might not have preferred. Kathleen Golden, who lived in Sausalito with Matthew Naythons, remembered the night of a dinner party and how he played for so long with the new baby of a friend. And he asked several times, even rising to his feet, if he might help with clearing the table. There were not many like that, few so gentle. When Matthew was away, she said, he would call just to ask how she was doing.

As a teenager Gilbert Hunn had been chubby, shy, uncertain of how to appeal to girls or what exactly to do if he ever should. He moved with a band of neighborhood boys who always stuck together, not one of them anxious to go out on his own. The sight of them often disturbed or discouraged young women, who knew their lumping together made it possible for them to be so unsociable, if not ominous. "We had the great reputation of party paralyzers," Dr. Hunn said. Not until he was twenty-two did he become intimate with a woman—rather late for an American male—and he continued to view himself, without endlessly revealing it, as being not very secure.

"I think I've found that, in many ways, being unaggressive is the successful technique for me to get what I want," Dr. Hunn said. "I do better not being aggressive." He remained unaware of his own surprising lack of conceit.

It was not his tendency to be scornful of any human interpretation of events, as long as medicine wasn't invoked, so in the museum that day, looking at the great bronze horses of San Marco Cathedral, I felt free to speak about death for he, after all, had come to my rescue.

There is this to consider, I said, listen. When the small son of a friend, a man who had been a foreign correspondent for more than twenty-five years, was killed in an absurd accident, the father knew a mistake had been made, that it was he who was meant to die—in the Congo, the father said, or in Vietnam, perhaps in the African country where its emperor ordered him arrested, perhaps in Lebanon. But Death, seeking to locate him, its finger moving, had been clumsy and touched the boy by mistake.

Men who were correspondents, a few wars behind them and more coming up, almost never ridiculed this theory and had some of their own as well but would not admit this to many people, as the pretense of being rational and unemotional had to be maintained. I believed it, too, but that was not so unusual for women, and told Gilbert Hunn my own death in Vietnam had been long due. Perhaps I was crying, the tears came easily enough after the meningitis. He said nothing but took my hand and, relying on the intimacy that bound us, led me back to the green horses for a last look at Venice.

He was thirty-eight and had never known a time as intense and rewarding and useful as those months at Khao I Dang. In February, no longer needed, he traveled to Thai villages to do what could be done for their sick and incapacitated. "Without being conscious of it, the day I went to Thailand in November 1979, I embarked on an irrevocable course. That is all that is clear now," he wrote a friend in New York. He signed letters to friends, as few men do, with "all my love." Coming home, he was strangely ill at ease in his old surroundings. The woman he loved, who even flew to Thailand to visit him at Khao I Dang and saw a child die the first day in the ward, said she was leaving, and left his house but stayed in Inverness. She wanted to stand on her own two feet, she said, and he smothered her. He kept reading aloud to his son, David, and took him on hikes. By then he had read aloud *The Hobbit* and all three volumes of *The Lord of the Rings* to David. The idyllic life hardly changed, only he had.

There were never disagreements with his former wife, a nurse who had coauthored a highly respected book on cardiac care, on how to raise their son. She had married again, which caused him no pain. He understood that women became exasperated by his passivity; in get-ahead America he was the oddest of men, and it threw people off.

"I never wanted to be a full-time professional, but she wanted me to. I didn't want to set up a practice, I wanted to live my life differently," Dr. Hunn said. "Responsibility? I try to avoid it. But when there is no one else around, I wind up doing what has to be done. I think I am a good doctor. But one of my difficulties is the fact that the women I am closest to look at me as being a greater, more important, person than I really am, and a better person than they think they are. My wife, who is very competent professionally, felt inferior to me. Yes, I'm a doctor, but more than that, people think I am smarter than I am."

His only income, more than sufficient for himself and the monthly payments he made for David's education, came from filling in on weekends in the emergency rooms of different hospitals. He was registered with a service that provided him with work. He worked more than twenty-four hours at a stretch; it was not enthralling. The seriously injured were usually taken to a trauma center, the critically sick did not often come to him. He saw people in a panic about bad colds, people on drugs, a few alcoholics, and others having anxiety attacks about a health problem he, a physician, would consider insignificant. Some came to an emergency room because they did not know a doctor they could call or were unable to pay the current inflated fees.

"It's very expensive to become a doctor; you start off with huge debts. You pay them off by making money, and the only way is to treat upper-middle-class or upper-class patients," Dr. Hunn said. "You start living in the way you're expected to live." This is what seemed wrong but, of course, no one in the country could ever agree on what *wrong* meant.

He did not think of himself as an imposing, aloof figure. He did not wear white coats or black shoes. He did not stride, he ambled. He listened. He tried to be courteous to the poor, the confused, and the incoherent. He had always wanted to dispense justice and be honest.

"Men try to tough it out a little more than women," he said of patients. "You can tell a man, this is what it is going to be like. Men get as anxious as women, but their anger and anxiety get turned inward and are more difficult to recognize, more difficult to alleviate. A doctor is more aware, more alert, with a woman because her anxiety is more obvious. Men tend to underplay their illnesses. A tremendous emotional bureaucracy builds up: what women probably expect is that if they become emotional, they are going to be comforted by a concerned response. A man is not going to expect that, a man would never cry on my shoulder. Maybe that is a pity."

Make voyages, that is all there is, the playwright once said. Gilbert Hunn set forth again, another odyssey, returning to Khao I Dang, which had drastically changed. No one there knew him, and an air of dreary permanence seemed as fixed as the bite of the sun. The new volunteers were not as recklessly generous, as driven, as the first groups had been, for the historic and monstrous crisis was over.

He moved on to Borneo and traveled by himself, taking photographs in color, quite good ones too; he returned again, went on reading to his son, and horribly missed the young woman, who now hoped they could just be affectionate friends. Inverness was so small they often saw each other. "I do not want to become an aimless world traveler, yet I am filled with the need to move, to go," he wrote in a letter. "At the same time I want the security, the beauty, the peace of my home, my family, my prosaic concerns. I am certain I cannot go back to my Thailand life . . . Why do I need a woman and of all women, why Sally? The questions and answers are terribly trite." It was no good advising him, as people were tempted to, that the conflict he knew was ordinary, had jarred generations of other men, and was without solution. He wanted to fall in love and was embarrassed to admit it. What he thought he needed was a huge entanglement that would not let him sleep or chew his vegetables so thoroughly. Nothing happened. He waited.

The high hopes held for his medical career were now limp and mislaid, and even Dora Hunn, his mother, could not keep them suspended before the eyes of a large, inquisitive, ambitious family. Her son did so splendidly when he chose, and once his career made her proud: medical school at Temple University, his internship and a year in a research training program at Duke University, a year as a research associate at the National Institute of Health, a fellowship in genetics for his doctorate in medicine, and a postdoctoral fellowship in clinical pharmacology at Stanford University, and then the slow change, the falling off, in California.

The family had disapproved of his marriage to a woman who was not Jewish—the two met at Duke, both not at ease in the South, each needing an attachment of some kind—then grew fond of her, fonder yet when a son was born. News of the divorce, in a family where divorce was seen as a violation or a neuroticism of the worst kind, came as a blow. The mother of Gilbert Hunn—who had worked nearly all her life selling expensive clothes, dressed well, and knew a nicely cut coat or suit across a room—did not want him to keep going to countries that were both dirty and dangerous. Why, she kept asking, what for? No answer sufficed. Once when Dr. Hunn said, on the telephone, "next year in Jerusalem" she misunderstood and had a vision of buses blowing up, bridges bombed, men without hearts aiming at helpless crowds, her son an easy target.

The standards held by Dora Hunn were unusually high and in direct opposition to his: cleanliness was a major concern and so, in her Philadelphia apartment, there were no wastepaper baskets in any room. You walked to the kitchen if you wanted to throw away something; all litter was considered distasteful. Visiting relatives in hospitals, she would take it upon herself to disinfect the sick room. Not trusting others, she sprayed herself, and provided another story for relatives to tell, laughing. She left no dish unwashed or wet before going to bed, no matter how late or fatigued she felt, and furniture was straightened and cushions fluffed up as if before dawn an inspection might be called and she held to judgment. Her daughter, Gloria, attempted to calm and reassure her about Gilbert as the years went by, but she was unsuccessful. All the laments about his beard, the pleas to be clean-shaven, went unheard. Gilbert Hunn was the light of Dora's life, the genius, the puzzle, the child who at the age of one had had bilateral pneumonia, which scared her to death, almost. No precaution went untested: when he played in the streets as a child, his mother would find him and pat cornstarch on his skin, fearing that his perspiration would lead to an oxygen tent. It was not the cornstarch she used that was unusual, rather the amount she applied. Her worry became celebrated, that small face quick to cloud.

His father worked for three decades or more as a waiter in a famous Jewish restaurant, Himmelstein's. He was always silent on his day off, Dr. Hunn said. The child was closer to his grandfather, whom he saw every week and adored. Grown and so disobedient to the wishes of the tribe, Dr. Hunn knew that his cousin, Rita, a principal of an elementary school, understood why Dora's dream of her son in a white coat, a large office, an imposing title at a famous hospital, was too dreadful to imagine.

He knew immense love for his sister, his mother, his cousin, his son, but would not listen to the women when he was home, for they talked constantly and long ago he had found out how to remove himself from a room without stirring. He simply shut down. Gilbert Hunn always knew what he did not want to be.

Go to work in Harlem Hospital in New York, a friend said. Another thought it should be somewhere in Appalachia or rural Mississippi, or that he must leave right away for Nicaragua. What all of us were saying to him was: You surely have no wish to be comfortable when you can relieve suffering in such places; we happen to be useless because we are not doctors, but you must feel it worthwhile to be wretched if you are able to do so much good.

But no, he did not. He did not want to live in a filthy, maniacal city, or in exhausted places where certain children were destined always to be underfed and needed protection from despair as much as vitamins. He did not want to live in a Central American country which might be bombed or invaded, so poor that a small bottle of shampoo, a sewing kit, or several cakes of soap were often seen as a fine gift. (But if someone gave him a ticket, said go in a week, you are expected, he might have gone for a while and come back.)

What he wanted was clear air, mountains and hills to go up, flowers he had not seen, encounters of great interest, adventures, some belief—perhaps even proof—in the newness of one's self, an awakening, not places of sadness when such sadness glazed everything and need not exist.

Once, years before, he had gone to San Quentin—the state prison on the point that extends into San Francisco Bay—when there was an opening for a physician on call, but he could not bear it. "The most depressed I have ever been in my entire life was that day in San Quentin," Dr. Hunn said. "Nothing could touch that." He was taken on a tour of the medical facilities, and afterwards remembered yellowing walls, the dirt, a horrid smell. In the faces of the guards and prisoners he saw how alike they now were, the slight grimace of their mouths, the tightened, wary look on all their faces.

A long time later, in the little library of Inverness, he noticed a tall, strange man in the room as he talked to the librarian, Lynn, which he did almost every day. The man moved in an odd and disjointed fashion, as if he lacked proper human sockets. Then there was his pallor, that white face with almost a tinge of green in the skin. "He seemed very pained; he seemed contorted, twisted, not necessarily an evil or demented thing," said Dr. Hunn. Lynn told him that the man worked in San Quentin, but he had already guessed.

On a single day in that prison he learned what he could not tolerate: to be within reach of such despair, among men whose faces and bodies were the diagrams of their ordeal, in a place of such awfulness that anyone could be contaminated and pulled down. He saw he was useless there.

Early in January 1982, what he thought would never change was taken away. A storm moved in and did great damage to Inverness. An astonishing rain began on the third day of the year, and the stream below his house, once three feet wide, swelled to five times its normal, pretty size. The deck around his house went down and the geraniums flung petals everywhere. A wall of water swept down falling trees and created a mudslide. Cars were pinned down by other trees, roads were useless, the landscape he loved turned treacherous; power, gas, electricity were out. A medical center was set up in the high school where he, the one physician, was posted, but there were none of the injuries expected, not a bad cut or a broken bone, just some sprains. "My house, the land is all gone," he said when it was over, and spoke like a grieved man who knows a huge injustice.

There was even less reason after the storm to stay put, for the house was uninhabitable and the view torn and disturbing. He went to London to study for six months at the School of Tropical Medicine, but he found the work too easy. He was without course until a missionary he met in England suggested he come to visit in northern Uganda. It was a casual invitation but sincere—a doctor is always of use—and there would be lodging and food. Dr. Hunn agreed, wanting to see the Ruwenzori Mountains, first described in 1879, climbed in 1906 by the first European, an Italian duke, and famous for its mists and curious plants. Back in this country, to say good-bye and to prepare for his life in London, he hoped for invitations to foreign countries, where he might work, for a very small salary, but none came. A few letters were written, queries made, the need for doctors surely urgent. There was Ethiopia, Cambodia, Nicaragua, dozens of places, but he did not want war zones and did not think he could manage extreme heat. He hoped for Zimbabwe but left without hearing. In Inverness the young woman who left him now promised to take care of mail, bills, his bank account, and all else; she could always be counted on and was loyal, no matter the imposition.

In Africa he followed whispers. He did not need clocks. He spent very little money. He kept a journal. He made friends and went to a wedding. Arriving in Kenya, he simply stayed on, not anxious to push on to Uganda because it was so pleasant. Carrying the blue rucksack and his two cameras, he went to Mt. Kenya and entered the park alone, which was forbidden by the authorities on safety grounds. It was not his intention to make the perilous climbs, to attempt the ice slope called the Diamond Couloir on the southwest face of the mountain, only to hike on the trails. At Two Tarn Hut, no more than fifteen thousand feet up—a small structure named for the two peaks in view—he passed an evening with a physicist from Oxford University and a graduate student at St. Catherine's College, both Englishmen and experienced climbers. On Sunday, the kindest of days, warm, bright, and without wind, he set out by himself, well equipped in the unlikely event he could not return by nightfall. He did not. The next day the two Englishmen, uneasy, searched for him and found the body lying face down, a large rock across his legs, no more than twenty minutes, an easy scramble, from the Tarn hut. The older Englishman, the physicist, later wrote to Dr. Hunn's mother and sister, whose names were provided by the U.S. embassy in Nairobi: "We had very much enjoyed meeting and talking to him; he was a very nice, charming, quiet guy with a gentle sense of humor. In our different ways Pat and I were deeply affected by his death, but we gained some comfort from the knowledge that he had died instantaneously, without any pain. That, surely, is worth something to you also," wrote the physicist.

Dora Hunn, unwilling to believe it was her son, wanted the coffin opened, to be sure it was her child. So at the funeral his face could be seen, still with a look of sweetness and the usual slight frown, even then. Two friends were asked to speak: the first the younger doctor Matthew Naythons, who was deeply shaken. A woman spoke next; it was I.

Gilbert Hunn was an explorer, the saved woman said, the map he examined was of himself, and by going forth in the world to strange places he made a voyage of the mind, it was not just his body which traveled. Wanting to know the world better, he found both joy and sorrow and was afraid of neither, she told them. Among the mourners were those who could not help wishing Gilbert had stayed put, done research, won a Nobel Prize.

There were letters. A professor of medicine at Temple University wrote: "He was a gifted, intelligent young man who had constructed a computer while still in high school and at a time when computers were just being born. Because of his intelligence he was frequently bored in medical school by sophomoric lectures. This boredom led to inattention and was interpreted by some as incompetence. In my judgment he was always superior intellectually and it is for this reason that I persuaded Dr. Eugene Stead to accept him as a resident in medicine at Duke University. Gilbert must have done excellent work there, because he received a fellowship to work with Dr. Joshua Lederberg, who had won the Nobel Prize. . . . Subsequently Gilbert became disillusioned with common practices of questionable repute in the field of general medicine. . . . I am proud of him and what he has done. . . . He was successful in what he thought was worthwhile doing . . ."

Such were the condolences. It was terrible to see the suffering of Dora Hunn, who could not stop asking why he was dead, and of the sister, Gloria. The young woman in California, who came east for the funeral, spent months sorting out the books, photographs, letters, and possessions Dr. Hunn had stored with friends in Inverness, and was, each day, reminded of their lives together.

No one was able to imagine how he might have spent the rest

of his life if the large rocks had not fallen, striking his head. The mystery of him made his friends sad; one woman thought a man so out of step with the spirit of the country in which he lived had been in danger all along and never knew it.

When jobs were so scarce that more than 10 million people needed and could not find work, the soup kitchens began opening everywhere in the cities. What was given out was not often soup; the free meals sometimes meant some meat, sometimes some chicken, which people were allowed to eat sitting down at tables, not standing outside in the street. In Kansas City, Kansas, at Fifth and Ann, the line began at 10 A.M. outside old Saint Mary's Church, even in the summer when each day seemed swollen with a hard, white light. Volunteers from different churches came with the food and kept cooking it. Some people waited for two hours before the priest, Father Richard Etzel, unbolted the basement doors, and in the heat the lines often grew a little fretful. One July day in 1982, 492 people needed to be fed lunch, but it was so punishing outside the priest tried to have the queue bunch and coil inside the basement so people wouldn't have to bear the heat as well as hunger. For a lot of them it was the only meal of the day and on weekends they went without (although later the kitchen would be open all week; it had to be).

Father Etzel handed out tickets for the sake of having a record, otherwise a correct count was not possible. The tickets looked like the ones you buy to get into a movie. Children were given a different color. But people put their hands out so quickly for the tickets, as if some first barrier must be swiftly overcome, that I confused the colors and tore too quickly from the wrong roll, muddling a simple task. It was the job he usually did, and the presence of the priest—the worn, still young face, the white plastic collar, the same dark clothes he wore all summer—had a calming effect while mine did not.

I was relieved of being at the door and went back to the kitchen to help hand out plates of food, but this was harder. You could not keep your head down and just look at people's hands; now you had to see them.

On the line young men did not yield their places to women,

even those with infants or several children, and no one expected them to.

Many of the men stood looking at the floor while they waited, as if they hoped to go unnoticed, to achieve invisibility so that others would not see they were hostages to the haphazard, waiting for a portion of frankfurter and beans casserole. It was the men who most often appeared ashamed because they felt helpless. Will was useless, because without work they could will almost nothing. "Women are more resilient and physiologically viable," writes the psychologist studying male and female development. "They are born more mature than males and continue to be more adaptable in the sense of having available a wider range of physiological fluctuation (the male being more constantly geared up for masculine muscular output). Thus men are physiologically more vulnerable than women. From the moment of conception onwards, the male is more likely to die or be defective." In his studies it is men who are seen as more anxious, more vulnerable, obsessed with their decline and death. In a church basement in Kansas City, even the youngest men seemed stiff and silent while the women, who knew panic and despair of their own, did not often appear to feel themselves disgraced. You could have conversations with them, a chat, while the men wanted no comments and gave none.

That week, hardly a special one, the newcomers included a young man from South Carolina driving across the country looking for work with his wife and four-year-old son, all living in the car. It was hard to see how she kept that blue dress so decent, how she found a sink and soap to do laundry. All the South Carolina man could manage to say was that Texas was now full up and the fuel pump on the car was broke, beyond his fixing. There was no work then in Kansas for a man like that who had only been employed in a textile mill. If you read the Help Wanted ads in the *Kansas Star* on August 1, there was some hope only if you knew how to be a data base analyst, an apparel saleman, a bookkeeper, a bank examiner, a candy store manager, an operator of a word processor, a cryotechnologist, a dental hygienist, a draftsman, a nurse, or a dry cleaner. The ad for Drivers said two years' experience within the past three years were required and you had to be twenty-five years of age, no older and no younger.

A few people in Saint Mary's basement grew agitated when

they suspected the food would run out just as their turn came, and it happened sometimes: once Father Etzel had to open cans of beef stew and those at the end of the line knew disappointment that the homemade casserole was gone. But still they ate the stew fast enough and some came back for seconds, which were only allowed if everyone had been served.

Standing behind the counter in the kitchen, passing out the paper plates of hot food, mindful that Father Etzel wanted the volunteers to receive people as guests, not as beggars or inferiors, you would try at first to speak to each person coming to the window.

Sometimes a man so famished could not wait to reach the table where the plastic knives and forks, the folded paper napkins, were laid out. When he held the plate of food that was his he would start to eat with his fingers, not caring if you saw. Two days in a row men did that. The women seemed more alive, as if free food was not a confirmation of moral failure, and they seemed glad to have a comment on how pretty a baby was, what nice eyes the four-year-old had. Conversation did not diminish them. "We come here, really, for the children," said Marla, who was twenty-one. There were four children, the eldest suffering from cystic fibrosis, to be fed on $251 a month in food stamps; the arithmetic of their existence did not seem to her to require secrecy anymore. Gary, her husband, let her speak; he seemed scarcely present as she explained that he had worked in the building trades until the layoffs two years before. Marla thought it was nice the day that one church group put bunches of flowers—sweet william and elderberry—on each of the sixteen tables in the basement covered by white paper, but he saw none of it—the old fan that could not do enough to make the room cool, the stained linoleum which the priest and other men washed with mops after the meal, and the walls that simply seemed old, with no real, familiar color left.

A photograph was taken of the family sitting in front of one of the high doors of the old church that no longer opens. The three children and the baby in her lap are barefoot and wear only tiny shorts. The woman looks at the camera with immense composure, the mouth curling in memory of what it is to smile. He is something else, not willing to be as responsive as she. His head is tilted back, the strong face defiant and shut, as if here is a man interned and not grateful for the surveillance of outsiders. Some money was given with a false explanation that it was a fee for permitting a photograph to be taken. But I knew better than to hand the money to him, and have to look closely at what was so distinct on that face; she and I conspired, without a word, so the bills could be slipped into her hand without his seeing or having to respond.

The Great Depression was often cited on television because the people who appeared on the air, usually smiling and chatting, on local stations would not imagine what other comparisons to make and their jobs, after all, did not require that they understand or even recognize the cyclical convulsions of capitalism or have knowledge of darker stretches of American history. It is believed to be better, certainly safer, if they do not. Drained and defeated people were interviewed on television and expected to describe their state in a few seconds, the time allotted them. Speechless dread was not permitted. Statistics flowed from television sets, took up space in newspapers; ratings were made of the states and industries in the most peril; some ministers and priests tried to make it clear their own congregations were really too poor to be able to provide food for all the hungry in the community; some denunciations were made of the government for permitting millions of tons of milk and cheese and butter to sit in warehouses when people were in need of food. Father Etzel saw days when the baby food ran out and the lines grew even more disturbing; in winter it was always sadder.

In some American towns there was no such thing as a soup kitchen, although boxes of food were handed out, and the expression "heat or eat" meant just that, for fuel was so high. There were no widespread disorders, Americans sank silently, denouncing nothing and blaming no one. There were a few voices of rage, unheard, and many explanations of the recession that contradicted each other. Several years later, when an economic recovery was assured, touted, and a cause for rejoicing, a report by the Physician Task Force on Hunger found that hunger was not lessened but worse. The twenty-two-member study group felt it had evidence that up to twenty million citizens may be hungry "at least some period each month."

In Lorain, Ohio, people led lives of greater caution but behaved as if it was not their right to expect to be spared such an affliction; unemployment in the county was running at 21 percent. Job applications at the local Holiday Inn were accepted during a few specific hours a week, the personnel manager was overwhelmed. A black woman, making beds, said the dental benefits were good, but since her husband was out of work they were no use to her at all; she could not pay her percentage. Younger men had known rage and now seemed worn out, fatigued, as if a toxic substance were making them weaker. All they said they wanted was what had been taken from them. A city of slightly more than seventy-five thousand at the mouth of the Black River on Lake Erie's southern shore, twenty-five miles west of Cleveland, the population stayed put. Men did not take to the road to find work, they held on. Men were out of work that November because of the deep layoffs at the Ford assembly plant in Lorain and at the U.S. Steel mill, which hadn't made its usual noises that summer, its old raucous breathing much too soft now. People in their backyards took note of how still it seemed. In the supermarkets, during the day, men moved slowly up and down the aisles, as if they did not now remember what it was they wanted. Once it was normal to see them shopping on Saturdays, but not alone like this on a weekday afternoon, paying so little attention to their lists. Their wives were working, but not in the better-paid jobs that men held. That was the month when 4,500 steelworkers were out, and the 3,000 still with jobs could not be certain for how long because it was rumored the mill might have a temporary shutdown or be closed for good. In 1980, when production was at a record level, 7,100 people had jobs there. The cuts began in 1982.

It was hardly better at the Ford plant, which had reportedly shut for a major retooling of its Thunderbird and Cougar X74; of 4,600 workers on the active roll that November, only 1,800 were still on the job. In May 1979, a good year, 7,200 people had been employed. Barry Whitfield, a thirty-five-year-old Ford worker in the third month of another indefinite layoff, did the shopping at a chain called Fazio's The Food People, the store in the Oakwood shopping center, with his two youngest boys when school was out. Since he did the cooking too, Mr. Whitfield found out quickly he could not spend less than ten dollars to make dinner for the five of them. The three boys ate so much and were used to meat, although he could do nice things with a macaroni and cheese casserole.

The children and the cooking took some of his time, but he had hours to kill off, so it was fine when a neighbor in South Lorain —a community of small and decent houses with wide streets and its own park of oak trees—asked Barry to help fix his leaking roof before winter gave him grief. All the men in South Lorain, considered too ordinary a place by couples who dream of big dens and two bathrooms, fix things themselves. They would not consider calling in a professional to do the job. They learn about roofs, engines, drains, pipes, motors, and boats as boys. So there was nothing unusual about three of them fixing the roof of a house on East Thirtieth Street except that it was a Wednesday and too many people were at home, their big cars bunched outside.

The weather held. All that week in November the sky was pewter but not dark, a day stiffened by breeze although the real wind from Lake Erie had not yet begun to bully people. Mr. Whitfield, deeply suspicious of heights, did not want to be on the roof, so he carried the shingles up the ladder to hand to the others. Since no one here ever walks, except the schoolchildren, Mr. Whitfield rode the short distance from his house on his used 1974 Kawasaki KZ 400 motorcycle, seventy-miles-to-the-gallon, which he loved more than his three-year-old Century Buick although that Buick was a very well made car, he said, but gas cost too much. The work had gone well; then it was time to get home right away to wake up his wife, Joyce, a nurse's aide then on the night shift.

That day, glad to have been in the company of other men, all of them young and out of work, Mr. Whitfield made a little joke about having to get Joyce up. "I let her sleep! I let her work!" he said, playing for a laugh. For a little while, as he stood there smiling, his thick brown hair raised in a wild ruffle, the thin face less tightly wired, you might not have known he was wearing out or how bad the headaches had been. He wasn't really touchy about his wife now bringing home the only paycheck. A lot of women in Lorain worked, had always worked in the more poorly paid jobs. They didn't want them for self-fulfillment or to show the world what they could do. Sometimes working was a means of getting out of the house or having money of their own. In Joyce's case she was earning four dollars an hour, $240 take-home pay every two weeks, Mr. Whitfield said, adding, in a burst of bravura, that he was not going to work for *that*. Not after the good days at Ford, not after those nine years he put in, not when he had come home with

$350 every week after a forty-hour shift in commercial, working on the Econoline vans, a utility man who could do almost any job. The truth is he didn't mean it; he only wanted to show faith that Ford would call him back.

The headaches had begun as a sharp, slow drumming inside the skull, a music playing to the beat of his panic. He had had only twenty-four weeks of work from October 1980 to October 1981. In 1982 he worked from January through July. That summer the pain became persistent and important. He went to a clinic in Oberlin twenty times during three months, "at fifty dollars a click," he says, all of it covered by his medical benefits with Ford. Only dental coverage was gone by then. Mr. Whitfield, who did not often seek medical advice, talked to a psychologist who explained the effects of stress and taught him biofeedback techniques. It struck some of the couple's friends as not only a weird but a useless thing to do; a few seemed shocked.

"I was just so worried constantly," said Mr. Whitfield, in the kitchen where the only luxuries are a Mary Proctor blender and a Brew Started coffee maker. "It made me feel better, it was relieving. You don't have to be crazy to go there. I know a lot of men getting into trouble now. I would watch television because I didn't have nothing to do; I had to watch soap operas during the day because there was not so much on. I would watch 'The Young and the Restless' at 12:30. I would watch a man in it, he lost his job, he's ready to cry, to fall apart, and I would see that's what is *really* happening, the men are losing their jobs and women are picking up while the men are crumbling . . ."

He had never quite considered women in this light, although he did point out that those who worked at Ford weren't pampered types, not like some others. Sometimes he saw one or two of them in Fazio's and they made fast jokes about when they would be called back. He thought that perhaps the pride of men, their needing to be the important providers, would make the misery worse when they were laid off. But he really didn't know very many women well, except for some widows like his mother, because Joyce was sixteen and he twenty when they married. Joyce did not get headaches when he was laid off.

It was a popular assumption—other men often said the same thing, making a little joke about it—that in a crunch it was the women who were ready when trouble came and who did not collapse. The men did not take into account women on their own who had families to carry, women who were shy and unskilled, growing more nervous and humiliated every month there was no work. The truth is that the women knew the same confusion and shame as unemployed men who felt themselves pushed out in the cold; sometimes, like the men, they even felt they were to blame when they were not. The difference was they did not see themselves as ruined women, suspect as females, people now exposed as profoundly defective.

Barry Whitfield did not know Karen Sue Dellinger, a thirty-eight-year-old divorcée, because they lived in different neighborhoods in Lorain, because they had never worked in the same part of the Ford plant, and because she was not a friend of his wife's. Mrs. Dellinger had lost three jobs in four years, so on most days her smile did not work as it once had and the threads of what she would say about her own life split and frayed as if her own narrative was too demanding to tell. It clearly did her no good to be brave, to be appealing, to be so devout, when she did not have enough money to eat twice a day.

Born in West Virginia, she came to Lorain at nineteen to visit a sister, then married a Ford worker, and now lives with her seventeen-year-old daughter, Tracy. The daughter has a two-year-old son, Jason. "Single parent" is not a phrase Mrs. Dellinger can bring herself to use, not this woman with copies of the magazine of the Lutheran Church of America in the living room who shows you that she is in one of the photographs taken at Our Saviour Church in Lorain. So she put it her own way: the strain in the family when her husband left, the divorce he wanted and then got four years ago, was surely a consideration, Tracy was deeply affected. The girl had heard it all before, she was not interested in this version, and she did not look at her mother; she was somewhere else. The child, Jason, sturdy and adventurous, made a rumpus and the two women, sitting together on the couch but so separate, still smiled faintly at the urgency of the boy, the racket he made. "On some days," Karen Sue Dellinger said, "we've had it so bad once I used dishwashing liquid to wash my hair; that's all there was in the house." She did not need to say that blond hair shows dirt faster. Something southern and girlish was still at work, so she laughed a little at the story to lift the strain in the room.

A son, fourteen, was sent to the father's household in September because she could not feed or clothe him anymore. Tracy picked tomatoes one summer, but it is not clear whether she helped keep the household going with that bit of money. The food stamps, $78 a month or $2.60 a day for two adults and a child, had been stopped, the reason unclear. The rent was $265, the unemployment benefits not much more. That month Mrs. Dellinger was working part-time for $3.35 an hour, the minimum wage, at the Gold Circle Discount Store in the accessories department, but knew it would be over by January however well she did. At Ford she had been in cleanup, then for a few weeks on the assembly line; for nine months she had held a CETA job with the Catholic Youth Organization, visiting the elderly at home and making herself useful to them. Her last job had been at the steel mill. "I was a leadman," she said, a hard job for her—a woman easily scared—working near the coke furnaces. She spoke of the larry cars; the thermal underwear you needed; the steel-toed work boots and the wooden shoes strapped on; some sign she saw that warned you about something, maybe cancer; and the day her hair caught on fire, despite the required headgear and a scarf. But the mill was too huge, too awesome for her to explain much, and I did not know what questions to ask about a coke furnace. After two months, she was let go in the fall of 1981.

What helped her most was having a friend—another woman, divorced and bringing up two sons herself on a small salary—and it was this friendship that kept Mrs. Dellinger pinned together and still on her feet. The friend was Susan Moralez, director of food distribution in the office of the Lorain County Catholic Youth Organization, which gave away boxes of a week's supply of supplemental food: rice, beans, peanut butter, hot cereal, cold cereal, canned vegetables, bread, flour, sugar, fruit, and, if available, coffee or tea. In the first ten months of 1982, 12,000 people had been given such boxes, the year before the total had been only 5,532. Every night, she said, she asked herself the same thing: "Oh my God, where is the food going to come from tomorrow?" That month she was urged to take a vacation for a week and went to visit relatives because her exhaustion was so visible a sister said, take time off. The Food Bank, a project of United Way and the Catholic Hunger Fund, was also helped by some large corporations, notably Stouffer Foods which had already donated as many as ten thousand boxes of their frozen Lean Cuisine, ordinarily $2.29 a box for the Meatball Stew, less than 300 calories, a product for people anxious about their weight. The portions are small. So Mrs. Moralez, who believed in God, and Mrs. Dellinger, who believed in God, spoke on the telephone and saw each other quite often—the first woman, stronger and wiser, pulling the other woman through.

Men, too, had friends, but often the other men were out of work too and they could not manage the effort to see those who were still on the job. And they dreaded seeing men who were like themselves, unemployed. It was simpler to stay alone because they knew a self-distrust as their lives began their deadly shrinkage. Some men who were friends were accustomed to doing things together, hunting or fishing or diversions like that—all of which required planning, cost money, and now even a beer in a bar cost too much for the ones whose lives had come down to the counting of coins. Most of the men had wives, but their wives were not their friends; they were something else altogether and knew too much to be a diversion or a fresh source of consolation. They were witnesses to the disaster, women watching.

It was Susan Moralez who had managed to get Mrs. Dellinger the CETA job and who made her a present of the pretty blouse she was wearing that day. That was the job that suited her the best, she said. People had been so glad to see her and grateful for what she did to smooth out their daily lives. She was very good with the elderly, not patronizing them nor finding them dull or pitiful. She made small friendships and remembered one elderly woman with wistfulness.

"I even did her hair sometimes," said Mrs. Dellinger. "You weren't supposed to, but it made her feel so good, you know."

That was the month when national unemployment rose to 10.3 percent, which meant that 11,987,000 people were jobless, the highest figure since 1947 when the government began to keep such records. The economy, one newspaper claimed, was suffering the worst recession since 1937. Wall-to-wall unemployment, a Houston newspaper called it. As had been the case since July 1981, called the beginning of the recession, the greatest loss of jobs was in the manufacture of machinery, automobiles, and steel. In addition to the 12 million out of work, there were about 1.6 million people so discouraged they had given up looking for jobs, said the Commissioner of Labor Statistics in Washington, D.C., and more than 6.5 million other workers were underemployed, working fewer hours than they wished.

Barry Whitfield, the Ford worker, did not know much about this or that American factories were operating at their lowest capacity since 1948, and he certainly did not follow the furious swings of the stock market or know that the number of autoworkers, like himself, on indefinite layoff reached 254,114 one week that month, yet another record, another nail. The endless analysis of the economy confused him so, he could not pay attention to the river of forecasts and endless theorizing, the charge that Washington had practiced overkill in the war against inflation, the words of men in white shirts and dark suits predicting "recovery" with guarded optimism, or the warnings of international economists that the world economy had been caught for several years in "a vicious spiral of contraction." None of it spoke to him, made anything clearer.

All he could think about was his job at Ford, getting it back and what might happen if the call did not come, how far he could drop and how fast. All that he understood with perfect clarity was that Ford was in trouble, that the Lorain assembly passenger plant had been shut down for a major retooling, and that it was his bad luck, after eight and a half years of working on the Econoline vans in commercial, to have been shifted to passenger when the vans were selling so well and those men were still on the job, even doing overtime. The shutdown had been too long. At first the workers in passenger were told they would be called back in November. That promised date had come and gone. The word now was January, and never before had the name of any month held such a peculiar and lovely glitter. He was not stone-broke: he had fifty weeks to go on his unemployment benefits and there were SUB payments, Supplemental Unemployment Benefits, a system set up by the United Auto Workers' Union and the Ford Motor Corporation to provide workers on layoff with a percentage of their base pay calculated on a system of credits. He and Joyce, who had both always wanted to own their own house but rented instead, no longer had dinner at McGarvey's in Vermilion, no longer took the children—ages twelve, ten, and eight—to McDonald's twice a week. But if a child brought home an A, Mr. Whitfield would still give him five dollars, which his wife thought was dead wrong.

"I was not intelligent enough to really keep in a college type of career," he said, explaining why he left high school. "I wasn't pushing myself, I push my kids now. My parents never even knew what grade I was in because they never cared, they never had an education . . . " His father, a coal miner in Pennsylvania, moved his family to Cleveland when he was small; both parents—members of the Church of God, sometimes called Holy Rollers—permitted no trace of frivolity, joy, sensuality, affection, or celebration in the household. The man died of black lung, a choking death at sixty-four; his mother—overweight by a hundred pounds, heart faltering, sickly because of "bad sugar"—sued, won, and survives. It was she who made her son learn to cook; now he does it better than his wife, even the children say this. During their marriage, Mr. and Mrs. Whitfield have always shared the chores.

"She used to cook dinner but on the weekends I would even run the sweeper," Mr. Whitfield said. "It doesn't take much for a man to run the sweeper. But most men won't touch that, they say that's the woman's work."

He began working as a spray painter in a tool and die company where the respirators didn't work and he began to fear he might breathe in lead and kill himself. Once a fifty-gallon drum of a highly combustible paint thinner blew up, splashing his face, and he kept hurling himself around the room, screaming because of the pain in his eyes. Other men caught him and washed his eyes out with water and he was sent home to lie down. In 1973 there was a boom at Ford, skilled spray painters were being hired. He stood in one spot, painting the door jambs and the insides of car doors, working in twenty different colors with spray guns attached to long hoses which the men pulled down and then released, using both arms to keep up with the line.

"It was hard," Mr. Whitfield said. "I've seen people at Ford go in there and actually quit an hour later because they could not take it. To work in an assembly line at Ford, in any auto industry, you have to be adaptable and industrious. You got to be able to do anything." Another man put it differently: "They trade people at

Ford like they trade stamps." But Barry Whitfield never minded that, he liked the variety.

After painting, there were other jobs: unloading rail cars, putting in seat belts in the vans, attaching the plastic grilles in front where the headlights go—a minute and a half for each job, sometimes getting sixty vehicles an hour—then switched to putting in seat cushions, building them up and steaming them. Now it made him angry that, with all his abilities, all his fine dexterity, he was at home.

Pork chops that day at Fazio's were $5.75 for 3.04 pounds, a box of Stove Top stuffing was $.89, frozen beans $1.65, a package of Chips Ahoy cookies $1.89. Sometimes, he said, Joyce would make her buttermilk biscuits, which she learned to bake as a child in West Virginia. In the kitchen—painted orange, decals here and there, plants by a window—he used tongs to coat the chops and cook them. Sometimes he thought about going to school to be a professional cook and how nice that life would be. But there were probably no jobs as cooks in good places like McGarvey's. He always tried for a certain engaging valiance, not wanting the remembered grimness of the Holy Rollers to seep into his household, not wanting the children to see him as a defeated, boneless figure. The headaches were better, Mr. Whitfield would say, because he could control his emotions and laugh at them, but on that night he must have felt an unnamed, mysterious defeat moving closer. Everything, perhaps even America, was in jeopardy.

"I'm getting like an old woman," Mr. Whitfield said, sitting at the kitchen table, talking to no one in particular, so softly that it seemed more polite not to reply.

In South Lorain people do not try to camouflage the branches of immigrants in their families, the foreignness of grandparents, as they tend to do in New York or in Los Angeles. It was not common for a man to change his name to something shorter, blunt, and easier to pronounce. You did not go from Zvosechz to Smith. There was still a dim respect for the forgotten, frail frontiers, the old geography of Europe with names like Galicia, Slovenia, and Macedonia. Once called Black River, Lorain had been given its name early in 1874 by a prominent citizen who remembered his travels in France in the province of Lorraine. The young city had drawn so many immigrants because there was work for all—in the railroads, on the docks, and in the shipyards. The first steel plant in 1926, called the National Tube Works Company, was later purchased by U.S. Steel, which continued to make seamless tubing for gas and oil drilling. In 1959, the Ford assembly plant opened and later a nearby one for trucks and vans in Avon Lake. Once the automatic steam shovel, used throughout the world, had been made here.

Poles and Germans came in large numbers, Hungarians, Slavs, the Irish, and Slovaks who still do not refer to Czechoslovakia as the country of their origin. So strong were the ties of each community that private social clubs were built for the different nationalities and many still exist. The Czarniecki Club, built by Polish men, still stands, its bar popular because the draft beer is cheap. There are tacos on the menu; a huge Hispanic community in Lorain, isolated from the children of the European immigrants, has made its food acceptable if nothing else. Once called Hunkies, an unloving name for certain immigrants of Europe, members of families who had owned and worked in small stores or businesses gathered together in October 1982 to celebrate what they had been and how hard all of them had worked. They called it the Hunkeytown Reunion and it made people nostalgic for the grocery store Czuba's, first opened in 1913, which gave generous credit, Kress' Candy Store, Goldberg's, Kucia's, Whalen's, Krupp's, Berger & Jacobs, and Shandarec's Picnic Grounds. Mrs. Slutzker of the Now Printing Shop on Broadway, once a bright ribbon of a street with shops everyone knew until the shopping centers ruined it for good, still remembers that Miss Janice Walchko was chosen the King's Queen by the graduating class of the Admiral King High School. And *The Journal*, Lorain's own newspaper, always runs a page called "With the Colors", items on who is in the armed forces and where they are stationed, as well as the honor roll in different schools, including those of the seventh and eighth grades. It remains a city of families named Luckowski, Mielcarek, Nagy, Shlapak, Stumphauzer, and Zsebik. Families do not abandon their own, they have holidays together, the children come home again, and if in trouble are taken back in.

So it was not unusual that Dave Sokol, for example, an unemployed twenty-five-year-old bachelor, moved back in with his mother, a widow with a small income who still had a job, although it made him sorrowful. He knew he was a burden to her now, being without money and in a dreadful state much of the time. What would have surprised everyone was if Mrs. Sokol, whose life had not been placid, had shut the door. Mr. Sokol will say that his mother is Polish and his father was Hungarian, although both were born in this country.

One man who left Lorain even joined the army and went to Vietnam to get out; he now teaches English and is a poet and loves Lorain as he never did when he was stuck there. He knows how Eastern European women spoiled their Ohio sons. "I think it may have something to do with the way sons come to represent a softer version of their fathers," Bruce Weigl said. "We look like our fathers and sound like our fathers, but something in us is tempered. My father, who is soft-spoken now, who is the man who will stop to change your flat tire now in the middle of an Ohio blizzard, was wild when he was my age, drinking and fighting. He once climbed a second-story hospital wall so he could see my cousin the day she was born; he got stuck in the window and hung there until the police came. . . . I don't think we're as wild and I think our mothers take advantage of that and share with us a tenderness that was never possible with our fathers."

Mr. Sokol, who is well known for his unusual exuberance and excesses, a certain extravagance and recklessness, spoke of his father when he wanted to make clear who he was and how awful he now felt. The father, who was a plugger at the U.S. Steel mill for twenty-nine years, died in 1972 at the age of forty-seven, cirrhosis a primary cause of death. "Big red-hot pipes come out, and he had these tongs to stick inside a pipe and roll it from one place to another," the son said. "I guess it was pretty dirty and hot. I do believe"—everyone in Lorain used this slightly southern expression—"that's what drove him to drink. When he came out he had to have something to cool him down, so he started. He used to hit the bars on Twenty-eighth Street, just all up and down Twenty-eighth Street. He used to drink boilermakers, but he always made sure there was a roof over our head and clothes on our backs." This was the point: men who drank were still the providers, that was the measure of them, not the alcohol consumed and the chaos it caused, nor the cruelties endured and imposed.

While some people without work begin curling inwards, having no language left to tell you how they feel, Mr. Sokol did not want to stop talking, as if he might purge his agitation by rushing ahead.

"I won't lie to you, the other day I came home, I broke down and cried," he said. "I just felt there is nothing, nothing anymore. Once I had things and now—well, I still have my car and a couple of boats. What did I do then? I talked to my dog, a hundred-pound Doberman, Samson. Me and him are great friends. Sometimes, I tell you, I could use a couple of Valiums just to calm me down. My Dad always told me when I was younger, if you want anything in the world, you got to work for it. I worked for my first car. I worked for my second car. I worked for my third car. You know, some people are born with a gold spoon in their mouth and I envy them. . . . I want to work but there's no jobs, especially in this part of the country." For fourteen weeks in 1982 he worked at Container Repair and was then let go. There was no place left to try.

He hated the Japanese and blamed them for his pain; it did not slow him down to be told that while the number one Japanese product, in dollar value, sold to Americans was passenger motor vehicles, followed by iron and steel plate, trucks and tractor chassis, radios, motorbikes, and audio and video tape recorders, America's top exports to Japan, in order of dollar value, were soybeans, corn, fir, hemlock logs, coal, wheat, and cotton. He did not care what significance this had, for Mr. Sokol's father had been in the Pacific during World War II—details were vague except for the mention of a boiler room on a ship—and Americans had been killed, friends of the father. "I'd starve 'em, that's what I'd do," he added.

When he and the woman he was going to marry quarreled in the spring and briefly separated, Mr. Sokol was so stricken he began to understand why people might find life unbearable. He mentioned a friend who used to go fishing with him and the times they drove down to the Toledo Bend Reservoir on the Texas-Louisiana border to catch bass and crappie. Mr. Sokol said the man lived to work; he had been let go by Ford, went to Florida, had a rattling breakdown, and shot himself. That was the one version he knew, and believed.

"He was an older fellow, he was thirty," said Mr. Sokol. "And I was on the verge of—you know, you think seriously—that you don't have . . . what the hell have I got to live for anymore? I mean it gets very depressing. You come very, very close."

At the St. John Ukrainian Church every Friday, women bake and sell potato- or cheese-filled *pirohy*. Each will insist that the Ukranian *pirohy* is the original and in all ways superior to the Russian *pirozhki* and the Polish *piroshki* which they scorn. It is the very old women, startling to see because they might be their own dead mothers in the Ukraine, who roll and bake the dough. Long white kerchiefs cover the hair, their skirts are long, the language they speak is not one the rest of us often hear. In that basement, with its comforting smell, the younger women have thinner wrists and polished nails and nice shoes. One woman points out her mother to me by the oven: she is eighty-six, wearing black, the hair concealed. She and her late husband came to Lorain after the 1924 explosion in the coal mines in Moundsville, West Virginia. The men never last as long as these women: they are damaged soon enough, their hearts and veins and lungs betray them, their arms and legs. If they live, each year makes them smaller and more fragile, so finally old men who were once strong are more like women than they ever thought they could be.

The President's Chief of Staff seemed to regard some Americans without jobs as malingerers. "We do know that generally when unemployment benefits end, most people find jobs very quickly," said Edwin Meese III. But he said it only once. When the inevitable comparisons were made between the recession of the 1980s and the Great Depression of the 1930s, it irritated some people, as if such comparisons were frivolous. In his column in *The Wall Street Journal*, Vermont Royster pointed out that the unemployed today did not suffer the same destitution as a far larger number of Americans had in that earlier catastrophe fifty years before. "There are 36 million on Social Security, 23 million receiving food stamps, 11 million getting special aid for families with dependent children. Nearly 4 million get housing assistance and 22 million are on Medicare. Some people get more than one of these benefits, none of which existed when the Great Depression hit."

Nothing he said could be disputed; what was omitted was any realization that recipients of food stamps, for example, were still hungry in unheated rooms and often ill. In Lorain, plenty of people over sixty remembered those years: eighty-seven-year-old Anna Grasa can tell you that the city once handed out sacks of cornmeal to the poor, and how she and the children opening their rough bag saw pale bugs moving inside, too many to count. Mrs. Jennie Olifar, whose parents worked long hours in their grocery store, Czuba's, remembers how credit was given to so many families who could not pay for groceries, how everyone in the neighborhood in South Lorain had to scrape for money. They were spared the sight of the rich, who lived at a distance.

But the stories they could tell did not strengthen the young; it was as if a veteran of the Western Front attempted to console a man who had fought at Khe Sanh or in the Ia Drang Valley by remembrances of his own, by speaking of lice and mud and trench mouth. Men who had once held well-paying jobs with decent benefits could not be certain they would have such work again or for very long, because of technological changes and a different economy requiring skills and aptitudes they did not have. It was too late to learn them and, even retrained, they might not find a place.

Michael Paslawski felt alone and abandoned: the President of the United States did not speak to him about fear and promise that help was coming; what the President spoke of was the recovering economy, how inflation was way down, the upswing begun, a corner reached and turned. Mr. Paslawski could see reflections of himself on television—although the unemployed were not a fashionable subject for very long—in the lines of thousands of people waiting to apply for jobs, in welfare offices or in food pantries. By that time it was quite common to read a little story in a newspaper that four thousand lined up in Ohio at the Sandusky County Fairgrounds to apply for two hundred jobs at Whirlpool Corporation's plant in nearby Clyde.

His life had once been as normal as anyone else's. He graduated from the Admiral King High School—named for Ernest King, a hometown boy, commander-in-chief of the U.S. Fleet from 1941 to '45—then married Debbi Smitherberger in 1977. The children, a girl and a boy, were aged two and a half years and ten months that November when he had been out of work for so long and did not know anymore if he had a future, if the children could expect anything, if the barriers would ever yield. He had been let go after a medical leave for a hiatal hernia plus a problem with an impaired heart valve, returning to the plant on a date he insisted he was given while Ford said he was overdue. The president of Local 425 of the United Auto Workers Union said the union was very concerned about the case and would press for his rehiring after the Ford assembly plant was in production again. His wife was expecting another child in April and it was to be their last. She did not remember anymore her own loveliness, because she was now just a quiet, deeply worried woman. But the face of her husband seemed frozen, his one expression suggesting sorrow, as if such a life could not possibly go on.

"It's just looking out the door and seeing nothing. It's the same old thing every day, just look out and think, but what's going to happen today? And you know, the way it goes every day, you just wake up and you get out and you look outside and after that there is nothing. All you can do is wait and see what happens every day," he said. "You just get up in the morning, you dress, you wash your face, you brush your teeth, you eat, and you get ready to hit the world, and then after that—" Their daughter, looking at a child's book, *Big Helpers*, with pictures of shovels, trucks, derricks, dump trucks and bulldozers, wanted someone to read to her.

He waited for dispensation, a release from the nightmare, an omen, a letter from Ford, a triumphant call from the union, but nothing came. The only work he could find was in the neighborhood, the jobs that any boy could do—cutting grass, cleaning yards, trimming trees, shoveling snow in driveways, or off sidewalks. There were elderly people living near him, some a little anxious about how much such a strong young man might charge.

"I tell them, by heart now, I just say, 'whatever you can afford at the time—you bring it out, I'll take it. Cash or food. Give me. I'll take it,' " said Mr. Paslawski. It was hardest for his wife when he was too long with the children, no matter that his daughter, Jennie, and Michael, Jr., were so pleasing, with round, creamy faces and immense blue eyes like his, children that people always mooned over. "His depression is when, you know, like the kids are screaming and I'm crying," said his wife. "You know he is not used to it and I don't think men can take it as much as women. It goes so much smoother for me when he is not at home."

Before the last pregnancy she had taken a temporary, low-paying job for a while and now said perhaps, after the birth, she should do that again. None of us then said, how nice, Michael could take care of the baby. All over America, men were learning that women, after all, were not *born* more loving parents, that men could take care of infants and children as well, but it was too late for Mr. Paslawski to want to heat the bottle for the new baby. You do not expect a haunted man to change himself.

Everything was going wrong, as if he were now a man attracting punishment, singled out for disaster, all immunity used up. The old Oldsmobile was on "its last lump," he said. There was no money for repairs, for the new tires it needed, and often enough they couldn't afford the gas, so they even stopped going to church. And the house which they rented for $185 a month and kept immaculate—twice he painted the outside white—was a new source of danger. The landlady, an elderly woman given to hysterical accusations, often reviled them for imaginary trespasses and threatened to raise the rent. Once he had earned a good wage from Ford, a lot of money when he worked ten hours a day, and their plan was always to buy their own place, then get a new car. Because the rented house lacked any insulation, their heating bills easily went as high as the rent. The Home Energy Assistance Program (HEAP) had helped them through a bad winter, but the place was always drafty, and Mrs. Paslawski said she still had to put a blanket at the bottom of the door to keep the cold out. The situation began to be so critical for many others as well that in 1982 the Public Utility Commission, like regulatory agencies in many states, declared a moratorium in shutoffs from December 1 to March 31 after state officials estimated that twenty-five to thirty thousand people faced a winter without heat. "We will not let Ohio families freeze to death," said the Governor, who was not re-elected.

The couple were eligible for $200 a month in food stamps, and every six months their case was reevaluated, in addition to $327 monthly in public assistance. His health was all right: the chest trouble was gone now and he was given a clean bill to go back to work when, as it happened, there was no work waiting for him. He said his job had not caused the trouble, although it required a lot of lifting.

"Most of what you do in Ford is strain," he said. "I was lifting springs, rear springs on the van line, maybe 150 pounds. You put them on frames, shackle them up, tighten them in with a hundred pound gun out of the air. You had to put the bracket on, put the bolts in it, then tighten them up." The union meetings at Local 425, which he always tried to attend, kept him going; the president Michael Pohorance was always nice, and here he could be with men who understood the tragic. And it was a man in the union office who helped them get food from the Catholic Youth Organization, which is why there were a few boxes of Stouffer's Lean Cuisine in the refrigerator. In the beginning he tried to go about finding work in a calm, reasonable way. Debbi had helped him make a list of places they found in the telephone book and every morning he would go "on the road" to seek any kind of work, even as a stock boy. Clarkins, Gold Circle, Gaylords, Figley's, all the auto parts stores—fifty places, his wife said, fifty places and still trying.

"It can drive you to craziness, to kill yourself at times, the way I look at it," Mr. Paslawski said. "I had a friend who just shot his wife, two days ago. He got laid off in the shipyards two years ago." The man, armed with an M-1, attempted to enter the apartment where his estranged wife lived. The woman expected him. The older child was out. She was alone with a baby when her husband opened fire through the locked door.

On his garage door there was a large sign saying Buy American. Mr. Paslawski blamed the Japanese for the economic crisis, but not with much spirit, and there were other stickers around that called for a new protectionism: Hungry? Eat Your Imported Car, or We Build Fords, We Buy American. He did not feel anger toward the President; he did not really know much about tight-money policies, or about the strategy to reduce inflation dramatically by letting unemployment rise, or about the projected deficits. In his confusion and dread, Michael Paslawski was beginning to think he was to blame; he had begun, as a psychiatrist might say, to "internalize" the problem, to believe something was wrong with him. It often happens.

"I just think about trying to make it, to see if we can't stick it out. Maybe them guys at Ford would give me a chance, I could come back and show them I could work again," he said. If you had been out of work at Ford for two years or more, the chances of being rehired were very poor. He might have known this, but he needed to say what a wonderful place, a marvel, the Ford plant was.

"I used to get up at 4:30 or 5:00 A.M.," he said. "At the Ford plant it was just like a big dream—*you are right in a big city*, you walk in, still half asleep, and you see all the lights of this big city —and all of a sudden guys are saying 'how ya doing' or 'what's going on?' and you got to know some of them like a bunch of brothers . . ."

Jack Flowers, who did not want his wife Cheryl upset, told her not to worry about the layoffs, that half the steel mill would be let go before they could touch him in the number one machine shop. He had ten years' seniority, a machinist in maintenance, which is skilled labor, when the cuts began in the spring of 1982, scaring everybody to death. In Lorain, the air was thick with figures and calculations, and his were that 4,700 people had been laid off or furloughed at the U.S. Steel mill while only 2,800 people were still on the job, nearly all men because the women lacked seniority and were the first to go. Mr. Flowers stayed on, but what happened to him was very bad. He was taken out of the number one machine shop, put on the night shift, and assigned to a series of menial jobs which he found hurtful.

Mrs. Flowers, a beautician before marriage, nicely made-up although a face like hers needs no blush or gleam, wanted to say how the work had changed him and tried to make it clear. Her husband did not cut her off or make light of it. For the last few weeks he had been a bander in cold shears and that winter, with so many willing to do anything for pay, Jack Flowers had no choices at all. "He would come home with his lips swollen, he couldn't move his hands, he lost weight, and I think of him being so strong. He said it was just terrible," she said. "His circulation—his hands would fall asleep, his arms, his circulation was cut off. Because he never done that before, and you know, eight hours of that, and almost not a stop."

"There's eight banders," said Mr. Flowers. "If you can imagine a bar of steel from two and five-eighths to, say, one inch, that they produce this in a bar mill, and after they make the bar they shoot it out on a long table or bed. It moves over a little bit at a time and hits rollers and then it comes down, someone cuts it up, and at the end of the line someone has to band it up and that's hot—not dirty, just hot, hot, hot. Because it's hot steel. You either have wire you wrap around it and twist up or you have bands you wrap over the top with clips on them. You have an air gun that runs it tight and you've got to crimp it on the clip so the band won't come up."

His wife sat close to him on the couch, intent on every word. Tell how you hurt, she told him.

"My wrists don't swell anymore, you get used to it. The strain is on the wrists and hands, legs and feet. An eleven-year-old boy could do the job I'm doing; I mean, he could figure it out. My job as a machinist was more mental."

It occurred to Mr. Flowers, who was thirty-six and nice-looking, a high school football player whose knees saved him from Vietnam, that what he endured as a bander was probably the equivalent of the workouts so eagerly suffered by people he calls health freaks. It was astonishing. He was accustomed to it now, no new part of him swelled, only his fatigue could be startling.

"I die when I go to bed," he said. He said he did not feel humiliated by the work he was doing now, only diminished and made ordinary. He was obstinate about this.

"I just feel let down. When I was in the machine shop, they would call, 'Jack, we need this out right away, we gotta get it out,' they'd give me a job, I'd hurry and do it. Put it together again and send it back out. You take pride in what you are doing. Now I am one of the boys that just comes in and goes home; it's nothing, just a simple job. It would be like they told you you can never write anymore, all you could do was stay home and dust. Just dust."

It was not pleasant when the telephone rang, because this was how the mill let him know whether he had work or not. As a machinist his net pay was eight hundred every two weeks, now it was considerably less. Since May he had been working on and off, only being out for seven weeks. The mill saved money by calling in men on the late shift, Mr. Flowers said; U.S. Steel was supposed to have saved $300,000 because utility rates were so much cheaper at night. He hated night work and sleeping during the day; even the children noticed how irritable he was, and were on guard.

"You never know. Every time it rings," Cheryl Flowers said. "They called one day and said, 'This is U.S. Steel.' When I called him to the phone I just knew he was being laid off, but they told him to come in early that night. Two hours later the phone rang again. It was U.S. Steel, this time the man saying, 'Don't come in early, come in late.' "

It was a shame, Jack was so smart, she said, her pretty eyes and mouth showing the worry she insisted she did not feel.

"We have so much," said Mrs. Flowers. "I know he is going to provide for us."

There had been 250 men working in the same machine shop with him; now the number was down to 46. In the shop he was sixty-third in seniority. The tension in the mill was often so acute that a man would refuse to break in someone else assigned to the same work for fear he might be replaced by that very fellow. The mill was old, huge, and always severe: inside it you could freeze or burn. When he first started there a red dust used to cover the buildings, all of Twenty-eighth Street and even more, but the open hearth furnaces had been closed for a decade now. The work was still punishing. Mr. Flowers knew—they all did—that other Americans tended to blame the steelworkers for the industry's sickliness and decline, as if such brutish men were being given too much.

"Oh, true, true, we have the best benefits. But everyone looks at a steelworker as a real rough, tough guy who goes around town going into bars and tearing them up. But they are everyday people," Mr. Flowers said. "Anything you read about steelworkers makes them seem really rough because they've got such a tough, hot job—big he-men, macho and no brains. But you can go on a college campus and see the same people there as you would in a steel mill; there's really intelligent people at the mill." That was the closest he could come to the real subject and then go no further. Few people in Lorain spoke of class or even admitted that any such intricate division existed, but their awareness of it had a deep place in their own private calculations of the world. Workers at U.S. Steel and Ford even now call those with authority and power the "bosses." Even the foremen, who spoke and lived and worked in the same conditions as they did, stood apart from them, a symbol of rule and of power to punish. Only the older ones, mindful of how once they had been looked down on as the laboring class, would bring it all up again. In a letter to *The Journal,* a man named Robert E. Roberts wrote: "Look at what unions have given to the working man. It used to be only industrialists and bankers could enjoy the things we have."

Jack Flowers was not the only man to be touchy about the complaints of other Americans, and the occasional report on television, that the cost of labor was ruining the country, crippling it for competition, hurting American go-get-it, and pulling us down.

"When they tell me that, when they say, well, West Germany, Japan, Canada produces a ton of steel for x dollars and we produce it for $3x$ dollars, how is it my fault we don't have modern steel mills to produce the steel cheaper?" Mr. Flowers asked. The mill was going to install a continuous caster, which would combine five processes into one; he heard there would be three hundred more jobs, he had signed on for a job casting. But Mr. Flowers knew that jobs would be lost once the caster was in operation.

Computers were already taking the place of people in preventive maintenance, he said; instead of inspectors, a computer now determined each month what machine should be checked. But there was still some time, some hope, because so much of the equipment was old that men would still be needed.

"The more he knows, the better chance he has of staying," said Mrs. Flowers. She knew of the pain of other people; there was proof of it in the papers and on television, and her pity for them was not false.

"I've never wanted him to intentionally try to get someone else's job. I wouldn't want him to do that. I don't want him to hurt anyone. But we have a family to think of—and you have to be petty. You know, I'm-going-to-learn-your-job-if-they-kick-some-one-out-of-here-they-are-going-to-kick-you-out-not-me," said Mrs. Flowers. "You have to think like that and, well, you don't want to have to feel like that."

But she knew, as you and I know, there was no choice and perhaps there never has been.

One by one the men were called back to work, so it was considered that the great recession, lasting from July 1981 until November 1982, was over and the national recovery begun, although in Lorain and elsewhere people knew there was no way now for them to defend themselves when more trouble came. In 1982, the Census Bureau said, those living under the poverty line rose to 15 percent of the population, or 34.4 million people. The official government poverty line in 1982 was $9,862 for an urban family of four, more for larger families and less for smaller ones. Some experts called millions of Americans who had lost their jobs and had little chance of gaining new work, or work at the same wage level they had earned for years, "superfluous" workers. Union membership dropped below 20 million in the recession, the lowest level in more than a decade. The National League of Cities, a group which lobbies for cities' interests, said that despite the economic recovery more than half of 388 cities responding to a 1984 survey called unemployment a severe problem or a substantial one.

In 1984 the Census Bureau reported the national poverty rate at its highest level in eighteen years, despite improvements in the economy—up to 15.2 percent. The official poverty rate was 35.7 percent for blacks, 28.4 percent for Hispanics, 19.8 percent for people living in central cities, 18.3 percent for rural citizens, 36 percent for female householders with no husband present, 22.1 percent for children, and 23.4 percent for single individuals. The Director of the Office of Management and Budget argued that official poverty calculations concealed improvements in the income of the poor by failing to include noncash benefits such as food stamps, housing, and school lunches. It became clear to some in Washington, D.C., that you had only to juggle figures to redefine poverty so it would not exist on such a scale. One million people had lost their eligibility for food stamps.

It is not helpful to collect such facts, no use at all, and people often think it is odd when you have clippings taped all over one wall of a room with figures that are no longer up-to-date. There are new facts, more newspapers to cut, the wall is papered with them. The income that defines poverty now is $10,718 for a family of four, not $9,862. Only one thing is certain, the information in a small story by the Associated Press deep inside a Sunday *New York Times*, way back on page 42. One hundred and twenty participants at a two-and-a-half-day conference in Williamsburg, Virginia, sixteen days before that Christmas, reached the conclusion that there was nothing in view that would lift an estimated 35.3 million Americans out of poverty.

This year the Congressional Budget Office estimates that 13.8 million children were living in poverty in 1983, some 4 million more than in 1973.

It takes some getting used to such an idea, but many people

have done so without having to bend too far to see a brighter side. There is talk of the world marketplace, of the "permanent revolution" that American capitalism brings, of our fixed capital assets, the cost-maximizing military economy, the trade deficit, the accelerated defense expenditures that account for the well-being of some states or talk of how such expenditures have strangled U.S. industry. A man in Pleasant Hill, California, writes in a letter to a magazine "just how barbarous and self-destructive the national cult of opportunity really is."

The 35.3 million Americans are acceptable losses and no longer considered news.

A few messages came from Lorain. Jack Flowers had an operation on his right hand for a condition known as carpal tunnel syndrome and still needed surgery on his left hand, the trouble caused by unusual and sustained pressure on his wrists. Back at U.S. Steel but not in the job he once loved, Mr. Flowers works in the bar mill, some weeks four days, some weeks six days. "My colleagues complain because they have to serve on too many committees," wrote his brother-in-law Bruce Weigl. "They will never know. They will die not knowing what it means to work for a living." Barry Whitfield was back at Ford, Dave Sokol married and was working, too. Debbi Paslawski wrote that Mike had only found a job in May 1984 in Elyria driving a ten-ton truck forty hours a week and doing shipping and receiving in a warehouse. "When he first got the job he was just driving the truck, now he got promoted into warehouse and driving all by himself," she said. "He also bought me a living room carpet and I love him so much more now." They had moved three times, with three children, and now had only two bedrooms. Mr. Paslawski was bringing home five hundred dollars every two weeks; Ford never wanted him back. The new job did not offer medical benefits, which was alarming. She was looking for work, the baby Erica was only two.

Unknown to any of them—although they might have guessed the results—was a study done by a Johns Hopkins University professor for Congress which claimed that the overall health of Americans is likely to be poorer for years as a result of the deep 1981–1982 recession. Three to five years after the height of unemployment, Professor M. Harvey Brenner of the Johns Hopkins School of Public Health predicted, there would be an increase in illness and the number of deaths. Bad times lead to increased stress and poorer medical care, he said. The report on the relationship between economic conditions in the country and the annual number of deaths, heart attacks, suicides, cases of cirrhosis of the liver and other illnesses was prepared for the Congressional Joint Economic Committee; the study concentrated on the 1973–1974 recession. Professor Brenner noted that it was reasonable to anticipate the impact of the latest recession on the basis of what had happened before. Attributing a 2.3 percent increase in the mortality rate to the 1973–1974 recession, he thought it reasonable to expect a rise in deaths at least three times greater than that from the more recent recession.

In the study, *Economic Change, Physical Illness, Mental Illness, and Social Deviance,* the findings were clearly stated:

> The suicide rate for prime age males is positively and significantly correlated with cyclical unemployment.
>
> Increases in the mortality rate for one group of prime age males (45–64 years) from cerebrovascular and cardiovascular disease peak slightly more than a year after the unemployment rate peaks.
>
> The unemployment rate is positively and significantly associated with mental hospital admissions and imprisonment at an appropriate lag.
>
> Life events and stress associated with negative life events are predictors of subsequent illness.
>
> Hypertension is exacerbated when job loss is anticipated.
>
> Job loss is strongly associated with depression, anxiety, aggression, insomnia, loss of self-esteem, and marital problems.
>
> Spouses of unemployed workers show psychiatric symptoms subsequent to job loss somewhat later than those reported by the unemployed partner.
>
> In a situation where many people have been laid off, increased job responsibilities for those who re-

main employed are positively associated with gas-
trointestinal problems, increased hypertension, more
frequent illness, increased anxiety and insomnia.

"The study leaves us with two messages: that changes in unemployment, real per capita income, and other measures of economic performance are correlated with crime, mortality, and a
number of physical and mental illnesses. And that a major deterioration of economic conditions will have a psychological impact on
hundreds of thousands of people, with a multibillion-dollar cost to
society extending far into the future," said Representative Lee
Hamilton of Indiana, chairman of the Subcommittee on Economic
Goals and Intergovernmental Policy in an introductory letter to
Senator Roger Jepsen, chairman of the committee.

Some of the younger people in Lorain knew enough to get out
before they were done in forever; it was often the women who
made the plans, pulling the men with them if they showed resistance. But there were just a few who had left long ago and wished
themselves back. Bruce Weigl, thirty-four, teaching English in
Norfolk, Virginia, does not look like most men in the South or in
the Eastern cities: his face is so sharply boned you cannot pinch
his cheeks and he must put a thumb inside his mouth to puff out
the skin for the razor. He thought his forebears had Slovenian,
Slav, Croatian, Serbian, and Czech blood. In Lorain no one
thought his face had a lovely foreignness to it, almost everyone's
still did. He misses Lorain now but longed to escape when growing
up there. Every year he tries to go back with his wife, Jean, a
painter, the child of Japanese Americans, and Andrew, their son.
He needs most of all to see his grandmother Anna Grasa. Some of
his poems are about her, and once in a while in Norfolk he cooks
chicken with vinegar and garlic as she once did. Cheryl Flowers
said that when Bruce came home from Vietnam there was another
man in his skin. His grandmother did not need to ask what had
been done to him. To show their joy, his father made a sign at the
foundry, *Welcome Home Bruce* in orange glow paint, and rented
spotlights so no one would miss it.

> Out of the car I moved
> up on the sign
> dreaming myself full,

the sign that cut the sky,
my eyes burned.

But behind the terrible thing
I saw my grandmother,
beautiful Anna Grasa.
I couldn't tell her, tell her.

I clapped to myself,
clapped to the sound of her dress.
I could have put it on
she held me so close,
both of us could be inside.

He always knew he belonged back in Lorain, all other places a
pretense, but it would be in another life. Sometimes he wrote
about it, typing letters to a friend here, a friend there, although he
did not have so many, for the war had done treacherous things to
him and ten years of medication did not always help. For a long
time he forgot how to be friendly. His best friend was still Rick
from high school, still in Lorain, but he was not used to mail.
Rick's wife, an industrial engineer for a steel company, made the
money in the family and wore nice blouses and suits to work, one
of the 6 million American wives earning more than their husbands.
Mr. Weigl didn't know any other women in Lorain who did that,
it was a most unusual thing. So many women worked, and he
remembered his mother going off each day and coming back.

When you spend your time waiting for your
mother on the stoop of Bunk's Bar, waiting for the
bus your mother rides from work every day and
you're seven years old and the city is spinning around
you, you don't ever leave that place. I went away to
the war when I was eighteen. A beautiful soldier
came to our high school in 1967 and gave us a pitch.
To run away from my father and from the slag stink
of the mill and from the immigrants who never
learned to talk right, I joined. Vietnam was a vague
and impossible country to me then. When I took the

oath, I hesitated for a moment before I took that step forward into loyalty. Something was pulling me back but I didn't know what it was.

In Vietnam my friend Charlie Fratt told long stories about growing up in Southern California, on the beach. He was tanned and he loved the heat, but the rockets made him shut up. But while he still talked, he described the beaches, the dunes rolling on forever and the beautiful women he swore would love you. I listened to Charlie, and to Kelly from a farm in North Carolina, and to Michael, the point man, who shot himself by mistake in the hand with a .45, and I began to think about Lorain in a new way: as a place, and how we drove the endless circles around the drive-in as if we could orbit ourselves away from our lives there. I don't know anymore what actually happened and what is made up. But there was always the stink of the slag from the mill and the rough love of my father and grandfather. My grandfather worked in the mill. Out of Ellis Island, he couldn't speak much English except to somehow lie his way into a crane operator's job on the docks.

At night the men in the family had come home with a stench, so as a child he thought it was the smell of all men; the friends of his father came home with that smell too. They had to really wash before dinner; Anna Grasa had bathed her husband and wiped him dry.

"In the blast furnaces, or in the pipe mill, or on the trains hauling ore in and steel out, they all worked the hard hours. The gas burned all night in a blue flame behind the bars that line Twenty-eighth Street, where we drank ourselves into believing it was possible to get out, night after night."

He hoped his father, the fathers of his parents, all the fathers, had not hated what was done to them, then knew better than to hope this but did not want them to be forgotten, pushed aside by paler men selling something. He had in mind the scented men with small and neat hands who did their drinking on airplanes and had fair skin that was finer than his own grandmother's had ever been.

Work

When I was a child we used to climb the slag heaps. They were like Charlie Fratt's dunes. And women wore babushkas against the cold wind off Lake Erie. We played war games in the slag heaps beyond the grind of the mill. We dreamed of being heroes and played war that got so real one of us took a BB in the eye and couldn't see for a month. In summer we played baseball in the street until dark. But most of us drifted away from that too. I don't know why we were so restless, the sons and grand- sons of immigrants—Serbs, Slovaks, and Poles—but we longed all our lives to leave. We swore we wouldn't become like our fathers, punching the card in and out every day until the grit builds up in the cracks of your face and your back is bent forever. We drank beer and roamed the city in loud cars. I think I spent half my life back there in cars, cruising the drive-ins, shouting love to women we could never have, chipping in when a buck and a half of gas would last all night, crazy to get out.

So that invitation from the U.S. Army was the first he ever had.

DUTY

*T*he old stories, told so willingly, are meant to amuse and to prove that, in his cleverness, the man was able to transcend the stupid and brutal bureaucracy of the army and triumph by his wits while doing what the country considers his duty. The evil sergeant might have had the whip hand but his story made clear he had felt no lashes. No man, wishing to impress, can ever describe other successes in his life quite the way he can illustrate how, in the arms of the army, he still had his way. When told to women, as such stories have been forever, women know to smile back. There are no such humorous stories from a generation of men sent to Southeast Asia, but older men keep on. The stories are exercises in wit and do not depend on suffering because that is not the point. After the movie on an American Friday night, eating pizza made by Greeks, the historian described how, more than thirty years ago, he was sent on a troop ship to Europe and because of a mistake, the usual negligence, the troops were fed nothing but cooked cabbage and candy bars for ten days. Seasick, he felt sicker eating a candy bar. No matter the ordeal, he ended up in France translating for an amiable general who did not know the language, able to fend off all the demands of lesser men, the sergeants, that he, a Specialist 3, perform the usual menial tasks. Some of the men with him in basic training were sent to the Korean War, but his Military Occupational Specialty, his M.O.S., was not infantryman but translator and, at that age, the year in

France was fine and his French became even silkier. Women do not have such stories to tell and, if they do, there is no one to tell them to for the same effect. If they join the army they are not apt to outwit anyone, usually not women who can speak fluent French and do the general's letters. They stay in the lower ranks and are obedient, deciding almost nothing, with men who do not know more.

Because masculinity is said to be on endless trial during the lives of men—never to be considered completed or fixed forever, even if its requirements may change or appear more lenient—men must ceaselessly convince themselves. In odd ways they do so, issuing bulletins that are nothing more than stories, anecdotes, or jokes. It sometimes makes them tedious or pompous or playful, sometimes deserving of love or memory. None of this do they seem to know or be able to acknowledge. The man can disparage himself only with humor and must maintain a conviction of his own worth; the army does not take this into account and sets other standards of its own. The soldier must be passive, childlike, re-spectful, and later, in a war, occasionally very brave. What is not asked is that he be nice, imaginative, curious, or outspoken. The success of the training depends on the man's wish not to be seen as a coward or weak; he is permitted to complain but never to say he will not bear it for another minute. Other men are watching. Sometimes it only means accepting cabbage and candy bars as the Atlantic heaves and thousands of men on a troopship have less room for sleeping than prisoners in a penitentiary. Much later, it can become a story, a small feather.

It is the country that decides when men must show they love it. Or this must be believed. Draft registration was reinstituted after twelve years in July 1980 and two years later, while a majority of young men had complied, a large number had failed to fill out forms—one figure put it at nine hundred thousand. Each year after, the numbers changed. Americans are never short of statistics whose meanings are not always clear. Failure to register was clas-sified as a felony punishable by up to five years in prison and a ten-thousand-dollar fine. The U.S government put its warning on tele-vision: a large man in a cowboy hat, dressed for the range or the woods, spoke in a southern cadence to advise the unregistered that they would find themselves in "a heap of trouble." The country has a claim above all others and young men, not wishing to be seen as shirking or timid, are expected to act correctly and prepare to suffer. All their lives male children know this might come about.

"The events of recent months have increased the number of registrations," the Director of Selective Service, Thomas K. Turnage, said at the end of 1983. "That tells me that the young men of today love their country." For some years such a statement would have been hard to make, when the young refused such an interpretation of love for country and their defiance brought on deep trouble. Mr. Turnage was happy. Required to register within thirty days of their eighteenth birthday—but not to enlist—or face a penalty not yet widely enforced, young men in greater numbers were coming forward and making themselves known.

When ten New York boys, all born in 1962 and expected to register that year, were interviewed by the *Soho News*, an irreverent and interesting newspaper now defunct, Americans were still being held hostage in Iran and all across the country people wanted revenge. Homemade banners called for bombing. It was all right to talk about war that year and to really want it. Ferocious Americans had their excuse. "I am in the tenth grade," said Luis Zuniga. "I want to ask Ronald Reagan that if I go away in the army for two years, when I come back do I have to go to the tenth grade again?" Richard Serpa played the tuba and intended to go into a military band. The *Soho News* man asked him, "Are you prepared to kill or die for your country?" "I just want to play the tuba," the boy said, but he smiled for his picture. The only one who would not put on a helmet or sailor's cap to be photographed was named Mosca, a very chubby, dark fellow who didn't want his picture taken, as if trouble would start as soon as he heard the camera's sharp little click.

"Any war is disgusting and terrible," he said. "I wouldn't go with any service. I would never go, no matter what, never."

"Even if you were faced with a jail sentence?" asked the reporter.

"I would run forever," the boy said.

Do or die, the small pilot called Watermelon liked to say, a joke because doing meant dying, not the reverse anymore. He was the pilot of a light observation helicopter, the brashest boy in school with a charming and terrible toy, flying it almost playfully, not ever letting on how much skill was needed. And in the end was too reckless, too cautious, too good, too careless, flew too low, too high, was grabbed by a tree, shot by a girl on the ground with an AK-47, tricked by fog, betrayed by the machine, and lost his life, not gave.

Coming back, many survivors of Vietnam spoke not at all except for those who called for an end to the war and risked being called traitors in the years ahead, or Reds. The men returning from Korea were silent, the men who had seen the worst of it in World War II were silent, except for those among them who could write about it. It is thought that men who have been in combat cannot speak about it as if the horror had rendered them mute or aphasic, but the real reason for such silence may be more simple. Perhaps they fear what they say will have no effect at all. The listener will try to humor or calm when something else is needed. Sometimes the stories are complicated for a civilian. Strange things are spoken of, a deranged language intrudes. Fire in the hole, *H* and *E* for high explosive, M-60, point, RPG, a slick, a track, fire base, 11-Bravo, combat assault, carbines, tracers, mortars, mad minute. But some stories have a clarity and a purpose that anyone can understand: a man wishes to be thought of as good, explains that decency was the last thing required of him and might well have only increased the danger to him and others. A kindness could be fatal.

There were never before, in this country, so many veterans, a majority of them from the three wars between 1941 and 1975. The April 1980 census revealed that 28,514,544 men had served in the military, although only a fraction of them had seen combat. So there was nothing extraordinary about Dan Loney, a white thirty-five-year-old male, married for fifteen years, then in the auto salvage business. What set him apart was the punishment of the war; it had reached to his child and maimed her. In the small dining room of his house in Upper Darby, Pennsylvania, he wanted to let you know almost everything. He spoke of his daughter, an appealing child then age one and a half named Jennifer, born without a right arm, and of a Christmas Day in 1967 when he had tried to honor the Lord, and how the lieutenant was to blame for Little Bit Garcia being greased. He went over the whole business again, racing and leaping, unable to slice up his grief in orderly bits, and so gave up trying. The child, whose undershirt had been taken off so you could see the little stump which she moved and touched, sat on the table with her father's immense arms around her, pleased to be encircled by him. Mr. Loney, who wore a blue bandana around his head, was not interested in being calm or stoic, or in maintaining the male pretense that pain and horror should be easily borne. He was already deep inside a decline and knew it; grief took over the room like an unnamed gas seeping into a trench. No one could breathe correctly.

"I'm history now, but she's got to live with it all her life," Mr. Loney said, as the child wiggled and babbled on the table. "And I'm deeply, deeply angry—you couldn't imagine. The worst thing for me was getting over the initial shock. I couldn't take her and go nowhere because people would say 'Your daughter has her arm caught up in a sleeve.' " But then he learned something new, and went to meetings of Vietnam veterans, all certain they were afflicted by exposure to a herbicide that drenched the countryside during the war. "Just her and me," Mr. Loney said, explaining that he wanted other people to see what had been done to them, and how all of the men had been sentenced with no pardon possible. Birth defects in their children were not so uncommon, but people did not easily forget Mr. Loney and his little girl.

Of this huge man whose face never seems shut, his friends like to say that unless you know Dan Loney you might take him for a barroom brawler, a bouncer maybe, so stunning is the weight of those bones. But if he was once a rambunctious, restless fellow, the kind of boy who might have worried his parents until the day he enlisted, Mr. Loney is not in spirit always a menacing man, often using the word "fishcake" to describe someone he holds in little esteem. He had once been interested in hairdressing and tried it. Perhaps being so big has made it hard for him, other men expecting his nerves might be wired differently, the large heart to be stonier than theirs. Long ago Alpha Company, which had been battered at Dak To and at Khe Sanh, was clearing a road near the Laotian panhandle with Mr. Loney walking point, creeping ahead of the others looking at everything. At the end of the road, he came upon the Vietnamese girl and was no less startled than she. Neither tried to move, so sudden was their intimacy; both trembled and were aghast.

"I didn't have killing in me," said Mr. Loney. "She looked about seventeen years old, holding an SKS carbine in one hand, and a big chicken or turkey in the other. I had the M–16 right on her. Then I said, 'Merry Christmas,' slow so she could understand. I said it twice. Mer-ree Christ-mas. Then I said, 'Di di maw'—get out of here. She dropped the weapon and split. When I did that I knew that she is going to tell that story all her life, that she will always tell her people how an American soldier saved her life on our Christmas Day."

It was a fine story, woven from that rough, bloody lace that so many of them can pull from their hearts as proof that in their misery they struggled not to become monsters, and it was important that day to believe him. He knew later that it was in Vietnam that it was determined his unborn daughter would be wounded: he had been touched, with so many others, by Agent Orange, which they all absorbed by mouth or by skin, never suspecting the punishment to come. It was the code name for a defoliant sprayed on jungles and farmlands from American helicopters to reduce the supply of food and hiding places for the enemy (or those believed to be helping them). Anything green was a threat. Agent Orange contained a deadly dioxin in the combination of two herbicides. Among the most calamitous effects making many Americans feel ill or fearful were birth defects in the children, often missing or deformed limbs. The military had taken no precautions to protect the troops from contamination, and the dosage for the war was fourteen times higher than permitted in domestic use. The troops were not told, only believing it would harm others, never them, not suspecting they would be made equal now with the people they fought, that American technology would do them all in, playing no favorites in its efficiency. Mr. Loney often worried what would happen if Agent Orange was now at work within him—a malignant tumor, another kind of cancer, disorders of the nervous system, the list of deathly troubles was long enough. The Defense Department, the Veterans Administration and Dow Chemical, makers of Agent Orange, were all accused of ignoring the problem. It was several years before an out-of-court settlement between the veterans and seven chemical companies which manufactured the dioxin, including Dow, settled for $180 million; most saw it as not a great victory, only the best that could be hoped for. In those years when he went to meetings of a local chapter of Agent Orange Victims International with his daughter, he thought it might do some good if people could see her small, imperfect body, but most of the other men and their wives knew all there was to know.

Some men had already begun their own deaths, and did not bother to deny it. The mothers of many of the handicapped children organized, protested, struggled, and had dreams.

When the Supreme Court ruled on the validity of the Congressional decision not to conscript women because the legislators felt they were not acceptable for combat, a few letters turned up from men in newspapers, but there weren't many. Kevin Welber of Arlington, Virginia, had his letter printed in a July issue of *The New York Times* and it caused a little local flurry. "Throughout the ages, women have never been drafted; they have almost never fought in a conventional war. Thus, a female with an arm blown off is unacceptable to our sense of values. Is this because we value a female life more? . . . The death of a woman in battle is not so horrible because it is happening to a woman but because it shakes us out of our stupor and makes us realize that war involves personal loss, not just statistics." The inclusion of women in the draft, he wrote, might make politicians a little more reluctant to commit the lives of eighteen- to twenty-year-olds. "Being a male I find it insulting that my Government has decided that my sister's death would be unspeakable tragedy while mine would merely be an unfortunate, but necessary, sacrifice." Dan Loney did not know anyone who wrote to *The New York Times*.

"I don't want them to do nothing for me," said Mr. Loney on that cold day, the light leaving the room. "I'm a Catholic. I went over there as an American soldier and I really and truly believed. There's nothing they can do to reverse it. And I feel deeply hurt about what our country did to those people." Tears gave his eyelashes a peculiar, lovely shine. He had called the man Garcia "Little Bit" because he was so much slighter than most of the troops. Little Bit had been in motor maintenance until the lieutenant, needing replacements, had sent him into the field. Garcia was not ready and Garcia did not last.

"They did so much over there," said Mr. Loney, the sentence you could hear ten thousand times if you wanted to hear it. But his wife, a handsome, dark woman of Italian origin, and her mother, who had come for a visit bringing a new dress, a pair of white gloves, and a tiny purse for Jennifer, did not say much. It seemed as if they could not, on that day, reveal themselves to strangers, so the visitors could not say how they stood it, but the women remained somber and quiet when Mr. Loney railed. "And who will want to marry her?" he said of Jennifer. A man could manage, he was thinking, but not a woman with such a war wound as this. It was of no use trying to console him, he did not want comfort. So the rest of us in the dining room could only watch the eager baby making those river noises and sing praises of her eyes, her smile, the shape of her head. The new dress, the doll-like purse were all admired.

"When I came out," Mr. Loney said, meaning when he came home, "I never thought anything could hurt me again."

On the train there is only a magazine to read with an advertisement from United Technologies: "Are we losing our fire, our drive, our initiative? Is daring giving way to faint-heartedness? Are we turning into a nation of milksops?" Surely it was not addressed to me, a middle-aged woman, but to men of all ages, telling them to rally, to push, to struggle, and to win. Women are not accused of being milksops; there are other ways to humiliate them.

That year it was not unusual for American females to work for construction companies, be lawyers, deputy sheriffs, bus drivers, marshals, runners, mayors, prisoners, advertising executives, physicians, scientists, war correspondents, revolutionaries, legislators, astronauts, brokers, venture capitalists, novelists, directors, and psychiatrists. Men stopped saying women were not good drivers, but when a couple was seen in a car it was the man at the wheel. Men pushing strollers were not considered odd or silly but seen as sharing parents. Engagement announcements ran with headlines that might have been unthinkable a decade ago: "Miss Weinberger, Major in the Marines, Weds Pilot." A man's military service, as well as his schools, was always mentioned in such announcements and a theater of war given. Women no longer wished to be held back or held down by children, no matter how they loved them. A New Yorker with six children, ranging in age from seven to fifteen, left them with her husband, who had a job, to open a chocolate shop in Honolulu. In an interview with a newspaper she said she would go home when she found someone to manage it. "And I know I will have done something and my children will respect me for it," the woman said. In New York the children seemed sympathetic and interested in their mother's career, but one of the girls said, "One lesson I have learned is not to have a large family."

Never before was so much attention given to the possible effects of hormones, cultural conditioning, upbringing, societal expectations, and the question of whether a boy's great incentive to be the aggressor is due to instinct or biology or psychology or even the differences, if any, in male and female brains.

I never thought anything could hurt me again, Dan Loney had said. But the pain of some men was of no consequence to many women who could point out, quite correctly, the harm men inflicted on them and their families. The number of husbands and fathers delinquent in child support payments rose to 2.13 million, a reason for sorrow and outrage. "My mother and I have always been at the bottom of everything," said a former marine corporal in New Jersey whose legs were blown off in 1971. His mother, who raised him alone, worked as a seamstress and waitress. In the Veterans Administration hospitals he complained of rats under the bed, indifferent care, and a shortage of the kind of artificial legs, stump hose, and wheelchairs he felt he needed. Men wanted war and got it, a woman told me, meaning they deserved what happened.

So pervasive is war in the culture, so accustomed is the population to war movies, to threats of war, to preparations for war, that it was scarcely noted how huge the population of American veterans had become. The veterans of Vietnam—first ignored if not reviled or feared, then forgotten—were forgiven and suddenly were noticed, no longer invisible, when large numbers of them went to Washington, D.C., to see their own memorial. Weeping, sometimes in each other's arms, they did not care who watched. No one who went to the wall, as some named it, would remain cheerful or bored. On a rainy night in Washington, D.C., when the press coverage had long since finished, delegates from the first convention of Vietnam Veterans of America went to the memorial and wedged a few roses between the panels listing the dead of the different years. The flowers leaned out on their preposterous stems as if they bloomed in black granite for 1965, 1967, 1968, 1970. One man, seeing for the first time the names of the dead in his very own platoon—there were three—first stroked them as a blind man might. Then, arms outstretched, he pushed himself against the wall as if he hoped to go inside it, to be with his friends.

All this became quite commonplace, almost ordinary, and was made safe and smaller by television programs whose actors, unknowingly, made a mockery of it until no response was required. In time the veterans became cartoon cutouts, the stereotypes of men held so long by great unhappiness; the monsters not of their making became a parody and could be dismissed. Films were not truthful, the actors older than the soldiers they play, and what was done to the war in Vietnam was what had been done to the other wars: Gary Cooper in the trenches, Frank Sinatra fighting in Burma, John Wayne at Iwo Jima, William Holden bombing in Korea. American prisoners of war in Germany were the subject of a successful television series considered comical. Americans then made up their minds to admire the veterans of Vietnam and pay honor of sorts; the veterans, no longer young, had grown docile, and fewer felt inclined to attack the government and its foreign policies. They had become weary of always being on the rim, so their own pacifications took place. The lost war, so confusing and unsettling, led almost a decade later to an odd surge of nationalism; a man in Minnesota wondered why his own father was again wearing an ID bracelet from 1943, with rank and serial number, but the father could not quite say why. It worried the son that he, someday, might want to wear his dog tags from 1965 when he was sixty.

The new spirit was good for commerce. War toys did well. On milk cartons the navy advertised the life of adventure it offered and the army recruited on campuses, unbothered, and said it would send you places where others just vacationed. Small boys, yet again, grew ardent for some desperate glory and would not ever learn about the Western Front.

It was the veterans of World War II who were always seen as the stable, strong men—only a few exceptions—who had come home to a Grateful Nation, and they were the proof that a man who fought for his country in the cruelest conditions benefited endlessly by it although this might not be apparent to him until he grew more mature. Life would be richer for the ordeal. "They have worn their memories of combat smooth with the retelling. They have grown easy with what they did for their country as young men; they won, and they are proud of it. The horrors that they saw—or performed—so long ago in other countries have been effaced by time, by the approval of history and of the nation they fought for," wrote one of *Time*'s most gifted essayists, believing it.

There was always a war, it seemed, or the promise of one. Soldiers kept coming home or thought they did.

Year by year, back from the ends of the earth, until in 1972 it was my turn too: some men, older friends, took me to lunch and dinner, dinner and lunch, to help me buck up, although the consolation, kindly meant, was curious. A novelist who worked in public broadcasting, a man of immense gifts, said very little about himself—at eighteen a platoon leader in the European theater, the platoon wiped out. Eight years later I heard it mentioned that this man had carried a dead soldier for some distance, believing him to be only dying. None of this was mentioned that day at lunch, and a warning, polite and firm, was handed over to me like an envelope. Get over it. And then, perhaps because he had children, he said, "Put it under your pillow," as if the tooth fairy would come to the rescue. "How long will it take?" I asked, since there was to be none of the usual "now, now, there, there," that men so often provide. "Ten years," he told me, certain of his accuracy; ten years it was, perhaps slightly more.

So the older survivors had things to tell me even when I did not wish to hear.

One summer a man explained how, in a hospital bed during the Second World War, he had been obliged to salute an officer by lying at attention; all the damaged enlisted men in the ward tried to straighten themselves. Yet another, a former bureau chief for *Life* in London and a next-door neighbor, took me to dinner in a small place, vanished now, where you could sit forever. He spoke in such a low voice I could not chew and hear him, but the face remained as it always was. It was not I who was to be cheered up, strengthened, given advice, prodded; it was he ready now, after so many decades, to confide. His were such small stories, no real beginnings and the geography not clear—that night he spoke of cold (while I remembered heat), the Rhineland, I thought, somewhere in Germany. His squad had entered the house of a German family, a real house, handsome, plump, and well loved. The occupants had fled. Such normalcy and privilege could make exhausted soldiers vicious and did; perhaps it was the curtains, the wood furniture so well waxed, and the library with its leather bindings. One of the soldiers began the murder of the table, his bayonet going in deep to make the slashes, back and forth, up and down. As if the table had hurt him, he kept on with the attack. As we ate our hamburgers, this man, my old friend, could still see the white cuts on that wood and made me see them too, although I had moved the table to Hue and Bong Song.

There are memories more terrible, never to be told, but the truth is that what men say does not put people off, never has, most of all not children who have come of age seeing some version of death eighteen thousand times before the age of fifteen, who even now can see an old film of a president's skull being shot off, of his brother dropping in a hotel kitchen, and more. The war stories, instead of repelling young men, bewitch them; the suffering is alluring and promises redemption. War teases them: the wounds they are ready for are painted on and can be washed off like graffiti; they believe the wounds will give them importance. And always they are led to understand what the American world, the biggest one ever, sees as manhood: a rifle, the lieutenant lifting a hand to signal, the men opening up, never such a chorus.

Some men grew moody who had missed Vietnam, deluding themselves that it might have made them better, stronger, more admirable; they never saw themselves in a wheelchair saying, "My mother and I were always at the bottom of things." A television reporter felt cheated. "It was the central experience for my generation," he said of the lost war, but by then it was almost fashionable to cultivate a range of behavior disorders. The television reporter thought that if disturbed by the war, he would have worked it through, a phrase in wide use; there was nothing a smart psychiatrist could not do if you were able and willing. A good book might have been written, there was that.

Fathers spoke, children heard, or thought they did. In the summer of 1975 Susan Armenti, going abroad for a year of study in England, cried at Kennedy Airport, for this was to be her first long separation from her family. She remembers how her father, wanting to console her, said, "What are you crying for? When I was your age they sent me to war." She was eighteen.

Raised in North Trenton in a stable and decent neighborhood that he has, for some years, seen as ruined and disgraced by those who moved in after the European immigrants prospered and left, Fred Armenti was from an ambitious and careful family. His father, a laborer, took work on the side to better provide for the children; the mother, a gentle and much respected woman, was never disobeyed or defied. The children—five sons, a daughter—were not taught Italian; although their parents had immigrated from the southern region near Naples, in this country they did not wish the youngsters to be thought of as "dagos." Mr. Armenti still remembers, as a teenager, being asked to leave the house of a seventeen-year-old girl he called on. Her mother put it plainly: no Italians. He went politely and, years later, will tell you that the same girl's mother became a friend of his.

After years of working as a milkman, in May 1964 he was able to borrow a modest amount of money from a bank to open Fred & Pete's Deli on Route 33 in New Jersey, which drew a large crowd of customers who for years have remained faithful. A proud and outspoken man, confident of his own charm and powers of persuasion, Fred Armenti serves fine Italian food and what some people say are the best lunch meats in the state.

A new customer, making much of the homemade pasta fagioli soup, said to Mr. Armenti's wife, working at the register, that it was wonderful. "That's Mr. Wonderful," she replied. Old-time customers, his friends, his children, and his in-laws all know that Fred Armenti's nickname is Mr. Wonderful and that if a man has lived by a motto his is: Onwards. A younger son, Tom, now owns the deli, as the father intended: Fred & Pete's was not created for a fast profit but as a legacy to his children, a business for one of them to inherit, a monument to the energy and passion of a father who knew he must and could do more than deliver milk if his children were to flourish. Of course he still works there every day; to quit Fred & Pete's would be to invite petrification. It took him eleven years, he says, to pay for the college education of his three children, including medical school for his oldest son.

On the fortieth anniversary of the June invasion of occupied France by Allied Forces landing at Normandy, no one eating lunch at Fred and Pete's, not even those of his own generation, were aware of the date. But Fred Armenti, veteran of the war which ended in 1945, knew and said nothing, for he was too busy. Over the years, Mr. Armenti, who operated a .30 caliber water-cooled machine gun in the 104th Regiment of the 26th Infantry Division, known as Yankee, keeps telling bits of stories to his children about the war.

But they are the corners of stories, the insides are not completed. Mr. Armenti does not speak of using his weapon, of the smell of certain wounds, of how astonished some soldiers look in that second when they are hit, of the longing for hot food, of the words the wounded try to speak, of letters written but never put on paper.

The stories have gusto, even humor, the reminiscences of a man who says, "I managed beautifully!" With wit, he explains at length how he and the troops were packed in boxcars taking them to Nancy in France, and how hungry the men were, their rations far too meager. The train stopped at Château Thierry where, getting off, making inquiries, moving fast, Mr. Armenti found his way to an Air Corps installation, where he was able to buy a steak sandwich. Hearing of his good luck when he returned, other men also wanted steak sandwiches, got off the train, and were left behind, not to be seen again by the others. Fred Armenti was never left behind.

No one perishes in his stories; he transcends suffering but does not boast of bravery. His grown children are a good audience, waiting for the next installment. Asked why he does not reveal more to them, Mr. Armenti was faintly surprised, as if the meaningful themes are clear.

"Well, blowing up a building, that's not so important," he said. "Everything got blown up, everything in Europe got blown up. I saw Nuremberg bombed for three days and three nights and our men were even saying, 'Please, I hope the airplanes stop coming over.' There wasn't a house in Nuremberg that had a roof on it. This was acceptable. I didn't mind.

"Youngsters should know what happened," he said. "They talk about the Revolutionary War, the Civil War—they should know the price of being able to talk freely, of being able to write what you want, and of being able to walk down streets, and they should be willing to pay the price today to do the same, whatever the price may be! And that could mean going to war and now even fighting crime! It's unbelievable. You have to lock your doors! Don't lock the citizens up, I say, lock up the criminals. I don't care if you have to build ten thousand jails. Build them."

Coming home, he says, he did not find himself embraced by a generous government; others used the GI Bill of Rights to go to school but his own plans were throttled. He needed a registration fee and partial tuition, in advance, a sum of $750, to go to a small college in Massachusetts. The money was not forthcoming. Trenton State College in New Jersey would not take him.

There was no place for me, he says.

"The Vietnam veterans think they came back with no recognition of fighting for their country, but I think some World War II veterans were almost treated the same way," Mr. Armenti says. "If it weren't for the American Legion, the Veterans of Foreign Wars, or the Disabled American Veterans, everything would have died for us." Furthermore, Mr. Armenti says, the war in Vietnam would have lasted three days, not all those years, if it had not been for the coverage by the "media," a group he intensely dislikes. It was always difficult for him to tolerate criticism of the American government and the policies of different presidents. He hated hearing it and held those who openly opposed their president or high office-holders in contempt; a patriot would not. Fred Armenti, above all, feels himself a man of the fiercest patriotism.

He never did join the American Legion because his tendency is to want to run things and not abide by the decisions of others, Mr. Armenti says.

A civilian again in 1946, he was not a haunted man and will not have you seeing him as this. "No dreams, it never bothered me, nothing ever bothered me," Mr. Armenti insists, meaning it. "I wasn't upset. I was young, well, war is only for young men. Today I wouldn't do what I did then."

His unit was sent to relieve the siege at Bastogne, where Hitler chose the Ardennes for a counterattack because the U.S. divisions there were widely spread, the hills and woods would provide cover for his troops, and bad weather in those winter months would hamper Allied bombings. By mid-December 1944, some historians have written, the Allied armies were coming closer to Germany's borders, and although their advances had been slowed—after thrusts across France and into Belgium and Holland in the late summer and fall—their commanders believed the end of the war was in sight.

It was not.

He knew nothing of the grand strategy for the Battle of the Bulge; soldiers do not go to command briefings or have the confidence of colonels. They are the last to know. His company, called Dog for *D*, was taken in trucks from Nancy to Wiltz, Luxembourg, arriving late at night at a staging area in the woods. Ordered to make no fresh tracks in the snow but to walk in the foosteps others had made, Dog Company tried to tiptoe, moving silently past the dead Germans scattered here and there, as if the dead were decoys who might suddenly sit up and fire.

The moon was generous and in its abundant light they were able to make their way, uncertain who was watching. Passing one German corpse, Mr. Armenti saw the moonlight shining on the man's eyeglasses, making it seem as if there were still vision in those eyeballs, as if the corpse were staring up at him.

"Weren't you afraid?"

"No," said Mr. Armenti.

"You can't be made of ice. It's not wrong or shaming to be afraid."

"I wasn't too upset. I really wasn't," Mr. Armenti said. "That's why my son is such a great surgeon, he's the same way."

All his life he had learned, and thus believed, that men should not show distress or panic or fear and that to do so, most of all as a staff sergeant in combat, was a disgraceful surrender. A male Armenti was held to high standards, always, and he had been faithful to them. Despite the demeanor he chose to present to the world, members of the family knew him to be a deeply generous and compassionate man, and also saw that as he grew older he was less apt to conceal his emotions, as if now his guard could be lowered from time to time.

It was typical of him that as a soldier on the day he said the last good-bye to his family before going overseas, all of them understanding what none of them could possibly know—whether he would come back, or when—Mr. Armenti preferred to walk by himself to the Trenton train station.

He remembers still the artillery barrages, the great searchlights far from their position raking the sky, how the men moved, stopped, moved, and near the Saar River saw German troops in uniforms as white as milk skiing to their pillboxes. The two armies sometimes came very close to each other, as was intended.

"They didn't shoot if we didn't shoot," Mr. Armenti said.

The weather was killing them. By the end of December the cold was so inhuman in the Ardennes it was said that the wounded who were in shock would die if left in the snow for more than half an hour. Two days before Christmas the weather cleared. On the ninth of January the U.S. Third Army launched the main offensive with four infantry divisions, including his. The Soviet winter offensive began in the East three days later and by January 27 the Battle of the Bulge was over, At Great Cost.

Throughout it all he had one pair of boots, which were leather, and a single pair of socks.

When the war in the Pacific ended in the summer of 1945, he was kept in Europe for another year, first stationed in Austria guarding a huge stockade at Langbach, a village near Wels, for German prisoners who, he believed, included many officers of the SS, considered the favored troops of the Third Reich, the *Schutz-staffel*. His job was to supervise delivery of coal to American companies in the area for their furnaces; five prisoners were assigned to him. An elderly German drove the truck the men used. He was known only as Fritz; any German could be called that. The American treated the driver and the SS men nicely and stopped carrying a rifle to guard the prisoners except when all of them went hunting in the woods for deer. The Germans scared the deer into the open field where Fred Armenti shot them. The animals were given to civilians who were short of food in a nearby town.

Fred Armenti bore no grudges.

"I had nothing against the Germans. Okay, say what you want," he said. "I went to war for my country. That guy, old Fritz, the truck driver, he loved me; other than my father no one ever treated me as warmly as he did. That guy was the nicest man you ever saw, I used to give him whiskey, I gave him anything he wanted. No, no, that wasn't the reason. He knew I was a good man."

There is more, there is always more, but all stories must shut down and he was needed back at Fred & Pete's Deli. There was only one visible reminder of the war: his left foot, strangely pale as if the snow of the Ardennes had seeped in and would not ever melt. The foot still bothered him; the circulation in it was poor, the toes numbed. But Fred Armenti was not interested in discussing such an impairment. He took off his sock and shoe but held back the history of the foot. There was something more important to be said about the war.

"It was the biggest thing that ever happened to me," said Mr. Armenti of World War II. "I got to Europe—I went to Vienna, to Paris, I went to Budapest!"

Of all things, feet were a grave concern of the U.S. Army during World War II, so the military steadily nagged those soldiers sent overseas to the European theater of war. The subject some times obsessed field and company commanders. What the army feared, and with good reason, was the prospect of chilled, exhausted, and immobile troops standing or sleeping in water and snow, unwilling to remove their boots or change their socks often because they lacked dry or clean ones to put on. The soldiers were often ordered to sleep with their footwear off, but this meant, as they knew better than anyone, there would not be time to get their boots back on in case of attack.

Orders on "foot discipline," memorandums, papers, and various medical dissertations seemed endless. The soldiers were instructed to do so many things—instructions that were not possible, merely ridiculous, or in the long run ineffective—that many men did nothing at all and took their chances. The huge numbers of men considered susceptible in the European theater to trench foot, a form of Cold Injury, Ground Type, as the Army classified it, were alarming. Well over 2 million men were shipped overseas by army ground forces for combat, and it was not acknowledged until quite late in the war that many soldiers did not have warm enough clothing and their various types of combat footwear were ill-fitting or unsuitable so it did not always matter how prudent they were. The army knew that a man with trench foot was as useless, and as much trouble, as a soldier who had a gunshot wound, and it was unlikely that after certain medical procedures were followed—there being no cure—the man with trench foot would ever be able to return to the line. So critical was the situation that in November 1944 Gen. George S. Patton, Commander of the Third Army, who mistakenly thought the enemy at its weakest, wrote a memorandum to his corps and division officers that was not unusual in its severity: "The most serious menace confronting us today is not the German Army, which we have practically destroyed"—the Nazis' terrible assault in the Ardennes at the Battle of the Bulge began three weeks later—"but the weather which, if we do not exert ourselves, may well destroy us through the incidence of trench foot."

The danger was aggravated from October 1944 to February 1945 by the coldest, wettest, and muddiest months that Northern Europe had suffered in decades, but not until many years later was the damage assessed. Two men, both once in the Army Medical Corps, each holding the rank of colonel, did a minor masterpiece of reporting called *Cold Injury, Ground Type,* which the Office of the Surgeon General, Department of the Army, published in 1958. They said that the total number of such injuries—mainly trench foot and frostbite, which were sometimes indistinguishable—was approximately 71,000, most of which occurred in the 1944–45 winter, and that the total number in all theaters for the entire war was 91,000. Cold injury was a wartime trauma that caused crippling losses. In a foreword to the book, another colonel wrote that contributing factors included: "1) intensity of combat, 2) the inadequacy of clothing and footgear, 3) the pressure of events which required that new troops be taught so much in such a limited period of time they were not taught the essential facts of cold injury, and 4) as General [Omar] Bradley himself has acknowledged, the taking of a calculated risk, for which a price had to be paid, when, in the summer and early fall of 1944, it was decided that gasoline and ammunition should take precedence in transportation over supplies of winter clothing." In the week ending October 15, 1944, 320 cases of trench foot were reported in the European theater, and the total rose steadily until November 17, when 5,386 cases were reported during violent offensive combat, heavy rainfall, and temperatures between forty and fifty degrees, although colder in some areas. Extreme cold was not the sole reason for trench foot.

The authors of *Cold Injury, Ground Type,* writing with great clarity and sometimes even a strange lyrical quality, were Dr. Tom Whayne, retired, and Dr. Michael De Bakey, who much later was to be famous as a heart surgeon in Houston. Describing trench foot in one campaign, they wrote: "Within 12 to 14 hours after exposure to wet cold, many of the men affected began to complain of throbbing, tingling, and cramping pain in the feet. There were frequent complaints of cramps in the muscles of the calf. Numbness became progressively more troublesome, and many soldiers said they felt as if they were walking on wooden feet. Some could not walk at all. Only 40 soldiers in a provisional battalion consisting of more than 350 men were able to walk at the end of 5 days; over the same period, the number killed and wounded in action amounted to only 30. Many of the men presented extensive lacerated, ulcerated lesions of the knees that they had sustained from crawling over the ground because the terrain and the tactical circumstances had made litter evacuation impossible."

The appearance of men's feet was never the same, although the symptoms of trench foot hardly varied: the feet dead at first, insensitive to pain or temperature, particularly around the toes, usually cold to the touch, swollen, and waxy white, with a few scattered bluish areas in the skin. If the feet were warmed up or rubbed, it compounded the misery: they became markedly swollen, red, painful. The soldiers called that stage the "hotfoot." Blisters and discoloration were common. Heat, walking, or any trauma to the feet increased the escape of fluid and blood into the tissues.

Men punished by atrocious weather, the fighting, and the misery of their living conditions—which were often not as good as that of hibernating animals—were told over and over how to prevent trench foot. Socks were to be washed and dried by "pinning" them to an overcoat or field jacket and if not that, for pins were hardly a regulation item, socks were to be placed on the shoulder under the jacket to dry. When feet were cold and wet and nothing dry was available, soldiers were to keep *moving* despite their fatigue, or the possible danger this might bring them. In a memorandum sent by Gen. Dwight D. Eisenhower, Supreme Commander of the Allied Expeditionary Forces, but probably composed by the second lieutenant named J. K. Roberts of the Army Adjutant Office who signed it, the instructions were as unrelenting as usual. In fact they were almost daffy. The memorandum said: "If troops have to keep in one place they should mark time or make vigorous movements of the legs. When sitting down they should elevate the feet higher than the buttocks, being careful that nothing is constricting or interfering with the circulation of the legs." But this seemed written for men who had decent shelter, a bed of their own, hot soup, water for washing. It must have seemed comic to troops who were moving and sleeping in snow or water, who were never dry, and who knew, as eventually the army did, that their combat boots or service shoes were not waterproof. Many of them also lacked sufficiently protective field jackets and enough sweaters, a serious deficiency since prevention was a question not only of warm, dry feet but of maintaining circulation and body heat. Overshoes, in short supply, were not the solution either, because they tore and leaked easily and because in order to increase their mobility, soldiers were sometimes ordered or chose to discard them before an attack. The combat boot, called Type III, was officially observed to absorb more water than the old model it replaced, and although the men were commanded to "dub" these boots—General Patton, among others, was adamant—it was learned that dubbing, or polishing, actually reduced insulation against the cold and did not in any way make the boot more waterproof, which was the purpose.

There were never enough dry, clean socks. The boots, too, were often too tight, partly because in basic training the Americans felt happier in tight-fitting uniforms and snug shoes and usually gave their civilian shoe size, not realizing how much their feet would spread. When soldiers wore two pairs of socks, the boots were even tighter and, when wet, the leather always began to shrink. So the demand in the European theater for larger-sized combat boots grew urgent and could not be met. When the men in the line were able to exert themselves—the effort was often inconceivable—to remove their footgear, they found their feet had swelled so much it was enormously difficult to get boots or shoes back on. It was not surprising that soldiers became unwilling to take them off to care for their feet, and it did not much matter if they were being disobedient, since no retribution worse than what they already knew was easily imagined. There were almost no records of men malingering by claiming they had trench foot. Unit commanders were reminded often enough that it was they who were responsible for trench foot in accordance with Section IV, War Department Circular No. 312, issued in 1944, which spelled out "the diligent application of the protective measures." It did no good at all to ask for sweaters, socks, or gloves.

When there was time to write the histories of various infantry units, Harris Peel, a private in the 254th Infantry, 63rd Division, described a night for the men in one battalion fighting the Germans near a place he named as Jebsheim in eastern France, the Alsace region. "Sub-zero temperature combined with a fierce north wind which whipped the deep snow into a frenzy of blinding ice particles slowed our advance to a painful crawl . . ." French troops had already taken buildings of the Jebsheim mills, now on fire, and many of the Americans, perfectly aware they were ideal targets as they hunched close to the flames, wanted warmth more than safety. At 10:30 at night, G Company crossed a river whose name he remembered as Blind. One company of the 2nd Battalion, after wading through the icy, rough water, was pinned down by accurate machine-gun fire. Contact with the others was lost as the drenched men crawled through the deep snow. Companies B and G managed to come within four hundred yards of the outlying German bunkers at Jebsheim. A patrol, Private Peel noted, sent to silence the enemy machine guns, "met with failure as frozen weapons failed to work for their frozen owners." It was believed by such soldiers that if a record was kept, if only for the sake of the survivors, a fitting act had been done. Private Peel was so persuaded.

"Undoubtedly this night was the most miserable the regiment ever experienced," he wrote. "Each man had carried only one blanket into the attack and most of these had been soaked when we crossed the Blind. All of our clothing was wet either from the stream or from the snow melted by our body heat as we lay in it. This had now frozen to our skin. No fires could be lit . . ." No one did exercises, as Second Lieutenant Roberts would have wished, no one thought about their feet as Patton and Eisenhower might have wished. "The following morning we counted our casualties," Private Peel recorded, "and met a new enemy, one who accounted for five times as many men as the Germans—the dreaded trench foot. Men who could hardly walk hobbled back to aid stations to be evacuated to hospitals. The First Battalion suddenly fell to less than company strength."

It was not uncommon to feel persistent shooting pains in the feet and the pounding sensation of a pulse, the posterior tibial. In the more severe cases, the authors of *Cold Injury, Ground Type* did not think it excessive to call the pain "exquisite" if the feet were touched, however gently. When the edema, or swelling, decreased, the physicians noted, the surface layers of the skin began to desquamate, or come off in scales. Some areas could turn black and become hard and mummified. The appearance of lesions sometimes signified dry gangrene. The scaling often lasted for a month or more, the nails sometimes going, with entire casts of the toes coming off. Those who lost the superficial skin on their soles were rarely considered fit to return to duty.

When the men were hospitalized, their bodies were covered with blankets, the feet sometimes slightly elevated on pillows and always exposed to cool air, the blisters undisturbed. Nothing was to touch those feet, which sometimes, in cases of acute pain and intense hyperemia, had to be cooled with great care by ice bags or refrigerated by other means. The bed sheets were always held up so they would never even lightly brush those feet, which always remained on view: peculiar, treacherous, hideous, and sometimes shaming, the skin behaving as if it did not have a human history. It was, of course, not a disability that impressed people at home; some of them connected it with World War I and the Western Front.

His was not such an alarming start: the older son of a widow in Gary, Indiana, he was studying engineering at Purdue University when in 1943 he was drafted, and dismayed. He had joined the ROTC at Purdue without any intention of volunteering for military service, although a different James Finn, now remembering World War II, says he would do just that. But the younger man wanted none of it; indeed he even thought the army might refuse him on the grounds he was sickly, perhaps find spots on the lung, and that once inducted he would be put on the farthest rim of the war and never considered for combat. He could not imagine himself doing real soldiering, he was not cut out for any of that. After basic training he was sent, to his pleasure, to the Army Specialized Training School at Harvard to study calculus, while other draftees studied French or Japanese or physics. None of the students there, so safe from the killing as they led the lives of privileged schoolboys, thought the war could come close.

But in the fall of 1944 the Allies were bogged down along the German border, although their advances had been for the most part efficient and stunning since they had forced their way ashore at Normandy that June. Many Germans were not willing at all to consider the unconditional surrender demanded by the Allies, and they believed, as one military historian wrote, if not in victory, in a kind of nihilistic syllogism which said: Quit now and all is lost; hold on and maybe something will happen. "Already the Germans had demonstrated the ability to absorb punishment, to improvise, block, mend, feint," wrote the historian, with the odd, familiar rhythms of a skillful sportswriter describing a football game with endless teams and rarely a recess.

James Finn knew nothing about any of that, but he was turning out to be all sorts of things he never expected or hoped to be. For one, although he never cared much for guns, in fact even disliked them, he had a talent now for taking apart, putting together, and expertly firing the M-1 rifle; marksmanship medals were won. At Harvard there had been nothing like that, just classes, four months of calculus, a bed with sheets, cups and plates, towels, showers, food, and meals eaten off a table and walks at a nice pace. All this went when the Yankee Division was sent to France, Private Finn with it. Then the bulk of the Third Army, to which they all belonged, drove eastward across northern France to the border of Lorraine. Mr. Finn can tell you very little now about dates, the roads have lost their names, the towns are without faces, the terrible geography of places where they were all so cold and murderous and frightened at first, then passive, indifferent, obedient, and efficient beyond belief, has dimmed and disappeared. But he can always see the fields with the furrows, the slight dips or bumps and those long rows, so as a soldier he knew they had been planted, but there was no telling what wanted to grow there. And there was so much walking that he learned soon enough there was no choice between mud and water, for the rain was unusually heavy and spared neither army.

Because he was calm and intelligent, good at judging distances and moving carefully, Private Finn was made a lead scout several times, sent out to spy on the Germans but not to kill them just yet. In the company each man carried half a tent in his pack, and had a buddy, as children do in summer camps when they go swimming, a safety precaution also used by the soldiers. His buddy was named Savage and the others called him Doc Savage, after a character in a pulp magazine popular in the nineteen thirties. The war really started for him when they were first sent out in the woods, whose trees made it hard to see beyond twenty yards. The soldiers arrived late at night and had to quick-quick dig holes to sleep in, not putting up their little tents, which came to be a refinement of sorts. Private Savage awoke the next day very early and, wanting to make sure that he and Private Finn had not positioned themselves dangerously close to German positions, stood up, looked around, and was shot in the stomach by a German sniper. There was nothing for Private Finn to do except call for the medic, lift the head of his friend, hold his hand, cover him, say it would be all right.

At any rate, sitting that day behind his desk at The Council on

Religion and International Affairs, where he had worked for ten years, Mr. Finn was not prepared to say much about the death of Private Savage or what a bullet can do to the abdominal artery that carries blood to the lower part of the body. The bleeding can be astonishing and some men, lying on the ground, have looked, for just a second, mystified to see it.

He is not the only one, of course, unwilling to tell the details of such a death. It is not because men do not wish other people to gasp or turn pale or show distress, it is because they suspect they won't. The only hope is to honor the catastrophe by keeping it intact, letting no one else diminish or trivialize it. He was right to feel this way; no good comes of pushing the event in front, of sharing it and seeing nothing in the faces before you that a good movie could not more easily arouse.

Mr. Finn told nothing to his children about the woods and what happened in them, nothing to his son. The boy did not ask but, perfectly aware of his parents' opposition to the Vietnam War, decided not to register for selective service in 1981, prepared to face the consequences. He knew his father's books, *Protest: Pacifism and Politics; A Conflict of Loyalties: The Case for Selective Conscientious Objection*, which Mr. Finn edited; as well as *Conscience and Command: Justice and Discipline in the Military*. But the father never spoke of himself as a soldier. "The memories do not carry over to another generation," Mr. Finn said, in his quiet, matter-of-fact way, a brown-haired man at the age of fifty-five, not at all aggressive or calculating in the admired American manner. Some of his friends thought he should not have refused, years before, the job offered as an editorial writer on *The New York Times*, but it would not have suited him. He had been happier editing the little magazine *Worldview*, in a smaller, more contemplative, more scholarly enclave.

When they start, some soldiers are not sure they can manage, but no one has the extra energy to imagine what war will make of them. When his mother, whom he loved very much, wrote Private Finn that she hoped he was not missing Mass on Sundays, he was still able to feel amusement, for in those woods there were no days of the week. He did not know a Sunday from a Tuesday. He thought much later that his father, who had been a policeman, might have guessed what it was like, but most people could not. They said, in their letters, how difficult it was to buy steaks and other meat at home, but it did not bother them because they knew it was all going to him and the other soldiers, which he also found amusing and strange. It was as if civilians imagined the soldiers eating sirloin on plates around a campfire when, in truth, they often enough had no food at all except what they managed to hoard. He was very prudent, saving bits of the government-issued chocolate with its thick, bitter taste.

Once when the company pulled back from the woods, there was a promise of hot food. What they were given—always a great favorite, pancakes—was not even warm. They were cold and wet now as well. But the soldiers devoured the congealed, limp, sodden cakes with rapture, and it spoiled nothing for them that a medic appeared bringing in a wounded man. Everyone who was eating ignored them and behaved like busy, deaf men.

"His back was very badly mangled and he was crying out, yelling in great pain and calling for his mother to help him," Mr. Finn recalled. "All that. We tended to turn our backs on him, and pay attention to our pancakes rather than to him and his suffering."

It was all denial, then deprivations and ceaseless demands. Even the woods, ordinary woods, became a demented terrain from which no one could safely escape. The soldiers, addressed so often as "men," had to believe that now was the great, useful test of their masculinity, when in fact it was often a mockery of just that. They had never been so helpless, existing in a state of predictable humiliation, required to be passive and obedient as women were once expected to be, then bold and daring when the orders said to be. Timidity, of course, had to be pushed away—an exhausting business—and so did the realization they could do very little for themselves. They were humbler now than they had ever been, even the poorest and dimmest among them, waiting for more powerful men to decide when there would be pancakes or warmth, or when, and how, their lives should be used up. Civilians, of course, imagined soldiers to always be strong, choosing the risks. It made the war wearing in a way that young riflemen could not specify, so all they could call their own were their wondrous, inflated longings and memories of an old lust and private recklessness and food. Because the soldiers found out soon enough there was no one to care for them, they cared for each other, inventing families inside their platoons. It made it easier to do the killing, they killed to save themselves and each other. All this has been written and said so many times, there is no excuse for not knowing it.

And despite it all men did not often wish to be taken out or to have their feet betray them. Private James Finn was no longer useful to his army the morning he tried to get up and walk and suddenly could not.

He was in different hospitals, in Europe and then in the United States, for nine months with trench foot and in the beginning was quite sure this condition would clear up and let him return to his unit. But in December 1944, his company in the 26th Infantry Division was on its way to the Ardennes to relieve Bastogne. It was the final German offensive of the war, as three of their armies attacked five American divisions on a front that stretched to fifty miles. All that time, as casualties reached the hospital in Bournemouth, England, every man not in a coma or running a high fever or deranged heard of the savage fighting and the weather, so cold at night that it was said some riflemen slept in their slit trenches piled on top of each other. His pleasure at being safe alternated with his feelings of guilt, sometimes as lacerating as the sensations in his feet, which were occasionally alleviated by codeine. In his ward were the combatants with problems with their feet or in their heads, as the men themselves put it. Thirty-seven years later, James Finn, the former infantryman who never thought he would be drafted, cannot remember the name of his regiment, or what those woods near Strasbourg were called where he had been so cold and wet he had not been at all certain he would ever be dry again, or the full name of the man he had given his rifle to, who lived through the Bulge and when it was all over chose James Finn to be best man at the wedding in Indiana.

But what he can remember, not always by choice now, are bits and pieces, fragments too embedded to be carelessly disturbed or plucked out. Some have worked their way to the skin—black slivers emerging when they will, without warning, a reminder of the old, real, unconquerable wounds that have nothing to do with feet, the injuries a middle-aged man is not supposed to have because it was a war that had to be fought, the nation grateful to them.

Word of the fighting seeped into the hospital: he began to have disturbing dreams, quite dreadful ones, and during the day there was nothing at all to read, as the hospital staff had other needs to consider. Sometimes officers came through, providing distractions that were both lunatic and ironic to Private Finn with his purple, ballooning feet. He was really not in good condition, his feet in a stage of some danger where gangrene could develop, his guilt worse, when a field-grade officer, a major, paid a visit. Before he began the tour, the bedridden men in his ward were ordered to "lie at attention,"—a command which meant no talking, arms at the side, eyes fixed on the ceiling, no twitching, no noise including groans—as the major went through, passing bed after bed, not making small talk, not smiling. Mr. Finn said he did not feel malice; years later he told the story only with a certain sad mockery, nothing else, and spoke of the young lieutenant who also visited the ward, a pleasant and sympathetic fellow—clearly not one who had been in the cold or ever used the .30 caliber M-1 weapon, a semiautomatic piece. This officer was almost too anxious to be nice and not at all sure of what should be done. He talked with Private Finn, then politely asked: "Aren't-you-a-bit-young-to-be-so-far-from-home?" It made the private laugh, he did not even bother to hide it, which made the nice lieutenant blush and move on.

The atmosphere on the ward was not healing; his own nerves seemed feathery, badly affected by other men's breathing. And there was always, among the feet men, a great hash of talk—bizarre, childlike, and sad—as they confided too much to each other. You could say anything; the intimacy which few of them would ever feel again was acute and not always helpful if you were feeling somewhat disordered. It did not restore him to hear about American witchcraft or sorcery either. One man, about thirty he thought, was southern and liked to recall the admirable gifts of his sister, who could talk warts off your hand and make a burning fire go out by itself simply by coaxing and telling it to extinguish. A younger man near Private Finn's bed had a father who could do just as much and often had. This enlisted man, up and walking about since his feet were now in sensible shape, said he would be home by Christmas because of his chest. What is wrong with your chest, Private Finn said, not really curious. Nothing, the man answered. But a fortune teller in Belgium had told him he would be home by Christmas because of a problem with his chest, and soon enough a hospital examination showed spots on the lung and off he was sent. Private Finn did not need to think about warts lifting off and fires suddenly refusing to burn anymore, or the visions of fortune-tellers, though Private Finn knew, with a dreadful certainty, that all these things were true. But he was not sure he wanted to believe such things, a young man good at calculus, who missed his mother, skilled on reconnaissance patrols and at firing the M-1, a catechist without enough to read, and who had been in bed much, much too long as the hospital vibrated to a new, urgent hum, the nurses working faster as the wounded from the Bulge came to them. It was the name the newspapers gave for the campaign in the Ardennes which was going so badly, and every day that December that it went on, he felt shame and relief each yanking at him, and such strangeness.

Kindness was nice but not to be counted on. Early on when he was new to hospital life, a medical officer made an inspection of all the afflicted feet, and then, suddenly, would squeeze them and move on. As the doctor went down the line of beds, the yelling and shrieking rose with each movement of his hand, almost as if flares were dropping on and burning the bed sheets. Soldiers tried to brace themselves to be men, but could not.

"The louder you yelled, supposedly, the worse your feet were. I don't know what else he was judging, or how he could do that," Mr. Finn said. "Oh, I yelled when it came my turn; it was really a scream of pain. It did hurt. It did hurt." When an ambulance took four of them to Paris, the driver was kind and drove around so the soldiers could see the Eiffel Tower or Notre Dame, but none of them, of course, could get out and walk about. He always remembered who was decent. After England he was sent to army hospitals where he had a Christmas and his twenty-first birthday, in one bed after another, until his release in July 1945. The last three months he began to walk. Once, when at FitzSimmons Army Hospital in Boulder, Colorado, he took the bus into town, then knew right away it was a mistake, wanted the bus to turn around and take him back.

"I was disturbed enough so when I got off and walked down the street, it seemed as if it was very far away, and at the same time I felt I could stretch out my hand and touch somebody across the street," Mr. Finn said. It was frightening. But then a ward boy

—a private from the hospital, the only person he knew—went off with Private Finn for a drink, so the panic eased and he was able to make the next trip more comfortably.

When, at last, he went home to his mother, he was unprepared for the jolts; there was no way of being prepared, no possible homework he could have done. There were a few questions, and sometimes it was this one: How-many-Germans-did-you-kill? He would never tell, not only because the question could still startle but perhaps because he did not quite know how many. It was impossible to know; soldiers usually fired not singly but with others, unsure what bullet had gone where, unable to know if they had fired too low, too high, or waited a second too long, the hand hesitating, a reflex harmful to what the army called battle efficiency. When he was still wearing his uniform, because he did not yet have civilian clothes, a woman who had taught him English in junior high school bumped into Private Finn at the post office in Gary. "What do you do for excitement now?" she asked with the unnatural animation of people who do not have a clue what to say.

"I thought it was such a stupid question; I don't know what I said to her, if I was able to say anything. If I did, it was some silly thing like 'I've had enough excitement for a while,' " Mr. Finn said. "How can you talk to people who ask such questions? And, then, people who still had sons in the army would ask me why I was out, since I could obviously walk around and I looked healthy. They were asking me, why was I not still there?" (I told him of the remarks that once came to me, how at a college in Minnesota, when I had spoken of the Vietnam war, a student pressed my arm, smiled and said, "I'm so glad a woman was *there* to see it." "Yes," Mr. Finn said, "all those wonderful things.")

The evening shortly after his homecoming his mother invited a couple who were her friends to dinner. Private Finn mentioned a few things that had happened, none of it too revealing or apt to jolt the guests. "The woman just burst out laughing at me and tried to tell me, 'Well, that's not how things are done in the army,' " he recalled. "So I didn't say any more."

He knew his own experience had been ordinary for a foot soldier, and that he had certainly not had a worse time than so many others. James Finn thought, without any way of knowing, that he was acting perfectly normal, or the way he remembered normal to be, which means he had very little idea of how to affect it.

"I was told some years later that for a period of half a year or so I did not seem at all normal, which surprised me," he said. "I thought I had done very well." The war was no longer the problem, other people in Gary were, as cruel and clumsy as the rest of us can be, but he was hardly up to that kind of revelation. He did not want people to think of him as exceptional.

Other men had known many more harrowing days, especially during the Battle of the Bulge, where his friends in his unit had been sent and most of them killed. There were such stories: the two lieutenants who spent the night pretending to be dead in a roadside ditch as German soldiers passed them, sometimes kicking their bodies. One man had a bad cold and could hardly muffle his coughs. When he fell asleep he snored and had to be aroused, for if allowed to sleep, he would bring on their deaths. The other man, a Lieutenant Peebles, imitated death as SS soldiers stripped him of his watch, rifle, ammunition, fountain pen, and his hunting knife. His performance was remarkable, helped by the cold that had made him so stiff he was able to keep his body rigid when they snatched his possessions. Later, when the lieutenants were rescued after eighteen hours in the ditch, the feet of Peebles were frozen. What was awful was seeing the dead men still on their feet; many remained preserved in such cold, sitting, crouching, or standing until you pushed them over. From a distance they were only men waiting, on the alert.

Thirty-seven years later, James Finn regretted nothing, saying again that he would now volunteer for that war although he had not wished to do it at nineteen. He did not go to reunions with other veterans and felt scorn for "old men telling each other what a wonderful time they had during the war," although that is only one way of looking at it; the other is that they do not always understand the stories they still tell, and need to master their memories. Mr. Finn still has his dog tags but nothing else, and he grew to believe that the troops in Vietnam in the line for a year might have had a more bitter time of it than the riflemen of his generation who fought for the duration.

He is a man of peace, of reason, of conscience, and of belief— and yet there is one memory, never beaten down, never explained, never without a power. It is the memory, oddly enough, not of brutality or slaughter but of a small kindness. The kindness was casual, brief, by chance, but you could say it was the greatest gift in his life. It was a small cup of black coffee.

What happened was ordinary: Private Finn and a few others were moving down a road in a straggle on another morning that was as wet and cold as all their mornings seemed to be. They must have passed by an American artillery division with its own kitchen which provided hot food. As they edged along, another soldier from the artillery division was crossing the road and by chance passed in front of Private Finn. Surely he saw something unusually forlorn on that face, for he stopped, poured some coffee in his metal cup, then held it out. Private Finn drank, thanked him, and moved on, never to see the man again.

Speaking of it in a New York office, he was unable to go on, his face and voice no longer working, but he did not cover his eyes or, as some men do, turn his face away so there were no tears to see. His wife, Molly, was waiting outside, all three of us were to have lunch, so I left the room with the excuse of saying hello to her that he might be alone.

"Now you know more about my husband than I do," Mrs. Finn said. When it is exceptionally cold, the feet of James Finn are very white, the feeling almost gone.

His regiment was the 254th Infantry which, in time, had 125 days of combat to its credit and in June 1945 received a presidential citation signed by the Secretary of War, George Marshall, as one of the seven units attached to the 3rd Infantry Division. Like most American men who lived on afterwards, Jack Newcombe, born and raised in Vermont—which happened to be the place he wanted to live, not New York—had killed off most of the details of the fighting in his mind. But his memory, unreasonable in many ways, persisted and defied such healthy intentions, although he never spoke of being a soldier. In the middle of April in the last year of the war, the Germans were attempting to reorganize on the banks of the Danube, and at times it did not look as if the United States Army could win what the Americans liked to call "the race to the Danube." By leaving behind small groups of their best troops, bolstered by SS soldiers, the Germans attempted to delay the

American advance, even if their own soldiers were annihilated, to gain time to form a line of defense elsewhere. Both armies—the holding troops and the advancing Americans—were obsessed with speed. So frantic and strange was this race that often there were no communications between American units; when elements of a front line approached a German town, the Americans were uncertain whether or not it had been taken. Some villages were captured by people in a single jeep taking the wrong road, and men were thought missing when, misled by maps or signs, they arrived at a town which they then had to defend. The first day of combat for the regiment was the first day of January 1945, when his company was in the Allied campaign in the Colmar pocket in Alsace, eastern France. On one occasion pamphlets, sent by a special shell, fluttered over the Americans, written in understandable English with a jocularity that was meant to be bloodcurdling. "Hello, pals of the Blood and Fire Division," the pamphlet said, listing the names of fourteen captured Americans from G company. "They send you their regards with a very special one for Kpl. Lening. With the wish that he take better care of his soldiers. Otherwise he will soon be alone. *The Krauts are rough playmates.*" They spelled *corporal* their own way, with a *K*.

The men with him were all high school graduates; his special friend, who rode with him on an antitank track as the infantry units moved with an armored division, was named Alex Traverso. What Alex Traverso most wanted was to be free to go to Harvard University, where he had been conditionally accepted. Jack Newcombe, then nineteen, the youngest boy in a family in Burlington, Vermont, was quiet, pleasant and then, as now, a person who seems unable to complain. Long after the war, when he was a writer and a bureau chief for the old *Life* magazine, London suited him as a post more than Washington or anywhere else. He was not unlike the English—restrained, orderly, a man fond of the small, wry bit of wit and patient behavior, the well-tuned weights and measures of things, and the occasional patches of eccentricity in his friends. Although generous, he appeared a man happily convinced that frugality was a benediction and showed a clarity of mind. Many people were fond of him; they did not see that he seemed covered with the palest layer of melancholy, perhaps because in the rickety world of journalists he was doing so well: working in the plummiest post most reporters longed for, London;

a most serious salary and expansive expense accounts; the nice house in Carlyle Square; a grand American wife, nicknamed Trip, and four children, although only one daughter was still at home. He smiled, not grinned, quite often, an equivocal, wistful signal which charmed people.

When *Life*—then thought of by outsiders as a club of reckless, gifted, expensive people of unchecked excesses because of its famous photographers—stopped publishing, he seemed slightly blanched. There was nothing surprising about that, for he had worked there for nineteen years. Its closing came when he was in Washington, and the next great rapture was a divorce, as if now all crucial connections had to be finished. He did not seem in the least bit unhappy or forlorn on his own. "Do you miss it?" someone once asked, meaning the magazine, and his response was oddly sharp and too emphatic, something to do with his unbreakable rule of never looking back. Although at his next job, at the Book-of-the-Month Club, the place seemed too sedate, the meetings too frequent, the memorandums and reports going over him like an endless river of white paste, he could barely complain and did not tell stories of more adventurous days, in London, Paris, Antibes, Lagos. He wanted to live in Vermont so much, do his own writing, but at that point the children still needed help, although they seemed no more extravagant or self-indulgent than their father and sometimes he looked happy speaking about them in his very quiet voice, his youngest daughter mountain climbing on college vacations, a strong and pleasing child who became his comrade, his buddy, his darling.

No one had ever asked him anything about the war, Mr. Newcombe said. Years after London, when he was free now of children's bills, the full-time jobs, he was working for himself, still the tidiest of men with the faint smile. It was he who had once told me, when I came home from Vietnam, about the soldier attacking the table, and the man in his unit assaulting the elderly woman, and there was more to tell although he had managed, as they all do, to kill off most of it in his mind. There was something from the war he had always kept, a souvenir of sorts, although he was the last man to want a German bayonet, a dishonored insignia, or a dead man's wallet. A book of poems, perhaps, seemed more likely.

"Where is it?" A polite question, no more, usually bringing the reply that it could not be found. In city apartments people hold on to very little, except records and kitchen equipment, no place at all for old letters and books and the real things that will give us away. His answer, then, was astonishing.

"Here," he said from the bedroom, finding it immediately, all those years of always knowing just where it was.

The photograph of the children is tiny, slightly more than two inches wide, still clear, the four of them all looking in different directions. The oldest, a girl with pale hair in braids coiled over her ears, her knee socks knitted by hand, the small boy in embroidered short pants with suspenders, missing a button in front, show they must be German children, nothing else. There is some baby fat on their legs, their shoes are old but leather. The smaller boy in the embroidered pants has linked his tiny arm through the arm of the little girl who wears a pinafore and has a scab on her left knee. She is the star child, with her thick, brown curls and heart-shaped face, her eyes shut as if she was holding her breath while the camera worked, holding a wooden clothespin in her tiny fingers. Only the wall of the building behind them speaks of the war by its holes and crumblings and lost pieces.

That younger girl, so shy, had made him happy; her sister, who knew some English, was able to translate the few words he wanted to say. He never cared how often children made the predictable demands for food or chewing gum. Their curls and the pinafores of the little girls, their shyness and round, small knees seemed rare and splendid. What he needed was the simplicity the children possessed, their inability to excuse themselves, declaim their innocence or guilt, be accusatory or cringe, or speak of what they had suffered. What he wanted was a shout or hello, a smile, and being able to see them play in that tiny village, forgotten now as they are not.

Before he reached that day of taking the picture, all he knew could be called hopelessness, all the men too pushed, too frozen and half asleep to remember that once things had been better. In parts of the Vosges he always slept with his boots off, as the troops were supposed to do so the feet aired, and tied them to his ankles so the poorly equipped and acquisitive Moroccan soldiers, serving with the French forces, would not lift them. Later, that simple precautionary act seemed the habit of a normal man and any sleep at all a privilege. During one operation eight battalions of American artillery firing for fifteen minutes made it possible for three companies to move forward, mistakenly believing it would now be a cinch to take another town. "The fighting," as one man wrote dispassionately, "was of the most severe type possible—house to house, floor to floor, room to room." On the race to the Danube, those 125 towns he believes the regiment went through have no names for him now, so he only spoke of this village, that road, the next town, the furthest village.

Heading south of Ulm, the old imperial city on the Danube, they came to a place of the most charming proportions and prettiness, deserving to be a good postcard, he said. German troops were pulling back, the Americans just coming, having forward artillery units send in a few rounds to soften the place up. He and Alex Traverso, who wanted so much to get to Harvard, were in a field, leaning against a haystack, when a round hit a street and sent people rushing and circling and tripping out in the open as the flames began to eat some houses. The American troops went from house to house, Germans had five minutes to get out, the orders were easy enough to understand. The people took refuge in a barn, all the Germans were now in there. When alone, he went inside, holding only a rifle, some of the children began to scream, at the sight of him. To calm them, he took off his helmet; somehow it helped if they could see his whole face, the forehead, the eyes, the unwashed brown hair.

"We were coming in as conquerors," Mr. Newcombe said, "and we had the wrong feeling." At night the troops began sleeping in real rooms after looking for wine and schnapps in the empty houses, then getting themselves out and on to the next place and the next. None of them ever knew what to expect, when to be ready for the worst. Often enough the other army waited for them in the dark, and this is what took place on the road which even now he can sketch for you. The others were waiting and caught them. When the shelling began he threw himself on the ground for the ten thousandth time, but this time the earth was fresh and loamy, surprising and pleasing him. He heard the shriek and rolled over to touch Alex Traverso, who had been chosen by a sniper.

"His face was gone," said Mr. Newcombe. "He could only see out of the left eye." What was not there was the right cheek, most of the nose, the right jaw and some chin, and in the blood were bits of bone and broken teeth. Out of the left eye, Private Traverso could see his dear friend bending over, taking hold of both of his hands, and not letting them go until the medic came and the two of them were parted.

The village was theirs, although not easily, and there was still bread and food on the tables in the houses, as if people had foolishly believed one last normal dinner was to be theirs. In the one house so much grander and larger than the others, his platoon made thick, sloppy sandwiches which they carried into the study to eat. It was a fine house: in the basement there were shelves of preserves, not just jellies and jams, but local fruits as well.

It was Wheeler who looked at the furniture, the rows of books, then the table which the man who once lived here had used as his desk, and went to work on it with his bayonet while the others rested. He would always see that table. He could always summon up, too, the face of the sergeant he knew and liked who raped the old woman and told him so; she was more than sixty, more cold and hungry than the American. The sergeant understood what he had become when he was finished with her.

It took some time to do a job on the table. "I got up and left," said Mr. Newcombe. "I must have said to him, 'I'm ashamed to be part of the American Army,' and I went outside and slept there, glad to be alone."

The war became better, then worse, never different, and his unit was sent to Rothenburg, where his duty was to guard an American military installation with a submachine gun. He would not use it and kept the clips in a pocket. Twice he was reprimanded and did not care. That spring he made up his mind on two matters: never to permit himself to live in filth again or to fire a gun. Many men made exactly the same sort of vows and only they know if they kept them.

Good things finally came to pass: he studied Victorian literature in an army school at Biarritz and then, once home, enrolled in Brown University where he majored in history. A Professor Armstrong, grateful to have so many veterans in his class, told them: "I'll hate to see you people go." Alex Traverso was given a repaired and beautifully stitched face and, finally was able to go to Harvard. Mr. Newcombe wept by himself in the hall of the hospital to see what a marvel had been done. But, so much later and so far away, remembering him lying on the road, they way the mouth was pulled over and how the one alive eye looked, remembering the Mississippi sergeant who drank and showed a woman how much more she could still suffer, and the wounds made on the German doctor's calm desk—all this brought the tears to his eyes and even worse, the imploring face. He turned his head from me.

"There is no great use one can make of any of it," he said, knowing this is not what the young are made to believe or what the advertising slogans would have you think. He thought they would have to find out themselves, that warnings were of little use.

Then he put the little photograph of the German children back in the drawer of his bedroom as if for safekeeping.

In the huge New York apartment where the psychiatrist lived there was a photograph of Anna Freud on one wall, in his own room where neither patients nor friends would ever see it. A generous man, his Sunday morning now interrupted, he made strong coffee in the kitchen and saw, instantly, that although I had come to visit with an old friend of his I had the air of the petitioner, the applicant, the intent of an investigator. He did not back off saying, Ah, war neuroses were not his specialty, as two American psychiatrists had earlier done; such an utterance would have sounded preposterous coming from him. He was a European, of a generation that remembered the continent before 1939 and knew what the victims had been sentenced to and for how long.

He spoke of his own father, once a hunted Jew in Europe, a man he remembered as being "unafraid," a father who admitted he killed a German while making an escape but said nothing else, never speaking of the other men he might have later had to kill.

His English had small imperfections, yet he spoke the language with such distinction, the eloquence so unusual, that others seemed present in the living room where we sat in big chairs covered in a blue and white print. He spoke of Europe's children, the survivors who would be almost old now. There was nothing expressionless about him. From me, he heard about the man who wept because once he had been given a few sips of hot coffee, he heard about the man who guarded the picture of children he had hardly known for thirty-seven years. None of it, to him, was unaccountable.

"Very frequently the human being has known intense deprivation and this bursting out—the tears—is a recognition that, after all, our very deepest wish, to be cared for, to be treated with tenderness, might be possible," he said. "The tears may be a relief of pain once there is restitution of our belief that there is goodness."

Then, perhaps, he was thinking of his own father again as he spoke. "And, always, in the trauma of war the man asks himself, maybe much later, how could I shoot and kill someone? The guilt is unmentionable. How do I face, he says to himself, what I could do? In the war films we are never shown that; these films do not tell us how the wish for kindness and care is violated. Also, if the man knows the feeling of victim, of being helpless, this is an intensification of the drama."

Some men, he agreed, find war wonderful, very satisfying, but he was thinking of those who had been so hurt. "One is never over it," the psychiatrist said. "I don't think anyone can recover." He was not certain at all that talking about it would help, that a cure could ever be found.

Yet scars heal, they shrink, grow pale, shrivel, are covered by hair, clothing, tans, and are no longer noticed. They are not injuries anymore. This must be possible, I insisted, insisting too much.

But the terrible experiences do not become scars, he pointed out, then again, with patience, describing them as reverberations, hammered deep inside a person and often too disorganizing to face. The father does not tell the children what happened, what he did or was done to him—not to save them from despair or shock, not to avoid their pity, but because he cannot. Some of these American veterans seemed to me to be in a state of grief, but he thought otherwise. "No, it is not even mourning," the psychiatrist said.

There is my own memory of the American medic in Vietnam, a conscientious objector who refused to carry a weapon. In one village in the Iron Triangle, where his platoon was on operations, he made friends with two Vietnamese children. He wrote his aunt in Brooklyn to send him two of Beatrix Potter's books and gave them to the children. Once he had sat quietly with the children, and knew they had no toys, no books.

The psychiatrist thought it was not because the medic wished to be a child again himself with his two small friends but a soldier's need for contact in a war, the human need to bring to a child that part of himself that also needed to be nurtured and respected. It explained the photograph kept so long by Mr. Newcombe.

"It reminds us we should care," the psychiatrist said.

Between us was the sudden and startling intimacy of prisoners tapping out a code with knuckles, he and I in the lobby of a nice hotel in Evanston, Illinois, where ten novelists and poets had convened for a conference on The Writer in the World. That day one of the writers spoke of the esthetics of morality, puzzling to a man in the audience. "What is that?" the veteran asked. "What does it mean?" It means wicked things may be beautiful; it surprises him that people go on like this. Sometimes in Vietnam the Americans in a convoy or on their tracks would pass the children lining the roads, doing little jigs as they called out for food, and throw full C ration cans at them. The ham and lima beans, the ham and scrambled eggs, the franks and beans, but not the fruit cocktail, their favorite, or the apricots either. At first, the man said, the soldiers tossed the cans out, but soon they began to pitch overhand, in long, hard strokes, aiming the C ration cans like baseballs at the heads or chests of the children, boy or girl, it hardly mattered. The children crumpled and bled and did not bother anyone again. They were not always stoned to death, but these lively targets exhilarated the troops. "I did that all the time," the man in Evanston said. Ask him why-why-why, or ask nothing, and he will tell you. The answer has always been suspended before us. "To kill all of it," he said.

There were no secrets, his wife knew everything and had paid attention. His was an army of men who were demobilized and then did not all keep silent as older veterans have done for so long, the silence such a convenience for the rest of us. Sooner or later, the younger ones knew when it was their time to speak.

"I am dying inside," said a veteran known only as Frank. "I really wish I had lost a limb there. I wish it was just a leg. But when it's inside your head . . ." He spoke about himself on a film which was shown on public broadcasting stations, first in Boston on Memorial Day, 1981. The Boston station set up thirty telephones, each answered by a volunteer, and 302 calls were logged for two hours after the broadcast, two-thirds of the callers combat veterans needing immediate help or advice. Speaking of the mutilations he saw and the mutilations he needed to perform, Frank remembered something else—how he and other Americans helped in the evacuation of civilians from a flooded area and how in the panic a woman drowned her child by plunging it underwater before his eyes. Here, in the film, he is for once innocent and aghast, the woman mad, the baby quickly dead. Nine years without a drink or drugs, he could not at first see the rough cut of the film, and finally, watching himself, wept. His father saw the film too, and afterwards could only say, "I didn't think they'd let you say all those swear words on television."

The death of infants at the hands of their mothers is remembered by some former combatants of earlier wars, who will raise the details of these deaths as proof that they found themselves outside the known limits of all human inhibitions and are therefore never to be held to account. On the popular television series, the last episode of "M*A*S*H" showed Hawkeye Pierce finally succumb to hysteria because he believes he saw a Korean woman smother her baby child on a stalled bus so the infant's cries would not attract enemy soldiers. The other Americans on the bus do not seem to know what he saw, something beyond belief when all cruelties and savagery now seem so familiar.

To see such a thing is to bring into question whether the man is responsible for cruelties he committed when there were women killing infants, if whatever he has done can possibly matter when such slaughtering took place, without reason, the war not calling for it. It is a decent defense, the last one.

In the nation, half-buried memories of different deaths provoke and menace; men sleep and are overrun.

An increase in the number of World War II veterans suffering from a recurrence of combatlike stress symptoms aggravated by conflicts simulating the original trauma is reported in the *American Journal of Psychiatry* by R. M. Christenson, et al. It is mentioned, this increase, in a paper written by James Hamilton, M.D., director of psychiatry at a Veterans Administration Medical Center in Wisconsin, called "Unusual Long-term Sequelae of a Traumatic War Experience" and the story is simple enough. A fifty-five-year-old white male was admitted to the psychiatry service of a V.A. Hospital early one morning after he had destroyed much of his apartment and furnishings. His lover, a twenty-seven-year-old woman living in the apartment overhead, heard the commotion and attempted to restrain him but was hurled against a wall and menaced with a gun. Police were summoned and took him to the hospital. Earlier that evening the man had been drinking—two beers and two brandies, Dr. Hamilton notes, over a period of several hours. Asleep he found himself once more in Okinawa where he had been a marine thirty-five years earlier in World War II. He dreamed only what he had witnessed: another marine killing an elderly woman. The patient said he had not reported it because the company quickly moved on. When his unit began taking civilians into protective custody, the man was explaining some procedure to a young Okinawan woman with an infant in her arms. Speaking no English, the woman thought he intended to harm the child and slit the baby's throat herself. This is what he said he saw, what he dreamed, what Dr. Hamilton heard.

In recounting the nightmare, Dr. Hamilton wrote, the man remembered feeling helpless when witnessing these two deaths in Okinawa, and "when he recalled them while in the hospital, he expressed much sorrow." In the period since 1945, he had had occasional nightmares such as this one, but none associated with violent acting out, Dr. Hamilton noted.

The patient had been married and divorced twice. One week before his admission to the hospital, he had learned that the young woman whom he had known for nine months was expecting a child. At first, Dr. Hamilton wrote, the patient strongly recommended that she have an abortion but changed his mind.

In his work with railroad freight, and before that as a fireman, the patient "always assumed the most arduous and perilous tasks himself," the psychiatrist wrote, and during the Vietnam war the man volunteered for military service despite his misgivings about the validity of the war.

"Mr. A's violent behavior immediately prior to his hospitalization was diagnosed as a dissociative episode precipitated by the stress of deciding whether or not his girlfriend's pregnancy should be terminated, which in turn had reactivated unresolved conflicts secondary to his having witnessed the senseless deaths of the woman and child during World War II."

The patient would not cooperate. The patient resisted any attempts to explore the likelihood of an emotional basis for his explosive reaction because he was not "introspective generally, utilized considerable denial, and completely discounted psychological etiological factors in his illness . . . ," Dr. Hamilton wrote. "Because of the intensity of his survivor guilt, Mr. A was motivated to seek work, first as a fireman and then as a freight train conductor, where he would be exposed to life-threatening situations that satisfied his personal sense of obligation and responsibility, and where he was always on call for emergencies, as in combat. . . . Because of his willingness to place himself in such jeopardy, his traumatic war experience could be contained or encapsulated through repression and counterphobic behavior, only to starkly act out in direct response to life-and-death matters having powerful symbolic parallels to the original trauma that had occurred thirty-five years earlier." Dr. Hamilton, a generous man, thought his paper might have important implications in the assessment of the delayed stress syndromes of Vietnam veterans who may undergo similarly lengthy periods before having to seek medical care.

After a neurological evaluation was completed in the hospital with no significant results, the former marine asked to be discharged from the hospital and refused outpatient psychotherapy. Nothing more was learned of him.

All his life he had tried to be what his country most admired in its men and required of them, staying forever in a ghostly theater of war, with no one he knew to lead him out.

After the wars, some speak, some refuse, some give up, some keep a hopeless vigil, some show pride and want due homage paid, often knowing it will never be good enough, and others despise whatever solace can be provided. Most say nothing but need to make the voyage back to the ground they once fought to take as if by doing this they could at last defeat memories. At the fortieth anniversary of the taking of the Pacific island by the U.S. Marines, the Americans and Japanese who fought each other held a reunion at Iwo Jima and a few men even embraced. Some of the Americans, so much taller, were obliged to stoop down to hug the Japanese they faced again. On television a Medal of Honor winner, a former medic, said quite slowly, that every day for four decades he has thought of Mount Suribachi and that by coming back to Iwo Jima he hopes the ghosts that have kept him company so faithfully might now be released. To the camera he confides and the camera does not answer. He is spared the false reassurances, the soothing reply, any tribute to his gallantry, the firm hand on his shoulder, the thanks of whoever is left.

Some men managed after a war, and no one could be sure which of them would. George Swiers, at thirty-five, a former marine, thought to survive in his war a man had to totally brutalize himself and yet, to keep being human, hold on to a sense of something he could hardly remember. He thought it could be called humanity, unless you knew a better word. "That meant a constant, weird shifting of gears, and in the last thirteen years I have met countless men who, having shifted too early or too late, are forever trapped out there on the fucking turnpike," Mr. Swiers said. Sometimes he envied women and thought that men are systematically, constantly kept in clamps by a series of tests imposed on them all their lives and that the Pentagon could always depend on this conditioning as a useful prelude to military training.

When his two daughters were born he rejoiced in not having sons that the military might claim and deform. Sometimes he spoke of returning to Vietnam for a visit, it was always at the back of his mind, an inspiration to be evoked when there was no other. "I want to see it peaceful and quiet," Mr. Swiers said.

Having done their duty, there are men held in and held back who cannot permit a woman to come too close, except in the easiest of ways, for they fear what might happen to her. It is as if she might discover the bad news they carry and cannot, even by silence, hope to conceal. So these men may only provide an imitation of themselves and keep watching. Just a few months ago, in a small town in Oregon, the prettiest of places, a man with a glancing humor and a certain grace, his name inspired by a Kipling story for children, put it as plainly as anyone ever could. (No one would know meeting him—seeing the intelligent face, the small smile— how far away he stood.)

I had been teasing him a little about a woman who liked him, who was only half joking when she said, out loud, the sight of him made her heart flutter. For eight years the two of them had been circling each other and smiling across streets and rooms, the town is that small. But he kept his distance as if a certain energy had deserted him. That month was the tenth anniversary of the end of the war he fought, but he did not watch the television networks report on it, or read the endless newspaper or magazine stories, suspecting at last the war could be made boring, all that was left to be feared. And the next month was to be the fortieth anniversary of the victory of the earlier war fought by their fathers, so the air was soaked with something that did not need to be named.

Sitting in his car—which is where so many American men feel free to confess, to repent, to reconcile, to reminisce—he told a soldier's little story. It was no more grotesque or sickening than thousands and thousands of others—except to him. There were only a few things to make clear: in the platoon a young black from a poor city touched off a mine and the blast ate his leg. Crawling on the ground, the man in Oregon said, he wanted to find the leg and easily did. He tried to tuck it back into the hip of the dying man, who could still speak and use his eyes. But he could not put back the leg even though he held it to the great wound, so it stayed on the ground and was left behind when the helicopters came. Leaning over, touching the face of the mutilated soldier, he thought he kept saying, "I am here, here, here."

Then, in the car, his hands resting on the wheel, he went a bit further: "I wouldn't want her to be part of the blackness I would bring and then see what it did," he said.

And other men, who have never been in a war, have felt the same, dreading a woman might be pulled into a place they know and find out things that were too much to bear. It is not that these men are unable to marry, or live with women, only that they must be more watchful than anyone else and maintain a certain caution if they are to keep hold of the world.

LOVE
AND OTHER
GREAT RISKS

*O*nce I heard of a man, an orderly sort, who on a summer day in New York saw a woman on the street and wanted to seize her by the elbows, although until then he had taken little account of women's arms, other parts of their bodies more to his pleasure. There was no explaining it, why the fat arms of a stranger aroused such urgency in him. He had no interest in speaking to her, in knowing the plain facts about her. She boarded a bus, the man knew brief suffering, moved on to stern renunciation, entered the subway, and read about Nicaragua in his newspaper. Other men, over and over, have found joy, or believed they would, in their visions of a woman's breast, stomach, hips, legs, buttocks, hair, skin, mouth, all of it. There is no end to what they imagine could bring them joy. Somewhere in the Midwest is a shy man who once made it clear that the small, rather prominent, ribs of a thin girl were the noblest sight he had ever seen, although it struck her as suspect that this preference was so steadfast, that he adored such an ordinary arrangement of bones when she believed she possessed other more compelling assets.

For nearly all their lives most men are unhappily sentenced: they see what they want and want what they will not have, in most cases, or should not even covet. What they must do, unless unusually lucky, is feign indifference or lunacy of some kind. The impossible desires—as felt by the man who wanted only to kiss the arms of the woman in New York—may be punishing and sometimes severe for most of their lives, or only a chain of annoyances requiring them to be specialists in disavowal. Whatever else a man may feel about his wife, or a woman he has loved, when he speaks of the first meeting the man will almost always mention how the woman looked, some physical impression of her, perhaps even a dress, her hair. It is expected that other women, his friends, will respond as eagerly to this loveliness. "She has this wonderful auburn hair and immense brown eyes and you will love her," a friend, not usually a fool, assures me about a twenty-one-year-old woman he wants me to meet. Their idiocy is unknown to them. It may be that men have loved women because they saw them playing the cello or arguing in court or reading blueprints or skiing very well, but this is not what they tell you. I once married a man who was introduced to me in a nightclub and stayed at my side because he fancied I had a narrow waist and lion's hair—his words—which were stunning inaccuracies he did not easily relinquish even when harsh proof was at hand. He heard nothing that night of what I and others were saying about the Congo. A hairdresser and a wide belt brought love.

The stories are everywhere to prove the point. "It was her face and the way she smiled," says a New York friend, a journalist, the father of seven, speaking of his wife, Louisa. He was remembering when he was a schoolboy of nine in the fifth grade and Louisa was a year older, a seat away. But the skin and eyes of the child and the lovely wide calmness of the smile set her apart from any human being, any female, he had ever seen or imagined. All the valiant and obsessed boy had to do, if you will believe this, was to wait thirteen more years until he finished Harvard and was employed so that at last he could marry Louisa in 1955.

And still now, although she wears no makeup and washes her face with her hands, using water and soap as she must have done as a schoolgirl, has borne so many children and lived in six countries with him, always peaceful and certain they were coming to a good bend in the road, he wants to get back to her after the smallest separation. Once, after a wearisome day, going by bus and train for three hours to the suburb where they lived, he intended to reach home by midnight in the hope of having her company at breakfast the next morning. But he understands, as most men do, the great lifelong reveries, and even considers himself a flirtatious man, not understanding that his flirting was slightly too witty and cheerful to count for much. Women saw he was simply diverting himself, there was no intimacy in it, no darker promise of how happy he could make them. That was not his intention anyway.

"Every man feels that it is outrageous that he cannot go bowl over any desirable woman he sees," the friend said. "It's easy to fantasize. What really hurts many men is not the pain of denial but the sense of outrage at having to endure such pain. I think men get so tired of the tracks they make in the world and on the women they've lived with that they want someone new. Light out for the territory." And it was he, long ago, who had once said, when such a remark held little meaning for either of us: "Men grow old but women grow older."

Once on Boulevard Montparnasse, walking once more with a man whose character was a gray and puzzling weave but who had been loved by many unbalanced women including myself, both of us saw an elderly couple, so frail they seemed to be holding on to each other as if moving on a tilting ship, not a pavement in Paris. Arm in arm, they gave each other ballast. Both wore black; the man's overcoat, very old, made clear that he had once been larger than she, which was not then the case. Each seemed certain of being the stronger while concealing it from the other. And then the man at my side, whom I planned to leave for the fourth time, said, "That will be us when we are old." Long afterwards, when it was no longer possible or necessary to remember much about him, only what a black fuss he had made about his boiled breakfast eggs, that remark seemed to me more generous than all the rash, exuberant pledges and promises men had ever flung out. That will be us when we are old, he said, and did not understand why I touched his cheek, all fury gone, the secret out at last. He was more romantic than I, it was all he could manage.

It may be true that a woman does not give up on a man because he grows ugly, loses hair, has larger pores, never thinks to wash his face at night, has the folds of a bulldog where a chin had been, if he will only pay attention, provide a life of responses, provide some proof that she still has some semblance of his attention. But that is not usually the case with a male. Because men feel themselves in peril if they are not pleased by what they see in the woman, reminded yet again of the capriciousness of the penis, they often make sharp, staccato remarks when they feel themselves in danger. Your head is too big for your body, a husband told his wife, who was actually quite beautiful, as if with some good will on her part she could correct such a defect and, while at it, make her legs longer. That he spoke this way while she was undressed did not seem to him to show malice. He might have been speaking of a horse.

Each night, on television, it is possible to watch men and women kiss, fondle, grope, moan, hug, or advance on each other; the new made-for-television movies, on one network, now permit a man to lie on top of a woman and show unmistakable movements beneath the covers of a bed. Sex is no longer furtive, fewer women profess that they must "love" a man before fornication, and some women, young, who have casual affairs in the apartments of men do not choose to spend the night there but get up, dress, and go home alone. Sleeping with them is too intimate, one said, a thirty-one-year-old physician. People speak of relationships, of communicating, of wanting someone supportive, and radio talk shows take telephone calls from the bewildered or uneasy with nasty problems, sometimes sexual. They want to work it through. Sex is no longer a serious act, no more intimate than a game of tennis whose players are earnest and mean well, expect pleasure from bolder strokes, higher serves, and expert volleys. Happiness and absurdity meet. The purpose is to have fun, to indulge egoistic calculations, to feel worthwhile and healthier as well.

It is as if the final worth of all else has been forgotten in an exhausted country where people are not treating anything as a joke, least of all themselves. There is quarreling about the poor. A congressman has accused the budget office of making 12.4 million poor people vanish by its specious statistics. A few bumper stickers say, El Salvador is Spanish for Vietnam. Because so much is told on television, people mistakenly feel they are being informed and grow bored unless a great tragedy is on the air. The weeping parents of a marine killed in Lebanon trying to explain that their son died for his country doing his duty, sacrificing for democracy, being a man, knowing that citizens must risk for the land of the free and home of the brave, and that he believed in what he was doing. This keeps viewers sitting still, pain better than boredom.

On a CBS television program about medical problems and treatment, doctors and patients speak of headaches and allergies;

it is interesting because the migraine sufferers have such hard songs to sing. A woman speaks of wanting to gouge one eye out when the attacks begin—a migraine affects one side of the face—and of lives in darkened rooms, children on tiptoe, speaking in whispers when they are let in. A segment of the program shows a kindly looking physician, who carefully points out that we live in a society that values youthfulness, giving a new type of injection to women with spider veins. Usually found on the back of women's legs, they are streaky clusters of dark blue veins which CBS's own doctor—each network has one now to advise us—makes clear are not similar to varicose veins, which are medically significant. Spider veins are not painful, have no pathology. Several women speak of the anguish their spider veins have inflicted: they can be seen through panty hose, they inhibit you from wearing shorts or a bathing suit, and one woman says even children comment on the marks. In the waiting room, a couple who are clearly in their fifties, both hefty and possessing an air of certainty which is not so common these days, appear patient and composed. It is the affable husband who speaks about his wife's spider veins, what a good thing the injections are and how, after all, there isn't any pain. What is not revealed is what his legs look like, whether the spider veins are only on hers. She says nothing, looking down at the carpet, perhaps feeling a headache, although headaches were earlier in the program. Spider veins mean shame, that is what the woman suggests, and shame of this kind dents a good American. The treatment is not believed to last for more than five years at the most, the CBS physician back on the air tells us, doing her professional duty. Next week, and every week forever, we can share more small, sad secrets and inspect our legs.

Everyone is telling everything; it is considered a sign of improved mental health. So there is no embarrassment at asking five men, all forty-five or older, what were the general reasons for their having left their wives and remarried much younger women. Love is not mentioned, sex is not mentioned—they are too shy, they are speaking to a woman of their own generation, they have lost the habit of confiding, most of all on the telephone—although a man in Boston speaks of his new wife, sixteen years his junior, as "agreeable" and makes the point this is a most underrated quality. What he means is the young wife, who loves him and is made happy, does not take him on or create great disturbances. All her plans are him. She is not going to law school; she does not want to write for *Newsweek* or operate on the brain.

Young women do not have spider veins, stretch marks, thickening stomachs, but this does not come up. Other explanations flourish. A man of some brilliance in California explains he did not leave his wife during a long and loving affair because of the children. The idea that his wife might remarry, bring another man into the house who would daily oversee or influence the children, was too dreadful for him to contemplate. The idea was appalling, but if it had not been for the children he might have bolted. As he remembered the meals in California with the young and attentive woman, he ordering for both of them, anxious to get it done so he might begin to talk, his voice on the long-distance call sounded happy. It was slightly startling. It is not commonplace to hear a man sounding happy. Normally their voices are determined or vigorous, even triumphant or sorrowful, but on the whole men do not sound happy unless they are at a football game or have won an election or a lottery.

"The wide-eyed stare of young women, it is the way they look at you across the table," he said. "Oh yes, you may be right, occasionally they turn out to be nearsighted, but oh my God, not only do they not know your failures but they often look totally admiring, as if you are the first man to have answered their every wish. They have their pick of men. You are not handsome but *wise*." It is an oddly old-fashioned revelation, as if he had never met a young woman interested in aerodynamics, knew no females who wore contact lenses and did not want to widen their eyes, was unaware he could not set his stamp on a new generation of women who did not want to make any kind of surrender.

But he goes on: "It is also being in the company of one without bitterness. They are not bitter about anything, and if they are young enough they have not yet been betrayed by men," the California man said, opening up.

Without bitterness, he said twice. Two other men hear these very words, seize them as if they could be held like a regimental banner, and do not speak of their own cruelties in leaving wives who, as they themselves applauded and showed pride, had, late enough, made careers, one in politics, the other in medicine. Nothing is said of that, nor do they speak of the fear they felt for themselves, knowing they must have change in their lives but all that could be humanly changed was their women. The despair is common enough; it is as Justice Wendell Holmes once said at a dinner in his honor, speaking of his years upon the bench of the Supreme Judicial Court of Massachusetts. "I ask myself, what is there to show for this half lifetime that has passed? I look into my book in which I keep a docket of the decisions of the full court which fall to me to write, and find about a thousand cases, a thousand cases, many of them upon trifling or transitory matters, to represent nearly half a lifetime. . . . Alas, gentlemen, that is life. . . . We cannot live our dreams. We are lucky enough if we can give a sample of our best, and if in our hearts we can feel that it has been nobly done."

The man in television, with his rich, roly-poly voice, is not in a profession that wishes work nobly done; his new wife, who is under thirty, fifteen years his junior, is soon to have a baby. His last wife was told abruptly of his departure just as she was to begin an internship. He was leaving her and her children from an earlier marriage whom he had loved.

"There is a release from feminist struggle now occurring among women no older than their early thirties, who are, of course, the beneficiaries," he says. "These young women are free of the ruses and scars that can manifest themselves. The cohort of women who came to their majority in the early seventies avoided many of the cuts and bruises of that half-generation of women who are five to ten to twenty years older."

In Boston, a man who teaches writing in a private school, an old and prestigious one, has recently married for the third time a woman slightly older than one of his children. She does not know the meaning of Selma or the Ia Drang Valley or what year Bobby Kennedy was shot in a hotel kitchen. It does not matter to him any more than it mattered that his earlier wife did not inquire about his back with its intricate scars that made the skin look as if it had been oddly crocheted, did not ask how such wounds came about and exactly where. Once in the kitchen he spoke of his new play and said to the young woman—they were not yet married—perhaps on this one he would make it, and she smiled up at him and moved closer. A more reckless, braver woman might have said "Well maybe not, but I will still love you."

"The shock troops of the women's movement would all be forty-five or fifty years old. It was they who flung themselves into battle, took enormous gains, went a great distance in a very short period of time. Other women swept in right behind them, as the logistics people, you see," he said, always preferring the military metaphor, stunning the way he did it. It made you see Shiloh and Passchendaele and A Shau even if you knew little about infantry tactics; he took you to Borodino.

"But they, the logistics people, weren't impaired or wounded. The women who advanced and were out there on the line—well, for all the good they did for society, the secondary results of the campaign had hard effects on them personally."

Although the father of three daughters, he was often surprised by what he kept learning about women.

"In my writing classes I have had a number of extremely able students; the majority of these are young women, not because they are smarter or put together more shapely sentences. The boys do seem to love to write about their childhood, about themselves, while girls are very eager, almost pathologically, to take their narrators forward three or four years, and the difference in the subjects they write about is, no doubt, because of their sex and psyche. The bottoms of their stories are infinitely more interesting." It startled him to read the short story by an eighteen-year-old girl who had written about a lonely forty-year-old man. He had been such a man once; he could not imagine how she knew what she did, how she thought of the idea.

It had not occurred to him, indeed came as a shock, to realize that his male students could only at this time, and perhaps all their lives, think of themselves; they were, after all, their own most fascinating subjects. But the young women were noticing and thinking about other people, as if their lives depended on it, taking in the little habits, expressions, and voices of strangers. He had never thought of this defect in males before.

A doctor from Denver who treats children says, "Don't you know? Hasn't anyone told you? Men marry younger women because they like to make love more than older women do." Others are not so sure.

A reason, one among many, why so many men who could call themselves middle-class do not feel it is indecent to leave their wives is that more women now work or are capable of taking jobs. Women are leaving husbands too, but men do it in larger numbers. The man can tell himself that he is not abandoning a helpless woman in a cold house with only one package of Stouffer's Lean Cuisine in the freezer, however poorly off she may be without him. He falls out. It is no longer a scandalous act. The husband who leaves for another woman, almost always younger, will not be ostracized by the people he likes, or seen by his peers as unbalanced or not trustworthy. His relatives will not scorn him. There is no disgrace, very little inspires that much excitement anymore. Often he will be envied by other men who do not wish to leave their own wives but are awed by the energy and riskiness of the man who does and has someone else waiting. And there is something else as well, rarely spoken of, almost never admitted. Needing hope for themselves, while obliged to pretend otherwise, the last clear, hazardous act of their lives—when little else can be changed simply by choice—is for men to shift women. Selfhood is more precious than stability, a severance long felt is not to be calmly borne these days. Men will do a great deal not to define what they reasonably describe or willingly acknowledge: a cloudy sorrow that moves closer to the bone as they grow older. It is not the depression women know and speak of, not anxiety, but a despondency of a different sort. They lose their hair and wonder what else is going. A younger woman often dispels this, gives men back, in some way, an authority that was never really theirs, provides a cheerfulness the man cannot muster for himself. In the lunatic American landscape, runners racing to reach nowhere, pleased by the assault on lungs and legs, it is thought unwise to stay still. Change is splendid, speed is essential, even if the reasons for it are uncertain. A clearer, cleaner life beckons if love is fresh.

The younger women often want babies while there is still time, and older men, who have already raised their families and thought themselves free of all of that, must usually agree. It is not immortality they hope for, as some people think, but the need to hold the younger woman.

For a man who had his first child when he was twenty, and his fifth and last child when he was fifty-eight, putting the facts on paper made plain the dilemma. He is Loudon Wainwright, a writer of great gifts whose gifts, as is so often the case, have not made him happy. Very tall and somber with a white beard—without it he would appear much younger but he does not choose to try for such an effect—he once spoke of being in boot camp when he was seventeen and hearing, for the first time, the ordinary vile language used to debase recruits. Until that day no one had ever said, in his presence, the word *motherfucker*. Decades later he was to say, "And at that time I happened to miss my mother very much." Only three years later, knowing almost nothing about how children were born, and keeping his distance, he had his first son.

A picture of the newest baby is up on the bulletin board in his office. He smiled at the snapshot of the infant, sitting by herself on a bed, thrilled at the commotion she is causing, by the voices and pleasure she gives. The baby is proof of his love for the mother, 23 years younger than he, although for some time the idea of being a father once more appalled and embarrassed him.

"I agreed—after months of pained argument and anxiety— that a woman is entitled to have a baby if she wants it," he wrote. "Especially if she's thirty-five and hasn't had one. I wasn't clear about my own entitlement not to have one, except it seemed at least possible that if I insisted on it, I might have to enjoy my freedom from babies either alone or with another partner."

There was a "graveyard cast" to his objections, Mr. Wainwright wrote in his column for *Life* magazine. He knew he could not be assured of a full life with this child. "For some reason, the idea of becoming a father again at this advanced age made me terribly conscious of my own mortality, threatened me with it, really. A kind of dogged morbidity took hold. I wouldn't live to see the kid into school, went my piteous fretting. I wouldn't be fit to play strenuous games with it, he or she was doomed to the early loss of one parent." And he wondered how to explain to his own children, and how to say to his grandchildren that they were going to have a baby uncle or aunt. But his children were kind, even happy for him. He obliged himself to be cheerful, but the final and overwhelming consideration was pleasing the woman, whose dark hair and pale skin and unusually buoyant spirits made it unnecessary for her ever to explain that she came from a very large Irish family.

It is accepted now by this father, and others, that he probably will never see the daughter begin a family of her own, but it is also not certain exactly who will. In the cities and towns people speak of the possibility of annihilation, and sign petitions and join marches, and sigh as they watch the evening news.

When his first child was to be born, Mr. Wainwright spent all night in the hospital waiting room, drinking coffee with a man twice his age whose wife was also in labor. There were the two of them, confined and helpless and ignorant, as all expectant fathers were meant to be, their presence unwelcomed by nurses anywhere else, most of all in the rooms where the women lay, sentenced to lonely and ferocious torment. The other man had waited so long for a child, knew many disappointments, was now close to the great happiness of his life. But a doctor came out to say that the man's wife was okay but the baby, a boy, had not made it. The man then turned to his younger companion, touched him and said he knew *his* baby would be fine. So many years later the kind and decent man had not been forgotten, still even now can be summoned up. "I hadn't realized how close all life is to sorrow," Mr. Wainwright wrote of himself at twenty.

Some men are happy, their marriages as crucial as the vertebral column, in the way of my friend who fell in love at nine and will, to this day, lightly hold the hand of his wife in public, which surprises other people and sometimes even makes them sad. At first it is always a physical quality about the woman that pulls the man closer, something that suggests a spirit or temperament, or a need he finds alluring and out of the ordinary, even when it is not. Often it is a suffering which attracts him, or simply her stubbornness, for men are quick to believe they can lead women out of trouble, be the guide, and that together he and she will make it to safer ground. The man wants to rescue the woman; an illusion will do. But more often than not it is the woman who rescues him by letting him find out what has lain hidden and subversive within him for too long, making trouble. What sets the happy people apart is the significance they give to each other, as if they each suffered an unknown optical defect providing a startling, unbalanced view of the other the rest of us will never see. Many men who have been married more than once are those who, for all the trouble it caused, said yes to the trouble and found impetus in the new woman, a reason for existence they had not realized before when they thought that what counted was their work or other things. They are usually the men who were once consumed by loneliness and did not know it because they were not alone at all but, as the critic said, were tired of the tracks they had made not only on the world but on the women they had married as well.

These are stories of what is commonly called love, always a word of some sloppiness, stories about men, and who and what it is they love, no matter how sorry or daunting the reason for it. Believing ourselves beyond surprise, their little narrations will seem ordinary but the commonplace holds the wonder: a man who falls in love and leaves a decent and devoted wife; the silent father who at last speaks his love to the grown son whom he would not rescue as a boy; the small girl being raised by a young widower with the most ardent hopes for her, in a culture he often opposed; and the love of a man who once played football and still feels for the game. Remembering being a quarterback in high school, then in college, still another man tells me how football was this mystery, for it let you lose yourself inside it while making a man larger and greater than life would ever again permit. It was almost the same thing a sixty-year-old man told me many years ago about the love he felt at fifteen for a girl named Joanne in Nebraska: he felt himself surrendered, yet never so strong.

Sometimes the love men carry seems almost unknown to them, but usually not, its pull too strange and persistent to be easily denied unless they have put aside their old selves and forgotten where.

But how they hate to say it, this coarsened, short word, as if only women should come right out with it, as if leaving the mouths of men it might shrivel or defile them before our very eyes. What many men do—the slowest among them or the most clever, all so skilled at certain subterfuge—is to wind stories around love. The stories contain a code you are expected to crack, no questions asked, and this is the closest they can come on ordinary days.

Sometimes men reveal themselves in the most unsuitable places, like women on airplanes needing to speak of betrayal or incurable illnesses, because this is where all of us feel safer. Once, describing a piece of land he had owned, farmed, and lost, a thin man on a train to Washington, D.C., a stranger of no apparent charm, his eyes not aligned and hair badly cut, talked and talked of the soil he had worked. It was as if he alone had been permitted inside the Great Inner Temple denied to most mortals. Proof was an old snapshot showing a bit of baked ground, the usual crooked house, a tree clearly bullied by heat and wind, surely in some county in Texas although that he did not say. But what happened to his face as he saw again what had been his privilege and his blessing was nice to see. His were not the ramblings of a man who was drinking, a man given to elaborate boasts, nor was he one of those who could not stop talking. In that paltry place he had known rapture and that night on the train he wished to be reminded.

Not all stories of love have such clear maps, a beginning and an end, call forth a face, a name, special words spoken and then taken back. Sometimes the love comes from horror, from an immense sorrow suffered for useless reasons, known only by a few men whose skin becomes one skin for all of them. The love must be honored only by silence. So you cannot blame me now, so many years later, if two men are confused in my mind—although not their faces—for they said almost the same thing when I asked the first question and intended many more. One of them had fought at Ia Drang and another had been eight years in a prison in Georgia, and what both must have said, turning from me, was something like this: "It was something sacred, you have no right to ask." Some days I am almost sure it was the man who robbed the store who said exactly that.

What few men have loved is an ideal and what it promised them they might be for a little while, although this is never what they are able to tell you. Ten summers ago, at a small birthday party held outdoors, the wives began singing the old songs from the Spanish Civil War, still remembering the choruses, even those in another language. Sitting next to a man who had, so long ago, fought in Spain, I asked because I was drinking the Bordeaux which song he had liked the best. He did not want his Spain to be reduced to this: a silly question, the pretty table with different glasses for the wines, the women in long skirts, our pleasure because Francisco Franco was at last dead and clearly we were not. So he only answered, "Who had time for singing?" Not all love can be translated and there are men, and women too, who will not permit any attempt.

Perhaps no love rattles so deeply, brings such a lunatic joy or such great disturbances, as the love a man suddenly knows for some woman when he believes his life is already in place, the pages bound if not completed, his allegiance to his wife permanent, and then finds all this untrue.

That summer when he was thirty-five, William Harrell, who had done nothing that could be considered exceptionally mean or even disorderly in his entire life, stopped being sensible and cautious altogether. He fell in love at the worst possible time with a young woman who was also married and had two young children as well, a situation so unpromising that he would often speak of dying and death when, in fact, he now seemed unusually alive. Her name was Maude. The plainest comment came out of him with immense urgency. He began sighing when he spoke. After a long residence in a university town in the East, he and his wife moved to the Midwest so he could begin a new job, teaching at a new university and editing. They bought their first house, later he saw its limitations. It was thought then that these two were calmly, pleasantly married, so nicely suited that they carried out a civilized division of duties. A modern husband, he always did most of the vacuuming and the grocery shopping because she held the full-time job. He thought this only fair and rather liked such an arrangement. She was a better cook but he kept improving, especially with chicken, and did not wander off when the food was still on the stove.

When he felt certain that he was not going to recover from this splendid, strange seizure, Mr. Harrell would telephone four friends, all men, across the country to explain that he was dying. He believed he would lose the marvelous new woman, or his wife, or both of them. He spoke as if he had become a hemophiliac, in danger from the smallest puncture. The friends tended to groan and say, oh my God, but they believed it inevitable, they had all guessed that something was going to happen to him, and it made some of them almost cheerful to have been right. One man even said, "I like it when someone grabs life by the neck and shakes it." Mr. Harrell suspected later, when he was calmer, that two of the four men had been in similar situations and stayed put because of children. "Oh you lucky dog, I don't care how much pain you are feeling, you lucky fucker," one man said. "You have to follow your passion," another man advised. "You have to trust your instincts." They all knew, however, what he meant by saying it was too complex to be borne. And later he remembered a much-loved friend in California who told him, "I knew it was coming. You have been performing too long."

None of this was plain to him, but now he says it all with the clarity of a man staring at his own old X rays, seeing for himself the surprising tumor he carried, its shape, its size, its exact position. Nothing could be denied any longer: not his boredom, or the way he always felt compelled to stop short with his wife from saying what he wanted to, or the exhaustion of the plain, neat thing known as the marriage. More than half my fault, he would say, at least half. The good years were not to be dismissed, he was not at any time willing to say they had counted for nothing at all. There were the years in graduate school, the year abroad on a fellowship, the trips on the side, and the calm, orderly years near the first university in a narrow house, dark green downstairs, his piano squashing the small front room. He worked well.

That last summer in the East, when he was still teaching creative writing part-time at the university and working at home on his poetry and Italian translations, he often appeared scornful and impatient at first meeting, a man clearly hoping for something huge to intervene, anything. You will hate it, he said to a woman he had just met at a diner on the main street. She was to begin a teaching fellowship and thought the prospect lovely. The students will look down on you, he said. It was not to be the case and it did not describe his own situation. Some of his students liked the rougher way he judged their work, not concealing either his expectations or his impatience when they only gave him their pale perceptions of perceptions. A man with a bit of a burr, one older professor said of him, remembering a certain impatience, his occasional disregard for the cautious, ceremonious ways of doing things, which often signaled nothing would be done. He seemed then not to know, perhaps to have forgotten, that his charm could be considerable.

His wife each morning went to work to a job of some rank; she had a lovely oval face which promised a lyricism, an interesting temperament that she did not possess. In fact, as in the case of many women who are almost beautiful and do not believe it, her looks did her no good at all and she often worried about her weight, which never spoiled or distorted that face. When they were together, an outsider might have noticed that the wife was slightly deferential and quite watchful; he did most of the talking. She was not given to impetuous behavior, operatic outbursts, and denunciations until he came clean that one morning.

It was close to 3 A.M. In the manner of all women slow to understand a danger suddenly made apparent by the staged evasiveness of men, she began her interrogation, all patience and reason going. And he, in his immense new pain believing himself abandoned by his love, thought of it as a ceaseless hammering.

They were not accustomed to such scenes and he had no idea how to spare either of them. The dear room grew dreadful. He did not once mention the name of Maude. It may be his wife feared he had a tumor of the brain or a terrible neurological disease. When she knew the truth, the dreadful and most predictable part began. Later she tried to make him read *Passages*, which he scorned, and another book, *The Seasons of a Man's Life*, described on the cover as "The radical new theory of adult development that shows how every grown man must pass through a series of specific age-linked phases which underlie his personal crises, govern his emotional states and attitudes, even shape his behavior." He read it, page after page, wondering, Where is the part about me? It was not to be found; none of what he felt were the foolish, wretched, nice men in its pages resembled himself.

Without a job or friends of her own in this new place, the wife had nothing but this husband and could not understand what had been set in motion. William Harrell was, after all, the only adult male she had ever loved and lived with; she could not grasp that such treason was possible. They were so deeply joined together any real separation could be ruinous, but in the last few weeks they would ever have together they hastened the ruin; her language became uncustomarily strong, slightly coarse—not by American standards but by her own—and anger and grief made him feel closer to her, a surging of sympathy even at the very moment he was telling her he must go. Never had they seen each other like this; their life had been so composed and complacent, he was surprised to discover how much he had resented it all along.

"Oh, yes, peaceful, a life of peace and order and routine and time for my work. And I couldn't stand the responsibility of so much peace," he said. "It's a hell of a thing to have to bear. Every little thing meant so much; it was just the opposite of the lovers' intensity and desperation, when everything has meaning too but everything is exquisitely meaningful. But the peace—it wasn't so bad that I knew I was choking. If it had been a little more extreme I would have had a clearer sense of it. In fact I was able to bear it. But it made me sick. I didn't understand why I felt so bad."

He wrote a poem about the hunger both of them knew, asleep or awake, eating or not eating. There was no chance that his wife, who had remarried and happily so, would ever see the poem, for she lived in another country by now. But a man who was a friend of William Harrell mailed it to her thinking she might still be pleased to see his work. This how stupid some men can be, how dangerous, how wrong their instincts.

The story of how William Harrell met his first wife was one of the few she always liked to tell, making a slight but charming recital of it, which embarrassed him because, like most men, he did not care to have others hear how graceful or flirtatious or tender he had once been. He was an undergraduate majoring in Italian when she came to the campus, a student from a small college in Ohio, to study Persian for a semester in a special program to encourage the study of uncommon languages. Both went one evening to a large lecture hall to hear Stokely Carmichael, and the place was so packed with students wanting to be thrilled and disturbed that he gave the dark-haired, serious girl his seat and found a place for himself on the steps. In a university where there were so few black students, no blacks on the faculty, Mr. Carmichael that night was never to be forgotten and later Mr. Harrell remembered the speech as "the most beautifully turned eighteenth-century denunciation," a thing none of them had ever heard before.

"You can't imagine how splendid the sentences were," he said. "Black liberation—they couldn't believe it. It was just awful for some of them and it was a wonderful piece of theater. He was wearing a sharkskin suit, a marvelous suit, it was iridescent. He was unbelievably elegant and articulate."

The year was 1966, not a bad year for him, the country changing in peculiar and noble ways, growing sweeter and more murderous all at once. The music was insistent. He stayed apart from the recklessness and defiance and disorder that were changing the campuses, readying himself to face a draft board in Texas and declare himself a conscientious objector. Rehearsals for the very same thing were going on all over the place. He had only to wait his turn, all young men were waiting their turn; the reason was called Vietnam.

His wife was impressed by the swiftness with which he gave her his seat and how he smiled and nearly bowed; his manners were nice at a time when such gestures were already considered reactionary by some. Because there were no women at the university, he was lonely for them. He found the student of Persian charming; she was steadfast, shy, and unfamiliar with harm. He pursued her. It is possible he believed she would be very good for him.

At twenty-one, still a student, he married, and after his graduation went with her to Berkeley, where he enrolled in a creative writing course and stayed on to earn his Ph.D. in English literature. (Once, after they were lost to each other forever, he needed a pilgrimage, a brief bit of concentrated mourning, and stood outside the small house in California where they had once lived and been so captivating to each other.) There was a year in Italy and, later, short trips abroad to Europe, and nothing seemed wrong at all.

Not even in his most uncomfortable moments or the melancholic ones would Mr. Harrell have it said that these were not fine times; he never denied it. The two of them were content to come back east, because she had been offered a good job in research. Her prospects were better. They both knew poets were meagerly paid and so kept humble. He did teach freshman English at a community college for a while to students who were not in the habit of writing anything, certainly not letters, and least of all short essays. In a strange way which he did not recognize, they won him over as no class ever would again.

"It was hopeless and the kids were so wonderful," he said. "After the course was over one of them came to me and said, 'My old man owns a liquor store. Anything you want just call me, I want to be the guy that gives you what you want.' " And the boy whose father owned the furniture shop said the price of anything would be knocked down if he would come in, anytime. And a girl who, although of ordinary appearance and comportment, astounded him. This extraordinary girl who had worked as a volunteer in a children's hospital, and wrote about it, describing how her father put together an aluminum Christmas tree for the small patients. He was so excited, he felt a kind of love for her, the shy girl who did not want to know the importance of her own talent and who might have feared it would only bring her trouble. They worked on making the piece a little bit better, he being patient and careful. "Now you must do something with this, this is really far beyond ordinary things," he said. He wanted her to send it to *Mademoiselle* or *Redbook*, the names of magazines for women that first came to mind. He began to explain how to address the envelope, how to write the covering letter. The girl backed down, wanted none of it, and never was he able to figure out the reason. He moved on, taught Italian for a year at a better university, and was then invited by a former professor to teach part-time in the creative writing department at his own university—a sudden salvation. He and his wife saved money and thought it an accomplishment. They could not stop saving.

At that time he looked fine. In a country of large men he was certainly tall but not of a height that made others feel timid, and his walk was clearly American, at its most engaging when he wore jeans and moved in long, loose steps. His hair curled and was not long, his eyes were a nice blue, never bloodshot since he did not drink or go without sleep, and his voice was so low and well pitched it sometimes made a few older people remember how they once loved listening to the radio. His mustache was thick and a little too long at the sides; it is even now.

Years later, at a literary lecture, he met the new woman, Maude, because by chance they sat side by side, and a long time later, when they were at last safe and together, her children's lives safely protected and nicely arranged, he remembered his first impression of her.

"She looked attractive, of course, but she also looked damaged to me and it made me very curious. You must realize how few women I have ever had that feeling about; there are very few that I've had the chance to meet," he said. "I've just known a few women who have confided in me and I always want to know what experiences they've had. Give me that. I want that, I need that, I am hungry for it. In fact most women have had something happen but will not tell. To me. That is the way it seems to me, that's what drives me crazy about women, and that is why it frustrates me enormously when they are of an ordinary sort. I want to shake them by the hair and say, 'God damn it, won't you tell me? Surely you've told somebody? You've never told anyone?' "

"I don't get to listen to women talk enough. What disappoints me is that I know a lot of women to whom I would like to be able to speak and to whom I would like to be able to listen. But they don't start it and I can't get it going because I wouldn't be perceived correctly. And maybe they are secretly afraid that as soon as I get a few things out of them I'll feel contempt for them, for their having talked to me that way." Like many men who are opposed in principle to injustice and cruelty but who rarely witness it, he saw, instantly, what had been done to her and knew a restoration was possible, as if she were a country whose gardens and farms and rivers had been damaged by nameless armies.

But Maude had no secrets from him. She told him all about her life, rinsing herself of two wretched husbands, those dank and vile marriages, remembering her coming of age, her family, the birth of the children and her frequent dreams of the children, so that after a while he knew so much about her life he could often tell her own stories of the crudeness and boorishness of those other men. Nothing was kept back and he adored her for this, each story a huge and trembling pinwheel moving constantly as she spoke. She was not self-effacing and he came back to life, cured now of the old anemia which left him so cranky and sad. They wanted only to swim inside each other. A dark-haired woman with slightly slanting dark eyes, who knew how to hold her head well, who long ago understood that most men thought her figure very good, she had a generous anger to match his own.

Until then he had not been convinced that he was attractive to women and did not know his own power. It was not only his bearing and his poems, what a few women found alluring was how he could keep talking. He did not, as other men do, say "we'll see" when asked for a decision. He did not have to rise from the table as soon as dinner is over, for he liked to root himself there, to go on talking, a man who spoke in strong, fast sweeps, knew a good deal, and expected to learn more. And he played the piano with such bravura that Maude, on the telephone with another woman in another city, held the phone out so her friend could hear him playing "Blue Skies." Once a woman who spent a day with Mr. Harrell remembered afterwards why the afternoon had such a splash to it and tried to make a list of some of the subjects he brought up. They were: the novel by Asturias, *El Señor Presidente*, which he described; how his father in Texas had been a salesman and seemed to have gone from huge to little things, from once selling immense sides of beef all the way down to olives and little ballpoint pens with names on them; how he did not know his mother's family was Jewish until he was over thirty and found out by chance; a poem he wrote about a woman in the supermarket running away from him; a Velázquez painting, *Las Meninas*; how Nero in his persecution of Christians had pitch poured over their bodies so they could be strung up and lit like torches; and the work of the Italian, Ignazio Silone. It was charming that he knew the normal pulse for a man was seventy-two while women tended to have eighty-four pulsations per minute. "I have a woman's heart," he said, meaning his pulse was high, an arterial arrhythmia the reason.

He did not ordinarily tell stories about himself as other men so often do. Nothing terrible had ever happened to him. He had not been taken by an army, capsized a boat, been in a car crash, climbed a mountain and lost his footing, been mugged and beaten, or gone bankrupt, although he understood all acts of destruction and survival, what drove people to lunacy or self-pity. His only tragedy was the way his first marriage had ended, his wife's face sagging and losing color when at last she understood, refusing then to ask anything about the woman he really loved, not her name or the color of her hair or if she, too, was a writer.

He did not realize until long after she was gone that his wife had been a deeply maternal woman (although they had agreed many times over to have no children). He was able to speak to Maude about everything, and she, hearing every low note, every disparity, every incomplete chord, pointed out to him all the short-comings and delusions in his own version of his life. Eventually he came to know the reasons for the old unhappiness and learned how to exert himself more wisely. Once, visiting the Eastern university with Maude, he sent flowers to a friend, then saw in her house that they were slightly withered and not what he ordered. Maude went back with him to the florist and rehearsed him on how to successfully complain. She let him do it. Instead of being cutting, and making clear how furious he was, he began by saying to the owner he was sure a mistake had been made. It worked. Fresh flowers were sent out right away, apologies given, a new girl in the shop blamed for the bad bunch. It always hurt him when such things went wrong, but he had never quite known how to correct them, to make them right.

He came to believe that his marriage was not at all the special thing it had seemed when he himself violated it and that it was harmful.

"I couldn't feel passion, the prohibition was too great. I also felt as if I had to be very tender and protective. When I needed energy, when I needed wildness, I couldn't get it from her. There was nothing for me to tap into because it wasn't there, because she was so afraid of it. And I don't just mean a sexual passion either, but another kind. Blowing up at the TV, at a story in the paper, whatever—just the vitality of the moment. But such a maternal woman won't have a great passion about anything, even about eating, about drinking a soft drink. And especially not in bed."

The night he told his wife, uncertain he would ever again see Maude, it was not with triumph or pity, only a confession of torment and helplessness which she heard as the recital of an atrocity. When his wife left their bedroom, he listened to her going downstairs in her slippers and caught the noise of falling. He found her on the floor, quite still, overcome, and gathered her up, which was all he could do.

Some men, who didn't tell him so to his face for whatever reasons of their own, were wary of his need for Maude, his appetite for her, as if such a need and so much feeling had unbalanced him or would hurt his work. He knew all about that kind of reasoning and he has his theories.

"American men seem to feel that work, or whatever it turns out to be, comes first, that there must always be something *before* a woman; it's not proper to admit that a woman can be the most important thing in your life," he said. "It's unseemly—really something for fools."

He knew of the grudges women held against their husbands, of the responses that were never given, the surprises that would never come, the words left unsaid, so he listened with patience as a friend complained bitterly about a man who did not celebrate when his wife finished five weeks of radiation, five times a week, for cancer in its early stages. The man, who had long ago forgotten how to rejoice or why, expected dinner at home in the kitchen, and the woman, who then provided it, was unable to forgive him.

"Well, perhaps he can't see taking her out to dinner as anything except this huge thing, when all it has to be is a simple, sweet thing to do. Maybe the husband sees it as a battlefield. Then if he does it, if he takes her out to dinner, it is to acknowledge and agree to this desperation of hers. Maybe he doesn't want to acknowledge that this desperateness for love exists." He thought it could not be said with any certainty or proof but believed that most American men were emotional cripples, damaged, and no one knew the beginning of it or the way out for them.

"Many men don't want their wives to be that desperate for love; it makes them enormously uncomfortable and resentful," he said. "A lot of the time that is because the husband has substituted dutiful compliance—rituals and outward signs—for any genuine feeling for his wife. Men simply don't want to make the effort because so much is attached to what the women want. Everything is attached to it. The expected, the demanded response will never be a genuine one."

Never did he dream of leaving his wife in their thirteen years together, believing himself to be that deeply attached, so early on he said to Maude, meaning it, although with sadness, "This can't work out. I can never leave my wife, it would be like cutting half my side out." One year, when his wife was in her office, he had an affair which he ended before the woman moved away, the woman always insisting she loved him. The chance to have another liaison came. A friend from Texas, whom he once made love to in a car when she was a girl who needed risks and flurries of passion, called him. Uninvited she came to his house during the day, wanting more than talk of old times.

"I just knew it was wrong. I could see how I could become dried like the crust of a cicada without wings. I would never write again, I wouldn't ever touch dinner again, and she would use me up and throw me away. She had been through so many men already, I could see what she was doing."

With both women he saw that he was in danger, that nothing he would do could ever be enough for them, that they might diminish him, put him in a stupor, render him infirm.

"They were going to be disappointed almost as soon as we got into bed and I really didn't want that. No one has a right to be disappointed in me, by God," he said. "You know it's not fair, you can't have that. No, it's much better not even to get it started."

His wife had not been disappointed in him, only slightly wary and inclined to question or correct when he spoke his mind on any of a dozen subjects, which he needed to, since Mr. Harrell saw bombast and deceit and stupidity often enough. "She would say, 'You are angry and you are so dismissive of these things, why is it?' She believed there was a different way to behave that was far more proper and suitable. And I simply wasn't going to be that way. I was too excessive. But I wasn't being excessive at all," he said.

He knew men who were; one of them in the Northwest had

just bought a motorcycle and said to William Harrell, "I'm thirty-nine years old and will soon know how it is I am going to go." The man was speaking of his own death. This was a man with an interesting marriage, who collected many young women, who spoke of having five guns in the house—including a .357 Magnum, a weapon suited for killing people making a getaway in a car, a policeman's gun—and who drove his machine very fast. His own wife did not wish to know of people like this; she was a censor. He wished she didn't disapprove of his friend. The friend's ways were not an issue with him or a reason to weaken his love.

"So we had our bargain, we had our way of doing it," Mr. Harrell said. "I was talking to her in a way that I could talk to her and she came back the same way. There was an enormous amount of material that never came up." The difference in his life with Maude astonished him, made him marvel at how free he now felt, able to say anything, pass any judgment, and have something come back. She heard, she answered, they talked and talked, in a reverie.

In the newspaper he read an article about the murder of a newly born infant whose father, a veterinarian, had seen it born, then had also seen the small, deformed mouth, a cleft palate, and had smashed the child as if it were no more than an impaired doll. The nurse, hysterical, could not stop him, and so the infant was killed before anyone could interfere.

"The courtroom was packed, all friends or clients who came as character witnesses, and his wife, too, all saying in effect, he's a wonderful guy, he's always treated our dogs and cats with great tenderness, so this should not be held against him. He is a wonderful guy, don't put him in jail."

He read the newspaper article twice and told Maude, "Can you believe this? This is what I hate about the Child Society, nobody understands this tragedy. The first impulse of everybody is to say, 'Let's forget it because he is a great guy.' "

And he went on, because Maude almost never grew restless or critical, they found each other's opinions exciting. "This is a society of people who are not adults, who don't understand that tragedy is a dimension of adult life, it is not a dimension of child life. A child wants to say, I'm sorry, let's forget it ever happened. But the adult must be held accountable. People don't want to acknowledge that events occur which are there forever, which must be remembered, which are irredeemable, which are, finally, tragic events. Someone is destroyed because of an impulse," Mr. Harrell told her. "The point of it is that a man should go on trial, he killed his own child. It's incredibly—barbaric. But if I had had this article in my hands when I was married and had gone on at such lengths, what I might have gotten was a very weary and exasperated kind of indulgence—a degree of condescension. My wife would sort of indulge my flights; it was indulgence, not a sympathy, not an understanding of what I felt."

He hid all the knives in the house after his wife was told he loved someone else, because he could think of nothing sensible to do, not because he imagined she would stab him or injure herself. He remembered what she had said when he first spoke of his feeling for Maude. "That's a relief, because at least I know it is something concrete. I really thought you were insane, that you had gone out of your mind and that I needed a doctor for you."

But it was not such a relief at all. In all the years of their marriage, he was always her scout, the first to go down all trails and then come back to report. His wife was very dependent on him, Mr. Harrell said; the world intimidated her and it was his role to do reconnaissance. That was not the most serious problem, for he liked the role of caretaker up to a point and Maude, as well, needed him, depended on a kind of strength and advice, but she was bolder, more curious, not so easily pierced or rattled or ever put down.

With him, Maude knew happiness and began to believe she was not unworthy of it. In a letter she wrote of how everything was now different: "Life with him is bliss. When I married before, each day led me into knowing I shouldn't have; now each day makes me larger. There is room for such happiness in me. I have an expandable heart." He did surprising things, never waiting to be asked. He fixed a lamp she liked, he put up hooks in the hall for coats, he cleaned up, and without being asked, he took the garbage out at night, which a psychologist in Baltimore thought was what most women wanted men to do. The psychologist was only being slightly humorous, or maybe not at all.

William Harrell worked too hard, came home with too much work, never gave up on it, and knew, at last, deep love. Happy, he was still not frivolous, not careless, but prudent as he thought men should be; women had more choices. "My duty is to be honest about everything I can do, not to shirk something just because I don't want to do it if I am the one who is needed to do it, if it really must be *me*. Then I must not conceal that I can do it, I *must* do it."

If his father did not beat him with his own leather belt he would tell the boy to go cut a switch. The child knew no vocabulary for his suffering. In northwest Houston—so rural then a neighbor kept a goat and a donkey nearby—the family lived near a ditch that had once been a creek and was still called the creek. It was here the willow saplings grew in profusion and here he fetched the instrument of his own torture. Sometimes if the switch was used he was beaten in the yard, but when the belt was needed he would always be punished in the kitchen. It was his mother who inflicted the early thrashings, then, when he was larger, only would say, Wait until your father comes home, so all day he was made small and sick with dread, a summer day suddenly made septic. When the father came home he would be informed by her: William did this terrible thing. In fact, he was not often a troublesome child. The father always changed his clothes at night and then he would have to go to work on the boy.

Years later, free of rancor but still unable to say very much about the beatings, William Harrell thought his father was so angered by the mother's incessant instructions and demands that he took the anger out on him, when the child wanted protection from the femaleness that might have overpowered or ruined him. There was no reasoning with the mother, her wiring so confused and overloaded; the whippings could not be stopped or a ceasefire called. In the family it was understood you could not be whipped in the dining room or in the living room; the kitchen was the place, although no one knew the reason and none was given. Even at thirty-six he was to tell Maude what peculiar torment he had endured because it had been such a temptation to bolt, to hide like an animal somewhere else in the house. But it would have been so much worse for him to run, to go under a bed, all the time imagining the moment of capture.

The whippings went on until he was fourteen. Other fathers did the same to their sons, he understood that; there was nothing startling about such punishment, no appeal possible. In Texas and many other places, it was widely considered to benefit young boys. He knew boys who were beaten until eighteen, until their fathers suddenly feared they might answer with their own fists, and stopped.

"I think that once I reached a certain age when I said 'Don't, please don't,' but I took it," said Mr. Harrell. He thought his two sisters, much less troublesome, might have been spanked with hairbrushes or wire hangers by her, and all of it, he thought, was devious and awful. The boys, he and his younger brother, were considered to be of far greater importance, capable of standing more pain, and thus in need of it.

The father, whom he now loves so much, had rules laid down, none of them silly or unexpected. The important one was never, never, never to point a gun at anyone even if it was unloaded. The rules began with the usual sacred inscriptions known in many American families: never raise your hand to your mother, never hit your sisters, and always the warning about the gun, repeated over and over. All the males in the family had guns, although the father did not much like deer or duck hunting and was not inclined to take the boys along when he went off. It was a .410 shotgun that William Harrell owned and once lent to a boy across the street who returned it, saying nothing. William wanted to show his younger brother, Gene, how to fire it, not dreaming the borrower had brought it back loaded, a sinful thing. It went off as he pulled the trigger, saying this is how you use it, until the fearful noise and the hole in the wall of their room made them tremble and lose their voices. For the first time in their lives they were hurled into shock.

"I still get chills, I feel quite bad remembering it," he said. "My brother would have died instantly if I had playfully pointed the shotgun at him when I pulled the trigger, as every other kid I know would have done." It was his father then who had saved him from an unspeakable crime, a life of punishing regret.

It happened that his brother was the person he most loved as a boy and even much later, when they cried at each parting. "We wrestled our way to a deep, abiding love," he said. "If you don't fight with your brother you won't be able to love him, that's all there is to it." Once so fierce and deep was their attachment that when he would fly home and go to see his brother in different little places in Texas where he was living, neither man was ashamed of the tears that came when it was time to leave each other. Away from home he thought his mother had methodically ruined his brother by drowning him in overindulgent affection and never permitting him to become separate from her, always letting him do anything. Let him be bad and be wrong again and again and again, Mr. Harrell said.

The brother was now a follower of an Indian guru, but it did not seem to have ennobled him. Neither conspicuous nor eccentric in behavior because of his beliefs, the brother did not look or act differently, except sometimes in restaurants when he ordered the waitress to find out whether the beans had been cooked in lard, or something like that. His mother had become a vegetarian, too, so together they kept watch, avoided all meat-danger, discussed the perils around them. "You would just think he was a little abrupt, and generally harsh and absorbed in himself," Mr. Harrell said; a description that could easily have fit several million people in his own country. "The last time I saw him I said, 'What is the point of seven years of self-discipline and enlightenment if it has made you into someone that's harder to get along with, more selfish.' I didn't ask it as a question, I just let him know that is what I thought. He and my sister are both lying in unhappy places now, but I can't get them out." And this is what he was good at: leading people he loved out of the dank, tiny bunkers they descended to, and requiring the poets whose work he judged not to indulge themselves or too highly value their own pain.

He did not go easy on anyone, because he thought a grown man should not be so anxious to please when something more interesting or significant was at stake. There were lots of ways not to make it to manhood, he thought. One of them was to stay home, to be a child forever, happy with such constraints, safe from nasty decisions and the possibility of offending others. He thought too many people took pride in being infantile, wanting only praise and nice things to happen, impostors who would be shocked to hear it.

"Everyone's a child nowadays," he said. "I came home from work one day and said to Maude, 'Jesus Christ, I'm so tired of children. All I want is for everybody in my office to act like an adult. Is that too much to ask?' And she said yes."

He had not stayed a child, he did not stay the furious sentenced boy sent for the switch so he could be flogged. As a grown man—so tall that even as a teenager his mother could walk under one of his outstretched arms—he told his parents, with some precision, the wrong they had done. He spoke clearly, and with passion, all the power in his hands now. He held them to account. Said how damaging the beatings had been. It was then finished for him, all of it, but his mother, whom he described as "shot through with guilt," could not believe this and became slightly servile, although no less demanding of love.

He had been gone from home for much more than a decade, a married man and a published poet, when he discovered who was the love of his life. His father, the salesman, the very man who had beaten him but never by denunciations, a quiet fellow from a poor southern family who twice married this woman from a Hungarian family. Years after, his sister found a clipping that said their mother's oldest brother, a jazz pianist, had died in New Orleans in 1929 and a rabbi had conducted the funeral services. They did not know more but they knew they must never ask: the Jewishness, which he wanted to be proud of, was a forbidden subject, might bring on another of her heart attacks. He thought his parents' lives, which seemed unhappy to him, nonetheless made a curious love story: a young couple who quarreled, perhaps about money, the man drafted in World War II, the woman sick from tuberculosis who recovered to marry again, the failure of that marriage, and the returning father who found her again and once more made her his wife.

The father spoke little during the years of raising the children except to enforce the universal command: Behave. He was a small, barrel-chested man whose voice sounded clenched and dry. After William Harrell left home on a scholarship to a prestigious university in the East—and nothing could have stopped him, not even his mother's tears and genuine air of bereavement—things went smoother between him and his father, but not between the son and mother.

He had begun thrilling them both when he was in high school, bringing home A's, a boy ahead of others. A few teachers in English saw that his gifts were not what he imagined, mathematics and science, both pumped into the clever boys like him during the Sputnik age until they could think of nothing else. At graduation the vice-principal gave him a copy of Ezra Pound's *ABC of Reading* and one teacher gave him a small black case with a silver plaque on top with his initials. Neither adult pounded on him to choose a literary life over the one he planned; perhaps they knew it would happen and their advice too soon would discourage him. But at the university, an alien and bewildering place at first, it took six weeks for him to discover he would never be able to major in physics. So many other students were ahead of him, it was not enough to get an A, you had to make an A without even trying, and other boys could do the work in their sleep. Knowing this was the severest blow for him; it made him totter, so, wounded, he chose Italian and aimed himself another way. All accomplishments, grades, honors, the smallest triumphs were noted in letters to his parents, although when he grew older and knew more serious accomplishments, he said he stopped doing that and felt ashamed that he once had. The truth is he still let them know he was moving ahead, working hard and getting attention. Once, well into his thirties, he sent a Western Union Mailgram to his father on Father's Day for the first time, and the older man, so pleased, said to him, "I should have it framed." The son said, "No, don't do that. Mother may resent it."

"What she wants is more than I can give, and she always makes me feel as if I am being sucked dry. But my father is grateful for the smallest thing—genuinely, honestly grateful, and not melodramatically. He's not a harsh man; he was, but not anymore. And he is an uncommonly sweet man."

But loving Maude, he was helped to remember the appealing things about his mother: how she always played the piano, doing Chopin waltzes quite nicely, so that he grew up loving music, as accustomed to it as he was to having dinner, needing it the way children believe they need Snickers candy bars or Twinkies cupcakes. Maude lit the good memories of the mother and the childhood he had hid: when all four of the children were still quite small the mother would have them put on socks and dance, to music, in the sparsely furnished living room on the bare hardwood floors, which she wanted buffed. Sometimes all of them would play house: he was the father, but his sister would have to be the family dog, getting down on all fours, willing to do it just to be included. And once, saying good-bye to him, his mother's head reaching no higher than his chest, she cried out, "Oh, your heart—it sounds so strong." One of his uncles told William that his mother had never understood why she was not taller; her size made life seem askew, if not perilous. That a daughter of hers grew five feet and seven inches was only because she willed it so.

All his life the father would say "Don't forget your mother's birthday" or "Make sure you remember to do that for your mother," but he did not remember her making such reminders for the sake of the husband.

"When I went away to college he was so proud of me he almost burst," said Mr. Harrell. "He didn't finish the ninth grade and he had Lyndon Johnson's enormous, naive love of education—without being like Lyndon Johnson—this sort of uneducated man's passion for it in his children, not for himself." In Houston he had sent for the catalogues of the Ivy League universities and used to pore over them at night reading course descriptions. The mother had great ambitions for the children, especially for the sons. When he was eighteen, she would take his hands and say, "These really are the hands of a surgeon." It embarrassed and horrified him, he wished her to be less hackneyed. What he was was a very bright and lively student who played the piano well and the clarinet almost as nicely. Even then he could not bear her speaking this way and years later had this to say: "She can't read any event in her children's lives as an event in their lives, only in hers. She's always insisted on translating their failures and triumphs into terms of their love for her."

In his mid-thirties he thought perhaps that there was something singularly American in the situation, that perhaps husbands are so disappointing to their wives that an inordinate amount of attention is given to the first son. He thought of his mother that she liked to get the maximum punishment out of everything. The father was a different story, always shy when they met, only able to give a small smile and say hi.

"Since I left Texas to go up East there's been an element of cautiousness and there's been a tentativeness in their approach," he said. "It's just the most important thing in the world that I love them."

Twice his father read a book by a literary critic on Ezra Pound because the son's poem was in the front of it, as a prologue. "He read the whole book about Ezra Pound, of whom he's never heard, because of this poem which is not remarkable," Mr. Harrell said. "He has read every word I've written, although he doesn't understand it, including things I didn't even write that he thought were mine."

The life of the father, so different from his own, was a cluster of rough patches, years of grinding work, of appropriate fears about money, of things not said. The father did not speak often, but one story was passed to his son that he loved, through another person naturally. It spoke of the valiance of his father as a child in Georgia who know his life depended on getting away.

"Aunt Elizabeth told me. Every morning in Georgia they had to hoe cotton an hour before going to school and on one of those mornings my father said to her, 'I'm leaving today, I wanted you to know, you are the only one I am telling. But I want a promise from you that you will not follow me. This time I am really going, I am going all the way to Houston,' " said Mr. Harrell. "He had tried this three times before and three times his own father had brought him back. He said to his sister, 'I do not want you to come with me. You cannot come until you finish high school, and after you do, you can come and live with me. Not now.' " The girl promised and did not tell. She held fast.

No such reminiscences ever came from his father, and in the house he did not say much, especially in the years when his wife was ill, her heart not behaving. "My father is a man without wants, needs, ideas, likes, dislikes, anything," said Mr. Harrell. "And my father will talk in the car, and nowhere else in the world." So, on one visit home to see how mother was doing, during the time when he could only think of himself with Maude, that is the place where they spoke. The father said he had to drive to a different county where he owned some property bought many years before with a veteran's loan and over the objections of his wife who said, with reason, they could not afford it. Now someone wanted to buy the land; it was to bring him back his investment twentyfold, but he did not expect this when they set off. So the son insisted he be taken along; he wanted to be in the car with his father.

"On the way down we talked about me and my future, that I was going to get married to Maude, and he was mostly the worried father, seeing me having a teenage stepson—it was ordinary stuff but I loved it," said Mr. Harrell. "On the way back I drove; it was after the sale and he was feeling good, so he started talking. I never wanted to get home. As we pulled in the driveway I said how I wished we had driven to California, just kept driving. I could have driven forever."

It was another day when the two of them, the son so much larger, were waiting on the porch for his mother when the father spoke in his normal tone of voice: "I have to tell you, but don't tell anyone else. You're the one for me. You are my boy."

Here was the blessing he was to have for the rest of his life: secret, indestructible, never to be retracted or made dim. Here was his protection against all disasters ahead and against the world's rubbish and deceits. It is no wonder that thinking of his father and the words spoken on a porch he suddenly needed, so far away and so much later, to wipe his eyes and rest his voice. That August he and Maude married and took her children—the small daughter and an older boy—with them on a little holiday. It is what he wanted, it is everything he wanted, and he knew it would stay fixed forever.

Nearly every man, you see, will have you believe he knows something about love, a bit, but only speaks of women, what he gave and what he took. So it is rare when men uncover remembrances of fathers who were absent, lacking, remote, indifferent, admirable, brave, dangerous, beloved, and sometimes tender. Dead fathers present themselves over and over to sons who dream of their return or would have them more deeply banished, the early battles still fresh so long after they were done, with no resolution or treaty now in hand. Forgiveness is not possible.

Sometimes this seems a country of lost fathers taken by armies or by work, by divorce or separations men willed, by their hearts that gave out. "I remember him in the most profound way," says a reporter in Washington, D.C., who has three children of his own. "He died at the age of forty-nine, which is what I will be in a year and a half." He would rather talk about the Pentagon or El Salvador, not his father; it is a Monday, the birthday will come soon enough.

More than fifty years have passed since, as a boy, Fitzroy Herbert found his young father dead in that small rented room, but he is always able to console himself that his own life has been all that the father wished for his first child. The father had no chance at all but still held the highest hopes for the boy, and has been proven right. Not the least of Fitzroy Herbert's accomplishments—his wife hung the five citations he earned as a civil servant in the hall of their apartment in Queens—is a marriage of such beneficence, the couple's love so apparent, their existence so harmonious that relatives still comment on this devotion. Friends praise. Acquaintances are awed, for such a marriage is not commonplace and the couple hardly young.

He is uncommon in several ways, not one of those men who hate being held to the birthdays of a wife or who will always forget an anniversary. Nor is he made morose or bored by celebrations, as some tend to be. A dignified and distant man, probably one who has never yelled in his life, who does not admire harsh or rough behavior whatever the reason, Mr. Herbert has, still, an ardor for Amy Herbert he does not choose to conceal. On his wife's birthday, for example, which is October 22, he has presents for her but then something more: he tucks away six birthday cards, all with different messages, in places where she will soon discover them. In a drawer, a closet, somewhere in the kitchen. What he likes is her surprise and pleasure when she finds the cards, one by one, as if the very idea was still new and delightful. And he watches as a young husband might. He knows how this sets him apart.

"I don't think my showing my love for Amy diminishes me," said Mr. Herbert. "But I think a lot of men feel that showing love, *and they do love*, diminishes them, makes them less worthy of being men." So it could be said that in twenty-five years together neither one had ever been hurtful, rude, or scornful of the other, not once. They still seem grateful and deeply pleased to be together.

All round them in Queens lie the wounded with the little stories we know so well: desertion, betrayal, divorce, depression, a hunger for work and money when neither are ever coming, panic, drugs, sickness, and a despair so unchanging it might be easy to believe the victims were born with it, much like a pulmonary impairment, so that as babies they never did have an easy, normal breath. But this couple, on the eleventh floor of a huge building in Lefrak City, each giant in the complex named for a foreign capital or country that is not of the slightest interest to its inhabitants, have their lives in good order. Their relatives, not so blessed, like proof of such a lovely marriage, and there is not a day when Mr. Herbert fails to make clear that his wife is a remarkable woman, and adorable too. You don't need to go, he told Mrs. Herbert on a Wednesday when she was leaving for her usual appointment at the beauty parlor, a fast wash and set. You are beautiful the way you are, he said, even a man this smart not understanding why women like to have their hair done. She smiled and came home, a scarf over the rollers, not wanting to wait for a comb-out. He looked delighted to see her back.

They met in 1957 when neither expected much more in the way of love: she, with one daughter, on her own, working as the floor lady in a sweater factory, her wages considered good. And he, parted from his wife and the father of two small girls, now says of that time that he was "fancy free," although he was working full-time as a claims examiner for the New York State Department of Labor, investigating the validity of applications for unemployment insurance, and also ran his own small insurance office in Corona, a pleasant residential neighborhood in Queens where people fussed over their houses and swept their sidewalks, noting who did not. She came to him at the suggestion of a friend, for advice, which he always gave, never charging people and wanting to help. He knows how. When first he saw her he admired the bearing of this young, calm woman.

"I liked her importance," said Mr. Herbert. "And her gentle voice. She was very forthright about what had to be said and she listened attentively. Then she followed through, things worked out, and I liked that. Besides, she did have beautiful legs and she still does." He is accurate, a man not given to excess or exaggeration.

There are two kinds of advice he dispenses: what Mrs. Herbert calls "technical," which uses his knowledge of rules, taxes, jobs, benefits, the law, restrictions, and the bewildering machinery of the municipal government. The second is "emotional," to relieve the anguish and confusion of the problems of those who come to him. Here is a typical case: a mild-mannered, uncertain woman, over forty, with two children, a husband who has deserted her, debts, and no education. Mr. Herbert heard about all of it, then was able to steer her into a city training program so she could earn the equivalent of a high school diploma and learn a trade. He helped her find a job in the CETA program with the Bulova Watch Company. But the story isn't really that tidy; the woman often despaired of herself, school seemed punishing. It required Mr. Herbert to use exceptional language, by which he means he had to speak rather sternly, for him, and tell her not to give up. The woman persisted, made it, and eventually the husband came back and the couple rose from the mess. What he provided for her was "technical" advice.

"Yes, a lot of people come to see me," said Mr. Herbert. "I am like that. An advocate. Sometimes, I guess, you might call me a counselor or a consultant. People come to see me and they very seldom go away mad." He knows how to listen; he likes listening and he is rarely impatient. People feel more peaceful in his presence; he is not intrusive or judgmental.

Even after he was gravely ill in 1983 and was sent home with an oxygen tank that sits by his bed, the telephone did not stop. His cardiac condition made early retirement mandatory. "They call in droves, everything from *A* to *Z*," Mrs. Herbert said, who had to monitor the calls so her husband would not be worn out.

Fitzroy Herbert, who prefers to be called Roy, is black with pale blue-gray eyes inherited from a Welsh grandfather who went to the Caribbean. His mother came to New York from Grenada, his father in 1919 from Saint Kitts and jobs in Cuba and the Canal Zone, both with the expectation of that generation of immigrants that better times were ahead. They were not. Only one of them survived and saw the children triumph.

In the year when it was reported that 50 percent of all black families in the United States were headed by women, sociologists, experts in family studies, and civil rights leaders were trying to decide what to make of this, the reasons for it. Fitzroy Herbert is not to be found in their sad calculations; he is invisible when the melancholy statistics are compiled. It is true that he has known poverty, the separation of parents, the early death of his father, military service in a segregated army, a disagreeable first marriage, and a life of racism, but he has endured and flourished and been of exceptional help to others. A generous salute is in the hall: the citation dated February 1982 from Angel O. Berros, mayor of the city of Caguas, Puerto Rico, where Fitzroy Herbert, as Associate Regional Administrator for the Employment and Training Administration, Region II, through his relationship with the municipal government of that city, the prime sponsor under the Comprehensive Employment and Training Act (CETA), showed his good will and concern for the needs of the community by establishing affirmative actions geared to the delivery of CETA-related services. That is the manner in which official praise must be poured, in sentences of cement, but the document is precious to Amy Herbert, who wanted it on display in the apartment. It is not certain that in fifty years people will understand what this CETA was, what affirmative action ever meant, but there can be no doubting the appreciation of Mayor Berros in Caguas.

He knew himself to be appreciated and admired, but so many other men could claim nothing, were doomed in different degrees, obliged the society by loathing what they became and did not know how to save themselves or what for. The "negatives," *The New York Times* said, were being examined. Unemployment, the culture of poverty, the psychological legacy of the past, the distance of black men from "any meaningful engagement" with the economy and education and the social system were all reasons, experts said in the article. There was no mention of the dishonored self, only of how many black women were left on their own. Many black men were quoted giving reasons for their becoming defeated, wandering men or ones who would not ever know their children. A young man said his wife did not expect him to stay with her and their child. Her own father had left. She had no reason to expect he would be different.

Mr. Herbert knows all about such casualties—one of them, his father, is always on his mind—so very little comes as a surprise, even though none of the boys he grew up with or his adult friends committed crimes, knew jail, or needed drugs. Here was a man who would not recognize a marijuana cigarette if anyone was unwise enough to put it before him.

"That wasn't going to happen to me," said Mr. Herbert. "I always knew I was going to be a force for something. Not politics, but a force for something." No one who knew him would dispute that he had been. He did not know helplessness, had never felt it.

It is not his way to speak of withheld justice, imperialism, the convulsions of capitalism, the wretchedness of the unemployed. He is calm, but he knows all this and how deep the injuries are.

"Black men have been muted and they feel muted," he said one morning. "Consistently the male has been conditioned to feel that he is the one that has to go out and support the family. If he doesn't do it to the satisfaction of the family, very frequently it causes a breakup with the woman. Either that or she becomes less of a woman than she was when they married. She becomes brutal-

ized and acts in a brutal manner. He becomes less of a man—
much less—and acts more brutal to the brutalized woman. Neither
the man or the woman know what is happening."

It is as if he was remembering something of his past which he
has, in fact, never forgotten but does not care to reveal with non-
chalance. He went on: The man must find work, he must make
enough money. When this does not happen he has no choice but
to begin wandering.

"Then he is said to have abandoned his family," Mr. Herbert
said. "As a matter of fact, what happens is that since he can't
provide anything, the family then resorts to the only resource it
knows, which is government welfare. And he purposely stays away.
If a woman acknowledges to the authorities that she knows where
the father is or that the father even visits home periodically, that is
going to affect welfare payments."

He did not refer to them as benefits, and explained why.
"Well, it is not a benefit," he said. "It's an alternative in the sense
that, I won't give you a job, I won't provide day care for your
children so that you can get a job, I won't give you . . ." Mr.
Herbert said. "The feeling is they will do anything they can to,
what they call, 'outwit the Man.' But they have fallen into the
Man's trap. That's what it is. Welfare is an alternative to opportunity and all that opportunity means."

After a light lunch with Amy, he would go to lie down and
sleep, or listen to the radio and read his paper, *The New York Post*
or *Daily News*. Amy managed the insurance business by herself,
but he had a second business, as an accountant advising people
how to file tax returns. His illness had not affected his manners.
When a visitor recently came to see him and stayed on talking to
Amy, when he was resting but heard her get ready to go, he came
out looking a little sleepy, and walked her to the door, a matter of
a few feet.

In the elevator, which moves wearily as if each stop inflicted
fresh strain, two women with children were speaking of food
prices. Too high. One of them complained that her food stamps
could not last the month and her friend gave a long, bitter reply in
total agreement. They were young and had energy, but time was
not on their side and they knew it. All over the city that bright,
cold afternoon people were thinking they would have to eat less.

"Exploitation is always deliberate," Mr. Herbert says, if you ask him for an opinion. "It's an effort to establish a group of people who are subordinate and subservient and subcultural."

Racism was not just a disease of the whites, he added. You could find it among blacks; there were those who were so proud of their lighter skins they did not marry or want their offspring to marry people who were darker.

As a child he was not pitied, although pity would not have been entirely out of place, but that much he was spared. His mother, with the three children to support, worked in the needle trade, as it was called, sewing women's dresses, not paid by the hour, only by the work she completed. There were frequent lay-offs in the needle trade; sometimes the family hung by the frailest of threads. At night the mother worked on her own sewing machine, doing the dresses long after the children had gone to bed, but she did not complain or ever alarm them. The children were not rebellious or defiant: the strong, relentlessly strict mother laid down the rules—come home after school, you may never play in the street—which were obeyed. As the eldest he was responsible for a brother, seven years younger, and a smaller sister. None of them ever dreamed of a mutiny. The father lived apart. There was no divorce, only silence and sadness.

"They broke up because my mother was—," Mr. Herbert laughs at his own understatement, "a very dominant argumentative person. I don't know what it is she wanted him to do or be. But obviously he couldn't do it. He was very quiet, intelligent, soft-spoken, and proud. Taking a pride."

The father from Saint Kitts, whose own father had been a butcher, was a printer by trade and had taught himself to play the violin so nicely that, in Harlem, churches and social groups often invited him to perform. The charm of the man was so affecting even the child felt it, knew others delighted in it. In those days, Mr. Herbert claims, a black man could not get work in New York as a printer; at any rate his father was kept out of his true profession, and did not make very much money at all. Perhaps the mother could not bear it, resented the charm of the man, grew desperate and unforgiving as she stayed at the sewing machine, but Mr. Herbert does not think it quite fitting to discuss the trouble in detail, and as a boy he did not know much, only that the failures of his father were not of the man's own making.

But Fitzroy Herbert was a successful child, as many are not, and so changed forever. He went often to see his father, living a few blocks away in a small room on 146th Street, the window facing an airshaft. The man did not say the room was not fitting. They talked of the boy's going to college, and both favored Michigan State because of its journalism school, for the youngster wrote well and had ambition. The other thing the boy wanted was for the father to come home. First the father wanted a better job, but in 1934 many men did and knew only refusals.

"He was always trying to escape," Mr. Herbert said. "He always wanted to escape from the jobs he had. He recognized that these jobs were not good for him. They were dead-end. They were dangerous in terms of his health. They were low-paying."

Because the father, who had such persuasive and unassuming ways with people, had been made a precinct worker by local Democrats in Harlem, he was now eligible to sit for a civil service exam. This promised everything: a good job and solid wages. In the small and dingy room, a Bible the only book, the two of them laid out the strategy, seeing brighter days to come. The man planned to approach his wife to see if he could rejoin the family, go home at last. This is what they both wanted—and for the boy to keep studying. No hopes were ever again to be quite as urgent and as exciting.

The last weekend of his father's life the children were taken on a boat ride by their mother, who planned the little outings with care; the poor are not often given to impulsive pleasures. Sometimes she was able to take one child at a time to the movies, each of them taking a turn. For the boat ride the father had given a bit of cash to his son to divide among the children; he always did what he could. The day after, the boy went to 146th Street to tell the father how nice it had been.

"I was the one who found him dead," said Mr. Herbert. The child knocked on the door twice, waited, then entered the room and saw the man sprawled on the bed. He said Daddy once or twice, tried a gentle sort of shaking, touched the skin and knew it felt too cold, and pulled up the sheet so the body was now covered. Then he ran fast to Mrs. White, the landlady, who so liked having this decent man as a boarder and who grew wildly agitated when she reached the room and knew what the boy said was true. His mother was even less resigned, unable to control her convulsions of grief and weeping, as if she had never loved a man so much as the one now gone. Her son never determined what she really felt after her first awful lurch, and wondered if hysteria was a sign of love and remorse, and thought, much later, it was not.

At any rate the death did not do in the boy named Fitzroy Herbert, it did not finish him off. Psychiatrists cannot tell you why some children, taking deadly blows, do not crack or come apart, while others, knowing so much more safety, have no resilience at all and stay crouched much of their lives, hiding somewhere.

"My father didn't get asthma from working in Saint Vincent, or in Havana, or in Panama. He became ill because the only job he could get here was a car washer in a garage at night; that's what got him." This is what Mr. Herbert says and believes. For some time he wished that the four of them had not gone on the little boat ride that day, that he had stayed in Harlem, that he had gone to see his father and saved him from choking. But he is only disposed to light, dry words, and fifty years later speaks so simply about the death you might not understand how real the father appears to him still, although the parent he summons is a young man, and he no longer so.

The mother, who went on working and became a passionate supporter of the International Ladies Garment Workers Union, reached her early eighties, not much changing, a stubborn and combative woman who knew all about peril and had, alone, kept the children from ever approaching the rim of ruination. During World War II she had prospered, for wages were not fixed and the hours were good, everything much safer. She bought a small house in Corona for seven thousand dollars, her daughter sharing it, the two of them alike. The mother always inspired his respect, a courteous and consistent devotion, but the love he felt was for the frailer and sweet father who had died because garages are so cold. Asthmatics are often affected by extreme temperatures. The father did not go to a doctor in those days—it was a luxury many people could not consider—and he may not have known if there was any real help to be had.

The mother often moved the children when the rent on an apartment could no longer be paid; Mr. Herbert does not say much about this. They lived by candles or kerosene lamps when the electricity bill could not be honored. None of this was unusual. Still the woman did not complain. When the children were older, Mr. Herbert said, the three of them finally talked about being poor —a touchy subject—and decided that poverty was not a question of income but rather a measure of spirit. Deciding that made it easier for them. He thought of his father and always finished his homework and held part-time jobs and sometimes went to school wearing shoes whose soles were fattened by cardboard. But he insisted that none of them ever did dwell on the deprivations which were, after all, not exceptional. Once, watching yet another so-called medical report on a television program whose subject was stress, its causes and methods of relief, he thought it all rubbish and that this stress was often, if not sought, self-imposed. And fashionable as well.

Junior High School 139 on 140th Street was named for Frederick Douglass, the American abolitionist born of a slave; his white father was unknown to him, so he took his last name from the hero in *The Lady of the Lake* by the poet Sir Walter Scott. The school was for blacks but the faculty included white people; its principal was Dr. Jacob Ross.

There is a roll call of names he can recite: Mrs. Hemstreet, who had been a nurse in World War I and who taught chemistry; Mr. Dixon, a music and French teacher; Mrs. Douglas, who taught algebra; Mrs. Brooks, who taught French; and Mrs. Segal, who was from France and also taught French. And Mr. Tines, who invited him to join the Negro History Club. He was the class of 1938 but more than four decades later could give you those names and spell them. Most of the students, in such hands, worked hard and understood what might be waiting for them if they were lazy or inattentive; what was waiting, in any case, was not a hospitable world. It was he who won the French medal for excellence and then went on to Peter Stuyvesant High School on Fifteenth Street, a place for some of the brightest boys in the city, usually excelling in math, ready to leap for the high grades. By this time the family, accustomed to so many different addresses, had moved from Harlem to the Bronx, settling in a new apartment in a five-story brick building, the rooms so clean he marveled at such purity. With its large Jewish, Italian, and black communities, the neighborhood on Prospect Avenue—they were at 1226—knew no friction; he saw nothing of trouble. It was the nicest of worlds, not requiring any of them to feel in danger. On Saturdays, even after midnight, he could, if necessary, make the five-mile walk home from the ice-cream parlor in Harlem where he made sodas behind the counter, his wages in his pocket, and not be scared. In the 1960s Mr. Herbert had reason to return to the Bronx, to go by 1226 Prospect and see for himself the wreck it now was. "How did this happen?" he said to someone, not needing an answer. And no answer was forthcoming. The tenants were now Puerto Ricans, whom he thought a very decent people, but this old building, and the others, were an affront. They were intended to be slums; maintenance and repair did not make the buildings more profitable, inhabitants did not matter. Old buildings lived in by too many poor tenants were not an appealing investment to landlords.

The ice-cream parlor was owned and run by a German couple, Mr. and Mrs. Herd, both the illustration of a new word for him, *Aryan*. They were always decent, approving of this reliable and quick young man, not someone to ever make a mess of things or cheat. Mr. Herd spoke often of Hitler, approving of the chancellor and what he was planning to do, but his wife, shrewder, saw fit not to comment. She was more interested in matters at hand, whether a customer was walking out without having paid. The Herds would ask him in German, so as not to humiliate everyone, and he would answer in that language, a sentence or two.

In high school, he knew a setback whose name was intermediate algebra, for no matter how hard he tried he never caught hold of it and until he did college was not a certainty. After two semesters the army wanted him and he went. At Fort Dix, New Jersey, the recruits were given paper and pencils and made to take a test, none realizing at first how important it was. He scored well on it, a basic aptitude test which determined who went into what branch, and, in a rare example of the military correctly assessing a man's abilities and temperament, he was assigned to the Quartermaster Corps and eventually made a staff sergeant. Black soldiers were kept apart from the white troops, some of them almost preferring it, being from the South and born into an earlier war where death could come by lynching or burning, but he was not easily intimidated.

It was his responsibility to make inventory of, have access to, and keep in a good state in warehouses supplies and equipment needed by infantrymen in his battalion. "I was very efficient," Mr. Herbert admitted. There was some trouble with a fool of a captain from Louisiana , who behaved offensively. But it was not Sergeant Herbert but his own men who by refusing to go to the mess hall for lunch and staying in the barracks made clear their disgust with the white officer. The captain saw all blacks as the same, deficient in intelligence or energy, but Sergeant Herbert, without risking the danger of insubordination, soon had the upper hand. He was simply correct—and formidable in observing protocol so clearly— in pointing out to the captain that the captain had permitted others to enter one of his warehouses without notifying him, Sergeant Herbert. The troops did not mutiny; they finally went to lunch, calmed, eager as always to eat. He always had the same attitude when whites grew imperial or attempted condescension.

"They were not putting me down," he said. "They were putting down what they saw, which is a young black man. When they realized this was *me*, then it stopped." His unit, the Quartermaster Salvage Repair, moved with its battalion to France, Belgium, and Germany, where he saw more things than his old teachers could have possibly prepared him for, but no matter. All of them then were suddenly sent—not home, as they expected—to the Pacific, as infantry to fight Japan, but the war ended and he was spared, exempt from the worst if you do not count the two typhoons in Okinawa, so severe that he and some other men took shelter in tombs where they found skeletons, he said. Whenever he took a stand—on behalf of the black troops if treatment of them was unjust in comparison to what the whites received, or for a black soldier he knew and respected who suffered inappropriate reprimand—it was he who always protested, sometimes on demand and often on his own, by going through channels, sending a letter with all the facts or giving a report to the proper office. It was the way to get results. And there were two lieutenants he liked, named Hardcastle and Street, both white, no grievances between the sergeant and them.

It was at Camp Lee in Virginia where he taught himself to type, practicing by typing stories from a newspaper, until his speed was 120 words a minute, which not many could match. He was twenty-six when he was a civilian again, first applying to Standard Oil in New Jersey, where his brother worked, for a job. What he wanted was an administrative job and the woman in the personnel office had not expected this. "Well, our boys don't do that kind of work here," she said. He understood perfectly, thanked her for her time, and got out.

It took him only eight days in February of 1945 to find his place. A job was his with the New York State Department of Labor, Unemployment Division, first in Long Island City, then Flushing, Brooklyn next, and then an office at Forty-second Street near Second Avenue in the twenty-two years ahead. A patient and precise man—"I always loved paper," Mr. Herbert says—he began, intending to do well. He always did. There were small triumphs of reason and persistence on his part. One involved a man, once ailing, who applied for unemployment payments because he had been treated by a chiropractor and now was fit to work, although unable to find a job, and was therefore entitled. The word of a chiropractor, however, was not taken into account or considered medically valid until Mr. Herbert intervened and said it certainly should be.

He interviewed people all day, asking them for facts that would be pertinent to the claim, then getting confirmation from other sources. He made sure applicants really were seeking work, in other words. In the beginning years he saw twenty people a day: men and women, black, white, Hispanic, and Chinese. He was always fair but scrupulous; pity had no part in it. Amy Herbert remembered how her husband once intervened on behalf of an alcoholic who was now sober—"recovered" is the current word. The man's former employer, although not objecting to his receiving unemployment insurance, was insistent that the fellow, with his dreadful history, would not hold up and could not possibly keep the next job. Roy Herbert listened and thought differently.

"I said he was eligible," said Mr. Herbert, the details coming back. "He was going to AA on a regular basis and he showed evidence of applying for work at a number of places. He gave me a list of them and I called up to verify. I said, and I put it in writing, that he was eligible, so let's pay him." He won.

It became clear, too, that the state had to do more to assist the Hispanics, handicapped by their difficulties with English. He raised this point and then raised it again.

Often enough it was the more educated people who gave him trouble—made him dance the maypole, as he put it—because they were more facile and knew better how to circumvent requirements. The atmosphere did not oppress the staff and, even when interviewing the most feeble or desperate person, Mr. Herbert did not dispense with procedure, treating all of them with patience and being fair. None of the unemployment offices were flooded with people in startling numbers. This was to come, rising above 10 million in the winter of 1982 when he was long gone. His views were the same.

"Unemployment is not predicated on need," Mr. Herbert said. "It is a right. It was never intended that unemployment insurance was going to take the place of wage income."

Once, only once, did Fitzroy Herbert do something out of character and act on impulse, a reckless thing for a civil servant to do. In Long Island City, on a busy day with absences among the claims examiners and the others in the office indifferent, he began to hate the place.

"The top parts of the walls in the office were painted light green and the bottom part was dark green. It was a very institutional-looking place. That one day I was most overworked," he said. "I think I was the only person in my unit and I was swamped. I just couldn't stand it anymore. Could not stand it. I couldn't stand the institutional look, I couldn't stand the fact that there I was, working my dingus off and not getting any cooperation or assistance." People had been waiting for three hours, he could not handle more than twenty. Mr. Herbert took his hat, his coat, and walked out. No one noticed or made comment. He thought later the people must have been sent home, told to come back in the morning.

In the street he felt immense relief, struck by the charm of a nice summer day, walked a while and went home. He stayed home for two days, not calling in, and then the weekend, without a moment of fretting. On Monday he went back to the green walls, but no one said a word or asked if he felt better, assuming perhaps he may have had a cold and the cold was cleared up by now. Things went on. He does not take complete credit, but he will bring up how later, the walls were painted in pastel colors, those greens gone forever. The initiatives of Fitzroy Herbert were not to be ignored.

Amy Herbert knew as well as he did how his career had progressed, as if each day and each promotion had been explained and described. The insurance business did well in her hands. She loved listening to him and he, in turn, gave her his complete attention, not the pretense many men affect, fooling no one. Claims examiner to senior manager, senior manager to office manager, and then, in 1968, transferred to the federal government payroll, an administrator-investigator overseeing funds allocated to the antipoverty programs, whose names changed, for New York State, Puerto Rico, and the Virgin Islands. The citations began going up on the wall in their apartment. The lives of their three children, all by their earlier marriages, did not always go as smoothly as might have been wished. One of the girls married too early, bore three children too fast, and was given no money by her husband, who simply refused and left. It was hardly a surprise that she gave up on herself and was only to be saved by the two of them who, year in and year out, would not allow her to go under. Mr. Herbert did not vilify the son-in-law, whom he liked; instead he provided support. The children, even grown, were close to their parents. They were the reason that the Herberts did not ever consider moving to the Virgin Islands, which would have been ideal for them.

It was Mrs. Herbert who occasionally provided a reminder of her husband's past, the memories of such women being more finely attuned. He talked to her so often of his father that she almost felt she had known the man, can tell you of the day the boy was taken by him to see the great Marcus Garvey in Harlem, who had called the First International Convention of the Negro Peoples at a rally in Madison Square Garden, and of a car Mr. Herbert's father once drove, details of ownership unclear, a touring car it was called, a convertible, Chevrolet, with a running board.

"I wish he was here," said Mr. Herbert. "And shared with me some of my plaudits. Then I say to myself, well, maybe wherever he is, wherever his soul, he knows. When I die, if this has not happened, if he doesn't, I am going to seek him out." He smiled, half joking, the very idea making something unnamed and delicate lift up inside his chest.

"He was crazy about me, yes," he added. "About all of us. But I was the firstborn, his first son." His mother died without speaking once of the father, even his name never came up, the subject not suitable for discussion with the children, or perhaps simply too tragic. There was nothing to be learned. Sometimes, on Mother's Day, she made flowers out of scraps of material for the children to sell in the streets. Some of her flowers were pink, and some of her flowers were white; people thought them pretty, and paid.

The memories men have of their fathers, of love given or love withheld, of what was promised and never provided, are often no more than a single story that is clumsy and short.

The son becomes accustomed to the remote or foolish father, nothing else is ever expected. So there is nothing startling about the recollections of a former marine, in his mid-thirties now, but not more than nineteen when he was hit, long accustomed to having just one leg but still leaping and running in the dreams that any athlete might have. What he will tell you, without making too much of it of course, is how his father behaved when the parents, pale and stricken came to the hospital in Philadelphia to see him. All his injuries were later to be neatly typed, with abbreviations, on a card from the Veterans Administration which he carried: below knee amputation, left leg; right peroneal nerve palsy; absence, acquired, spleen and right testicle; shell fragment wound, left thigh and buttock, right foot, neck, both forearms, penis and scrotum, anterior thigh right, both iliac crest. And these words too: psychoneurosis, anxiety depression. On the card his last name was misspelled. In the hospital the father did not hug the son, touch his face or smooth his hair, but rather busied himself by looking at charts or inquiring about the treatment in chats with nurses or the occasional physician. It was up to the mother to talk, how she talked: the son was looking better, he had been missed so much, he must eat all of his lunch. When it came time to leave the hospital, and the corps, the father told him, Wear your uniform home. But the son would not; he had learned now how to refuse all sorts of commands, and was even defying the last instruction to have a regulation haircut at the barber before leaving, a final defiance. He meant to go home with long hair and one leg pinned up on his blue jeans. This was his plan. What was meant by the father's request was perfectly clear: in that uniform he would still be respected, not seen as a pitiful or impaired man, someone who might just have had a terrible accident. But the idea of putting on the uniform—the revered symbol of maleness—made him sick. He left the hospital with his curly hair over his neck and no hope at all, having started his addiction to drugs right there on that clean, well-supervised, strictly run ward. The other patients provided them.

At the unveiling of the gravestone for Gilbert Hunn, the doctor hit by a rock while hiking on Mt. Kenya—a poetic woman friend chose to believe he had raised his head to see a beautiful, fretful bird, then began to fall while the bird hovered near him—the family and relatives gathered afterwards, other deaths also in mind. One of the older men, a relative who had made a success in coin-operated machines before video games, spoke of his own brother, named Harry, who had died just a month after Gilbert, and what a decent man he had been. (Gilbert had been young, the brother in his sixties.) The relative wanted to say what sweetness Harry had but did not know quite how to put it. There had been four boys in his family, one just a baby of a year, and an older sister when their mother died and left them to a father who was powerful, strict, vehement. There was little money in the nineteen thirties; the father was a painter and often worked at night. It was Harry, said the brother in coin-operated machines, who had made his three younger brothers hang up stockings one Christmas, although they were Jewish and really too poor to expect anything at all.

It was Harry who stayed up and filled their stockings, which happened to be very worn socks, with tiny, cheap presents he paid for himself. All the boys worked. Now Gilbert Hunn's relative thought of all of this while the rest of us ate salmon and salad, but a younger brother heard it, the one who had been twelve months old when their mother died, and snorted. "It was coal," he said. "He put coal in." But the older man said, no, Harry had put in *gifts*.

All the brothers had spoken often of their father and the youngest, who is now a successful Cadillac salesman, wanted to show what an admirable man he was. The word of this father was law. The night that Harry came home and said he just bought his first new car, the father hit him hard across the mouth right at the dinner table. The car was a Ford. Old man Ford backed Hitler, the father said, none of them should ever buy a Ford and they knew that. Even now, at Gilbert's unveiling, the Cadillac salesman still obeyed his dead father and did not care if Henry Ford was innocent or guilty. "We idolized our father," he said.

That summer there was war in Chad, war in El Salvador, war in Nicaragua, war in Lebanon, war in Afghanistan. The expression "get real" was often heard in certain circles in New York, usually among the young who were overworked and wanted to make films, an unrealistic ambition. The dollar was too strong. Hundreds of young Americans, male and mostly minors, using names such as Cracko and Red Rum and Stainless Steel Rat, had roamed without authorization through some of the country's most advanced computer systems, and faced severe punishment if they kept it up. The trespassers worked on home computers in bedrooms or in basements without their parents' knowing their children were acting as highwaymen. More people were going hungry, although it was often repeated the economy was booming. Soup kitchens and food pantries kept drawing longer lines, and a woman in Seattle said, "We're getting a whole lot of people who don't know how to be poor. I mean people who have never had to cook beans from the dry state."

In New York, the doctor who was thirty-six and on the teaching staff of a hospital in New York was not buckling from the heat that was becoming dangerous for the elderly and some animals. He was willing to talk about tears and love, about women and the sick. In his small apartment on the West Side there was no air conditioning —he did not require it—and the garden in back, although wonderful for such a grimy, muddled city, was filled with the loud breathing of a huge generator that made it possible for those in more expensive apartments to stay cool. The doctor's bed, in a tiny alcove, was not made, and there were roaches in the sink, exploring an unwashed plate and cup. In the hospital—a place of such continuing crises there was once no codeine at all for the cardiac patients—little came as a surprise to the staff, which at that time included five women physicians, all young, all accustomed to forsaking sleep and food, exactly like the male doctors.

The doctor, who was very large, said he played football and that it made him happy and still provided him with the most glorious dreams. He could stay silent for an unusual length of time, as most doctors are able to do. And he had the glaze of a private school, the good vowel tones, the perfect grammar giving it away. At the private school in New England, then only for boys and most effective in imposing on all the children the age-old, honored ideas of masculine leadership and control, he had been lucky. A few of the more interesting men in the faculty had known better and made him see there were choices he would not have found by himself, that he need not be obedient to the old rules.

"It opened me to the idea that it was all right to weep in front of women," the doctor said, "even though I am still pretty bad at doing that kind of thing. But at least I don't feel as if I would be disgraced. Women my own age, who are my friends, do not expect me *never* to cry."

His pretty mother, who had wanted five children and who believed vivacity was the highest form of moral courage, began to drink when he was at boarding school, and the drinking became not the enemy but the purpose in her life. The father, in despair, would ask his older children—the sons, really—if he should leave her or stay. As if they knew. But the father stayed put, hung on, kept working, behaved with dignity and hope, and the woman recovered. The doctor had proof of it, a photograph of the two of them, outside, smiling very brightly. The father deserved to be loved for it and was, although he was never told.

"I don't think I would have been able to do it," the doctor said. "But he did, and I think it is wonderful that he did, although he is not wonderful in a lot of other ways. But in that way, great. I tried to tell him that—well, now that you mention it, it may be that I have a harder time telling him than he would have hearing it. Men are not used to this. The emotion that is involved is almost an admission of weakness, for both. And the father might feel disconcerted if the son spoke in this way. I think it would be more embarrassing or discomfiting to me if I tried to tell him something like that. But as I get older the idea bothers me less. Men don't really talk to each other thay way, it's true. Hardly ever. They talk in more general terms, vaguer, more nebulous terms, much more indirect. It's acceptable for women to behave another way, to speak of love and of loving, and it's quite pleasing when they do, that is how they are supposed to behave. But for a man to behave that way—it's as if he is behaving like a woman. Yes, even now. I am sure that's part of it—not to act like a woman. We are not really equal, only a little bit more; there are still too many barriers, too many differences."

When the telephone began to ring, he did not move or stop

speaking, so successfully ignoring the summons that it was clear a woman was calling. It was the woman who had last lived with him, was now somewhere else, was calling for the second time that evening. He was quite used to this, to women wanting more than he chose to provide. and he has his theory.

"If a man is half-desirable at all he has that experience. Women want life to be planned. If they are interested in a man, they want to know he will be there. Women are generally quite monogamous. They like a certain amount of independence, but at the same time they want to feel that someone is attached to them, that they are attached to one person. What woman wants to be left alone?" It was easy to name one or two mutual acquaintances, but he felt they were exceptions.

"Most women seem to want a man always there. All the women I've known seem to want a boyfriend—it is a steadiness, an intimacy, a warmth, someone they can hold on to and get hugged by. Why they can't do that intermittently, why it has to be all the time, I don't know."

He did know. Everyone knows. It is a small if disconcerting truth: women fear being older. To get old, then, becomes a calamity. To be lonely and old was discouraging beyond belief; it made women still young do odd things, hold on to men they might not have chosen if they did not see themselves at fifty, forsaken and starved. The doctor had only to look at the covers of the magazine *Vanity Fair*. When the black-and-white photographs for the covers, taken by the famous photographer Irving Penn, were of male writers—an Italian and then the next month an American—every pore, line, vein, crevice, hair, and pouch could be seen, as if these dark male faces were the better for it. When a woman writer and philospher and filmmaker, very beautiful, was photographed for the cover of *Vanity Fair*, her face was so airbrushed it looked slightly ill, as if for years she had been eating only flour. The photographer was quoted as saying, perhaps incorrectly, that it was too cruel to photograph women at such close range, in such revealing light. But men benefited by any wreckage.

A few of the women doctors in the hospital, while admiring him professionally, did not like the doctor's badinage, found his obsessive flirting to be heavy-handed and monotonous, so constant it became impersonal. He did not know this, it was simply the way he reacted to women. He did not, after all, overpower them, nor was he a bully. It was himself he did not treat with respect. The women patients in his wards he found less reticent than men just as sick, better able to talk about themselves, their bodies, the exact position and frequency of pain, the times it came, in short waves or dull, and how often. He was inclined to be more generous with the sick women, although he knew the male patients, who interested him less, needed his attention every bit as much, perhaps even more. Black men with their bad hearts, black men damaged by high blood pressure and smoking and cholesterol, and, most of all, butting against life. It all led to such trouble for them, and the hospital was where you saw the end results. Alcoholism was as common for the doctors as the ordinary cold or a light summer rash for a pharmacist.

"I just love women," the doctor said in a sudden glow of animation, although it was late at night, and his working hours were appalling. "It's more pleasant to talk to women, in general, and there is nothing I enjoy more than a flirtation of some kind. That is actually true professionally. I find that with both men and women I get along best with them if in some way, when I first meet them, I sort of make love to them."

What he meant was that he needed to ingratiate himself and that with the women in the hospital, always black, always poor, he would in a very quiet way begin flirting with the girls they once had been. And then the telephone in the apartment began again, sounding more insistent now by the fifth ring, as if the woman did not intend to let him go to sleep without speaking to her, wanting a promise, his saying how much he missed her, before she would let him go. He knew it would happen with different women in the years ahead, again and again. The doctor had been in love once with a European, lost her, loved her more for leaving him, and then understood that he was alone beyond belief but would manage.

It is not that he never felt love, you see. He once knew it when he played football in school and he often knew it in the hospital when a patient began to recover, despite all odds. He never spared himself in his work, in teaching younger doctors, and every so often the memories of football would give him the echoes of elation. But he saw that was not something I would easily understand and gave in to his tiredness, asking now to be excused.

A brutish and dull game, nonsensical or murderous at times. The tackled halfback jumped on by so many other players his flattened body cannot be seen, the incessant interruptions and delays, the fumbling or incompleted passes, the broken runs, the crudity of blocking, makes football a tedious and clumsy game to watch. But not to all: every November a sweet suspense stirs the country and lasts, scores are sought, television sets stay on, people drive great distances to see The Game. Defeat does not discourage, hopes are always high, the power of the game eases something clenched and dulled, men are free to jump, scream, roar, beseech, plead. Football lets them be playful when little else does.

Some women love football but most, like me, do not care or are suspicious and haughty about it. Only the sight of one man alone, poised to kick the ball over the crossbar, rising on his toes, is of the faintest interest. So mythical is football, so immense its legends and the virtues the college players should have, so warlike and childish its speech and its attacks, so emphatic the insistence on seeking and bearing pain, that at the Phillips Exeter Academy in New Hampshire a few years ago, fifteen- and sixteen-year-olds knew how to mock all of this. A member of the class of 1981 recalls with a smile how she and dozens of classmates would holler at the school's annual match with its great rival, Andover, "Kill, Kill, Hate, Hate, Murder, Murder, *MU-TI-LATE!*" They yelled it in cheerful contempt of football, the competitor, the disapproving faculty, and the terrible lives they felt themselves obliged to lead. In assemblies the students would be ordered to restrain from such unbecoming chants, and at the next game with Andover, she said, they happily disobeyed.

"I don't know why it is beyond you," the man from Vermont tells me, teasing a little for we are old friends, comfortable with each other's stubbornness. "Sports in this country and for me is always football, it gives people immense relief from ordinary, dull, programmed lives. Sports provides figures we can admire and sometimes even love, it gives us great theater and sometimes tragedy, it throws up immense surprises when not much else ever will."

This has long been apparent to any American, it was exactly

what a sports reporter once said. All my life I have heard variations from other women, amused or bewildered, on the story told by a friend who was walking in New York with her brother-in-law, a husky man who long, long ago played college football in New Jersey. A stranger paused in front of them, looked hard at the brother-in-law, and said, as if it were too astonishing to be true, "Why you are Mighty Graham." And Mighty Graham it was.

In the taxi from Kennedy Airport to midtown Manhattan, there were four of us sharing the ride, prolonged because of rain and traffic, and found our silence unnerving, almost un-American. The three men began to speak, the subject Doug Flutie, the quarterback. They bickered about his height, whether it is five-foot eight and a half or five-foot nine and three-quarters, then one man said Flutie feels football is a *mental* not a physical game, which set them off wheeling. His size, his arm, his running, the touchdowns he scored for Boston College, were lovingly argued and discussed as if by uncles who want only the best for their boy but cannot exactly agree. The men in the taxi did not want to discuss the President's foreign policy, as reported in that morning's papers, or why the squalor of 125th Street we could see from the windows was unchanged. This Flutie was sweeter to them, mattered more, and gave them the illusion of ownership of something they would not ordinarily ever possess.

In Princeton the man from Vermont wants to take me to Palmer Stadium. We will pretend to play football, I will make a touchdown, imagining the interference, the roaring crowds, and adrenalin will do the rest. In this way I will appreciate what skill and courage the game calls for. It is not my idea of a grand Sunday, but we set off.

Princeton was, he said, the perfect place for my indoctrination for here, in the 1840s, in ordinary clothes, students played rough, impromptu games behind Old Nassau Hall. In November 1869, the first football game was played in New Brunswick between Princeton and Rutgers, in which a Rutgers student scored a goal for Princeton by forgetting to kick in the right direction. Seven years later, Columbia, Harvard, Yale, and Princeton met and formed the Intercollegiate Football Association, the ardor for football spreading. Donating a large plot of land to Harvard University to be called Soldier's Field, in honor of the dead in the Union

Army, the philanthropist Henry Lee Higginson said in 1896 to the undergraduates that sports would make "full-grown, well-developed men able and ready to do good works of all kind."

Without people Palmer Stadium seemed immense, quite unfriendly without the smallest human rustle, not a single face in the stands. Finished in 1914, it has the U-shape of the ancient Greek stadium but is longer and considerably wider, seating forty-two thousand people and another ten thousand when wooden seats are added at the open end.

He kept the instructions simple. My handbag could be the ball, to be thrown to me as I started running; I was told what goalpost I must reach, where I was likely to be tackled; and the curtain rose.

It rose on nothing. The sun was in my eyes, the wind against me, the silence of the stadium, my shoes not right, the bag just the everyday lump. But hunching slightly, I began the forty yards, weaving and winding as if malevolent Chinese ghosts might lunge and spit and shout from the cold air. Touched, I would break an ankle or, worse, the nose. The sight of me could not have been encouraging. And then a maintenance man employed by the university appeared, asking what is this about, but my friend and I were without an answer and took our leave. Triumph did not touch me; my coach saw no change had taken place, the imagination long dried, the handbag all wrong.

Once inside a prison in San Salvador I was ready to make a throw—never so ready—that would have pleased my football friend who never witnessed the conversion he hoped for. This was a man who always believed women could be taught to throw as well as most men, I had only to pay attention and give myself up to the idea. But it seemed a senseless talent, giving no pleasure.

Visiting El Salvador with a delegation of journalists concerned about the freedom of the press, or lack of it, we held a list of those Salvadorans imprisoned without being informed of the charges or having benefit of counsel or a date set for trial. The others had gone but, staying on, I intended to worm my way into a prison and, surprisingly, did, because of the unusual beauty and fluent Spanish of an exceptional twenty-seven-year-old American freelance reporter, Anne Nelson, who once studied to be an opera singer at Yale. By insisting to each prison guard who tried to block us that his immediate superior be called at once, we at last, after some imperial impatience, reached the office of the warden, who was watching television, in color. Asking to see two Salvadoran journalists, uncertain of whether they were even alive, we settled in for a long day, deaf to the warden's excuses. He was not displeased at all to have his television program interrupted by our visit, for the young woman, Anne, was of greater interest. As the conversation grew monotonous—his refusals, our insistence—she picked up a guitar in the office and began to sing, in Spanish, an old love song, "En Qué Nos Parecemos." Guards bunched in the doorway, faces now full of love, as her voice curled and soared throughout the prison. The warden was visibly moved, charmed even when as an encore, she sang in English "We Shall Overcome." There was applause, the warden as pleased as if he himself had arranged such a performance.

Permission was granted for the next day. We were permitted fifteen minutes alone with the two Salvadorans, whose skin seemed now the color of the oldest, most dingy, sheets. The eyes of one man leaked, so he was glad to have my eyedrops, which did little good. The men said they had been tortured immediately after their arrest by the Treasury Police the day their newspaper was seized and shut down by the government, but in prison they were not beaten or interrogated. Anyone could see that these two needed food, but she and I had come without, not thinking of that. When they were led away, handshakes all around, we saw for the first time the huge, heavy ring of keys left by the warden when he last came out to fuss over his flowers, a source of considerable pride.

Picking up the keys I stood back and looked up to the gallery on the first floor of the prison, wanting to throw the keys up. Once I had seen American soldiers lob grenades, pulling their arms far back, turning a little at the shoulders and letting go. It was the soldiers I remembered, not the men throwing a football on Channel 2 television, which I occasionally see while waiting for the evening news, often delayed by a game.

Someone would appear, hold out his hands, catch the keys, conceal them, and that very night free the prisoners. For nearly a second I was not my usual self; lifted by a fine madness, I was certain I could use the arm to pitch the keys up, ready now.

No one came out on the gallery, nothing moved, the movie flickered and failed. (It is not just men who dream of daring.) Then the warden came out, took back the keys which I was holding, said good-bye, inquired where Anne was living and said to her, in Spanish, that she and I should watch out—*Cuídense.* He had known all along that we did not have the permission of the Defense Minister to come to the prison, as we so earnestly and repeatedly claimed.

A pleasing boy, athletic and well-intentioned, the kind who made older men smile and pat him on the back after watching him play football, Thomas Charles Fox was precisely what the philanthropist Henry Lee Higginson had in mind long ago when he proposed that martial sport could prepare some young men to lead lives of strenuous social service. In his case, unlikely as it may seem, this is what happened.

Choosing a football scholarship at Stanford University in Palo Alto from among the twenty-six offers he received from colleges and universities, Mr. Fox went from Wisconsin to California, an immense leap, the distance far greater for him than the mileage would suggest. Here he met pacifists, organizers, radicals, a few revolutionaries, Joan Baez, draft resisters, students opposed to the rigidity of academic institutions and the war in Vietnam, an exceptional dean of freshmen whose views may have put his career in jeopardy and, at the Newman Center, Catholics as devout as he who practiced a more "liberating form of Catholicism," as he put it.

Football, he thought, was now a waste of his time. He gave up the game which had brought such brightness to his life and never knew regret.

He spent time at the University of California in Berkeley, where confrontations between a rigid administration and the student body over civil rights on the campus led to the creation of a Free Speech Movement. Its leader, Mario Savio, whom he knew, said: "There's a time when the operation of the machine becomes so odious, makes you so sick at heart, that you can't take part. And you've got to put your body on the gears and upon the wheels, upon the levers, upon all the apparatus, and you've got to make it stop." This was 1964. In the spring of 1965, at Berkeley, twelve thousand people came to a thirty-six-hour teach-in about the Vietman War. The great turmoil started, and he was paying attention.

But years later he could not bring himself to belittle football and see it as a harmful sport, one which illustrated for some people the preposterous and violent longings of Americans. He would not say football was bad because, in fact, it had been so wonderful for him.

When he was twelve years old and not yet very tall, this agile and agreeable boy, who was a quarterback for Saint Sebastian's School in Milwaukee, had a rapturous ordeal. It was a test; although requiring nothing unusual from him, it was one which made people quite sentimental, for they saw it as proof of his spirit and gumption, when it was only an accident. All that happened was that he was running for a touchdown—always a pretty thing to see since he had exceptional balance and did not lumber—but just as he was lunging across the goal line, another boy, trying very hard, brought him down. He must have flipped over like a diver strangely interrupted, landing right on his head, suddenly becoming no more than a child lying very still on the field. Later, the parents of Thomas Charles Fox said how people on the sidelines cheered and applauded him as he was carried off the field, out of it, taken straightaway to a hospital where he revived soon enough and felt immensely cheerful.

More than twenty-five years later, a happily married man living in Shawnee Mission, a suburb of Kansas City, unusually devoted to his own three small children—it was he who usually tucked them into bed at night, never cross or in a rush about it—he could still trace the outlines of such splendor. "It was an ecstatic feeling, knowing you had come through, that you had come out on the other side, still okay, with people wanting to give you all this attention," Mr. Fox said.

In Kansas, so many years later, he still held the glow of the boy who was always singled out as one who would certainly rise. It may have something to do with the perfect jaw, the fervor in those eyes, the thick brown hair, the height, and the face without an apparent flaw. His looks, although stunning, did not work against him, and his manner was without conceit. He might have been seductive but earnest men rarely are. Mr. Fox was not frivolous or playful.

In Marquette University High School, his playing was so exceptional that his father, a professor of neuroanatomy, began coming to every game.

"I was competing against my older brother, Jim, who graduated second in his class; he was going to Harvard. My sisters and I always thought of him as 'the brain,' and my father, because he was a scientist and an academician, looked on that above anything else as the highest achievement," Mr. Fox said. "Or that's what I felt. I remember his saying, in 1962, that he was very proud because one of his sons had been chosen to be a Rhodes scholar and another was chosen to be a football all-American. In an important and maybe even more intimate way than my brother's pursuit, I was winning his affection."

His own life was so absorbing, the demands on him so intense, good grades so important—he was in the top 5 percent of his school—that the boy was aware of, but not transfixed by, the nervous collapse and frequent agitation of his father when Dr. Fox suffered misunderstandings with other people in the academic world. The father was not a supple or sociable man, his manner harsh even when he wished to appear humorous or friendly, although his son did not appear to notice. There were three sons and three daughters, one of whom was obese, with startlingly small hands and feet, suffering from a rare condition known as Prader-Willi syndrome and confined to the house.

The mother, never disagreeable or too discerning, keeper of the peace, was the historian of the boys' achievements; it was she who collected and preserved all the clippings from the *Milwaukee Journal* and the *Milwaukee Sentinel*, having them laminated so that grandchildren could read the headlines and stories about Thomas. The trouble was the process was so new the plastic turned yellow and the stories in time became nearly impossible to read. He kept them anyway, with a copy of the high school magazine, the *Flambeau Monthly*. A blurb about the cover photograph, showing men watching a game, their faces transfixed, on an issue of the *Sunday Spectacular*, 1960, said: "There were moments in the St. Catherine game (always a tough one) when offensive efforts seemed to bog down. But the superb defense set the mood and soon the galloping Fox was off to the hunt. The crowd rose with a roar. In an unforgettable photograph, the victory scene was fixed: Three blocking backs and an all-conference guard leading the famous and familiar march around left end." The magazine also mentioned that the school's football team had won the Catholic Conference Football Championship for the second consecutive year and how, during that year's game against St. Joseph's, Tom Fox had scored five touchdowns, including "an unbelievable 65-yard punt return."

As a boy he understood the unspoken: not to show any fear of being hurt when the reason for an injury pleased adults. Football was a good reason, while jumping out of a window or getting hit by a car were certainly not. There was pain that adults permitted and expected you to transcend, and pain that did not make them proud, only agitated. Nothing was easier for him than to be knocked out, to be shoved, to be bruised; no test was ever again to be so simple and rewarding. Never again was he to know such admiration, such praise, each success leading to more success in the years from twelve to seventeen when he played football and knew only tension, not fear. And everything in Milwaukee conspired to make Thomas and other boys, even those not as gifted, want the praise and loving attention that football could bring them.

It meant a bit of gore, of course, but at twelve or sixteen you did not really expect your collarbone to be smashed or think about a damaged spinal cord, because you could not imagine such things. Bad bruises, wrenched knees, banged-up ribs, a broken bone once in a while—that was all right with them, the bargain seemed totally fair. And he loved the game, being able to memorize plays when still small.

"Football was just something that every child did at Saint Sebastian, every capable male nine or ten years old," Mr. Fox said. "In sixth grade you go out for football. You learn how to have fun, how to work together, all working together, and in many cases that is what life is about." He has this manner of speaking: earnest, straightforward, without surprises, almost a parody of a very nice man whose nation does not require children to learn graceful speech.

Now, when more young women are playing in high school and college sports on their own teams, it is not startling to read in a campus newspaper that Kelly O'Dell, a leading goalkeeper in women's collegiate soccer, played one year with a broken thumb or that Natalie Bocock, a forward in field hockey, is playing defense, a flier who must disrupt the other team's shots without regard for her personal safety. But, whatever progress is made, pain will not be so useful to them as it was for Mr. Fox and for all the boys who came later. In Marquette High School, first made a quarterback, then named the sophomore best player, he became a halfback because of his speed and running. Once, as expected, he hurt his back by injuring a ligament, so he was taped and the trainers used heating pads before the games. The suffering, because it was real and always recognized, with a distinct beginning and assured end, made his adolescence tidy and often thrilling. He had very few secrets and lacked interesting impurities.

"I was good for football and football was good for me," he said. "It taught me a great deal—how to have fun. It kept me busy and out of other things, and it was a lot of hard work. I'd come home from practice, I would be bruised and aching and very, very tired, but I'd go to my room and try to do algebra. And I felt good and I got the homework done."

He remembered that his father, seen by some as a domineering and eccentric man, would prefer not to sit always next to his wife at the games. Mrs. Fox was apt to become distraught if she thought Thomas was hurt and cry out in distress, which deeply embarrassed Dr. Fox. The boy was rinsed with honors—named to the all-conference team, the all-state team, and the Midwestern team. It excited Dr. Fox. Years later, when few people knew, or cared, that he had been such a brilliant high school player, Mr. Fox was a stringer for *The New York Times* in Saigon during the American war. When the arrangement was terminated through no fault of his own—he spoke Vietnamese fluently, his contacts were better than most correspondents had, his stories often important, although he wrote like a man who has never really loved a single novel—it worried him to think of what his father might say when he learned that such a promising connection for Thomas was finished. A correspondent in the bureau, seeing his distress, volunteered to write to Dr. Fox that Thomas had worked well but the Saigon bureau was cutting back.

The Marquette University High School football coach, a history teacher named Frank Kopenski who was not a Jesuit, once called him "the most coachable football player I have ever worked with." The coach, of course, was often abusive, theatrical, unreasonable, and clever, but the team did not mind, for his reputation only meant they were exceptional because they could take such a temperament and not buckle. The defense was known as the Rough Rocks. Thomas was spared the taunts; he was nearly perfect, no coach would have wanted to grate on him. It was Fleet-

Footed Fox, after all, who once made so many touchdowns against Saint Joseph.

"We would start practice August 15 when it would be somewhere between ninety and a hundred degrees, very, very hot, near an old building being torn down next to the school, in a field filled with rocks, stones, and rubble. The field was so dry you would breathe in dust, and when we fell the rocks would cut us," he said. "It was very useful."

The coach saw the engine of his team running on a mixture of anger and honor, cooked up by him, and it never worked as efficiently as when Marquette played their archrival, Saint Pius.

"Once when we had lost to them the coach told us he went over to their coach on the field after the game to congratulate him and to ask why Saint Pius insisted on keeping their first string in all the time," said Mr. Fox. "The Saint Pius coach took out a quarter and started flipping it in front of our coach as if to say 'you're begging.' Our coach told us this story as if he had been deliberately humiliated, and our effort then was not just to win but to redeem his dignity. The coach took a quarter and taped it to the bulletin board in the locker room to remind us of what we must avenge. By the time we played Saint Pius we were so eager, so desperate to go out there, we not only won but the score was something like twenty-six to six."

None of them had ever been invited, let alone challenged, to redeem a grown man's honor, and the responsibility elated him because all Thomas Fox had to do was what he did best. The simplicity of it was a great relief, the easiest of all burdens.

After a game he and his friends, Todd Bruett and Michael Harrington, would dress and then drive to Giles in Wauwatosa, where they would eat custard, standing up, ringed by clusters of high school girls from Holy Angel and Divine Savior. There was always a crowd of several hundred people milling around outside the stadium too, waiting to see the team come out, the players always identifiable by their wounds or bits or burnt cork still on their faces. The cork, used around the eyes to cut the glare of the sun, made them look like special units of rangers going out on patrol.

The comparison would not have been of interest to Thomas Fox because, for all of it, he was a peaceful person, surprisingly humble about the attention he created, made a bit shy too because he did not have a special girl of his own in high school. He was too busy with football and being a star pitcher on the baseball team to understand how to have a girl, so he did not consider the whole complicated matter of women. "I thought they would always be there," he said, quite nicely.

Before getting dressed for a game, the football team would go to the school chapel and sit quietly for a short while. No one spoke to them of maximal effort; they were free to pray, or to dream.

"We were smart enough not to pray that we would win, because you don't pray to win. If you have any kind of education at all you realize that you are not to play with God that way—that is not the function of prayer—but you could pray that you would do your best, you could pray that you wouldn't be injured," he recalled.

He received the twenty-six offers of football scholarships from colleges and universities, choosing Stanford University because it had immense prestige for a Milwaukee boy. Football was not fun there when he was a freshman; its demands were ceaseless, the varsity coach extremely serious about complete devotion to the game, and it was not a year in which football players were much admired. In fact they were suspect. No one had ever spoken to him about pacifism before, or about resistance; he heard Cesar Chavez, who was organizing farm workers, speak; he heard Bob Dylan sing. Ira Sandperl, a local activist, was among his acquaintances. The great and stunning rumbles from Berkeley spoke of landslides, volcanoes that would soon erupt. The man he deeply admired, Dwight Clark, dean of freshmen at Stanford, decided to lead a group of freshmen and sophomores to Asia and asked Tom Fox to come. His father said yes, go, and he thinks his parents may have been obliged to borrow the money needed for the trip.

"Football was now irrelevant," he said. He left the team, spent ten weeks that summer in the New Territories in Hong Kong working with refugees and laying cement for a tuberculosis sanitarium, and spent his junior year abroad in France. In Tours he read in *Le Monde* an account of the American bombing of Haiphong. Few Americans had ever heard of Haiphong. After graduation, he went to Vietnam, not as a soldier, but as a volunteer for International Voluntary Services. He was assigned to the area outside of Tuy Hoa, on the coast of Phu Yen province, where the villages had been leveled by fighting and U.S. bombing. The displaced Vietnamese were living on sand, in tin huts that made the heat insufferable. He tried to help them grow their vegetables in the sand. He tried to alleviate the malnutrition and the significant medical problems, but the situation was too typical, too extreme, the necessary help not possible. He went back to study Vietnamese for two years at Yale, then returned to Vietnam wanting to write about the war, believing that his work might make a difference. Long after the rest of us held no such hope, he was possessed of a certain persistence and did not easily relinquish it.

Years and years later, when a liberal friend in the East said football was the illustration of the war fever growing in the nation, a preparation for the real thing, he was able to argue. Football has nothing to do with real war, he said, it is just make-believe, and officers do not really have the time and inclination, in combat or just before, to talk to their troops, as Coach Kopenski had once talked to the Rough Rocks of Marquette. Mr. Fox thought there was no way you could really prepare yourself for war, certainly not by a game.

But always before that, and long after when he was in Kansas, the editor of the *National Catholic Reporter*, he would say good things, if you happened to ask, about his football life, always stressing the value of teamwork. "And pushing yourself very hard is not necessarily a bad thing," said Mr. Fox, who runs three to four miles most mornings. So persistent is the illusion that teamwork is an American virtue, when the country's deepest chord is competitiveness, that an Outward Bound Management Course for grownups now exists. Long famous for providing teenagers with wilderness adventures to create self-confidence, Outward Bound offers executive training courses for five days, or a weekend, to strengthen "managerial self-confidence and problem-solving capabilities: through rigorous physical challenges." This passion for physical punishment is what used to puzzle Jack Flowers, the steelworker in Lorain.

"When, for example, you suggest the best way for your group to cross a deep, churning river, you will be reminded what your personal input is worth. Or, finding yourself poised between one colleague boosting you up a thirteen-foot wall and another pulling you over the top, you will be grateful for group dynamics in a crucial way," said an article in an issue of *Esquire* called "Man at

His Best." It was as if physical adversity were a purge, a restorative, a line to something large and lofty, much more than a metaphor for solving career problems.

Thomas Fox would not argue the other way, believing as he did that running and falling on a field of stubble and rocks those summers in Milwaukee had been good for him. But some of the bigger, more famous college football teams sometimes repelled him. In 1981 Mr. Fox and his Vietnamese wife, Hoa, saw Notre Dame play Georgia because he was on a business trip to Indiana. Years before, Notre Dame, wanting him, had flown Tom Fox to see a game when he was still in high school.

This time something seemed dreadfully different and he did not like the chant he heard some people shouting. He had forgotten it was commonplace for the crowd to yell: Kill, Kill.

"I was disgusted. Notre Dame is living in a mythical land," Mr. Fox said. "That its football team is bigger than anything else means the university is living in the nineteen-fifties and teaching a rather parochial, outdated system that is ugly. They're still teaching the 'win, win, kill, kill' line—what in God's name does this have to do with anything that's going on in the world?" His wife had never seen such a game, she was equally disgusted.

In Milwaukee, he was invited to speak at his old high school on the topic of El Salvador, the role of the new church in Central America, and a book by Penny Lernoux, *Cry of the People*. It would not have occurred to him to miss a visit with Coach Kopenski, who no longer had the team at Marquette, and who did not show any interest in El Salvador.

"The point of football is to have fun, to work together, to be part of an endeavor, and it depends on how corrupt that endeavor becomes. That can be the difference between high school and professional football," said Mr. Fox. He did not intend to urge his son, Daniel, to play football unless the child showed a passion for the game, which was unlikely because the boy, half-Vietnamese, was not going to be very large. He does not want a Coach Kopenski to work on Daniel, either; he would not push the child as he had been so happily, incessantly propelled.

"It was manipulative and I don't intend to manipulate," Mr. Fox said. "I intend to explain, to be open." He let his three children handle his trophies—more than a dozen of them for football and baseball—as if they were toys; only one remained intact and sat on the top of the refrigerator, serving as a jar for odds and ends. When Daniel Clement Fox, age nine, played baseball in the Little League for boys, he and his wife and the two younger girls did not miss a game. The boy always did well and his parents were pleased although not emphatic. All the parents of the children paid attention to the league games, sitting in the heat on bleachers as the tiny players with the child-sized bats went forth. There were girls' games too. "It teaches about winning and losing," said one woman, whose son was the same age as Daniel Fox, but she could say nothing more; it taught some children only how to pacify their parents.

"Don't assume that I was simply a child trying to please a stern father," Mr. Fox said. "I was trying to please, yes, but it was he who instilled the values which set me on the course I have taken since. He was a radical in a politically conservative Milwaukee area. He supported Adlai Stevenson and found great comfort in knowing the Democrats could produce such a leader. My father suffered a great deal at the hands of narrow-minded people, mostly narrow-minded Catholics in our parish and even at Marquette University Medical School where he taught. I say this because my father's views—so progressive for the time and place where we grew up— had an enormous impact on me. From our earliest childhood he was teaching us to beware of jingoists, generals, businessmen, and Republicans in general. He was, with the exception of some close Jesuit and Dominican friends and scholars, largely anticlerical." His mother was more pious and devout, more traditional in her Catholic beliefs. In him there was something of them both. His father did not trust most Catholics because he felt their beliefs led them into "anticommunist crusades that were destructive and foolish," Mr. Fox said.

Dr. Fox, a Catholic, an intellectual who read *Commonweal* magazine, who dared to challenge some of the Church's general assumptions, used to say, "Contrary to popular belief, Jesus Christ was not baptized in our own Saint Sebastian's Church." Such remarks often angered people.

"And in the period of Senator Joe McCarthy, he suffered. Remember that McCarthy came from Wisconsin and was ushered along by some Milwaukee Jesuits," Mr. Fox said. "My father was considered 'pink' because of his strong labor views, his antimilitarism, his progressive politics in general."

When the son wore a button for Adlai Stevenson, the eloquent and unusually intelligent Governor of Illinois who first ran against General Dwight D. Eisenhower for the Presidency in 1952, Thomas Fox had the first fistfight of his life with another second-grader. The button offended the other child, it offended grown-ups.

"The Jesuits, and others, at Marquette High School used to frighten us by saying if we went to a non-Catholic college we would lose our faith," Mr. Fox said. "My father answered that if we lost it we never had it to begin with." Such importance was given to the children's reading that Dr. Fox discouraged Thomas from taking summer jobs, although often enough the cash would have been welcomed.

This is how he preferred to see his dead father when he himself was nearing forty: a man who was not silenced by the mean-spirited or the petty, a man who did not falter in his own beliefs, seeing his effort, in those years, to map out the brain's nervous system as simply an attempt to better understand God's creation. It was not significant that his father's nerves often went awry; the gruffness that startled the rest of us was not a true measure of the man and did not require excuses or explanations from the son.

And he, in turn, was gentle and without a temper. The *National Catholic Reporter* was his banner and he loved it. He wanted the children to see suffering, a world outside the Kansas suburbs, and not be frightened or apathetic. On Thanksgiving Mr. Fox and his wife and the three children spent the day in the food kitchen run by Father Richard Etzel in old Saint Mary's Church where the hungry sat down at tables and were served by volunteers. No one lines up on this day; the poor are to be served as you and I are waited on in restaurants.

He thought it not possible for a man of conscience to be peaceful in these times, but there was very little he wanted for himself, his own gain. He did not believe it wrong or morbid to be sickened by the misery of others.

"I will never be able to describe the anger and helplessness I felt at Stanford in nineteen sixty-five and nineteen sixty-six when President Johnson ordered the bombing raids over North Vietnam," Mr. Fox said. "And do you remember being at Quang Tri, seeing those mangled bodies coming back from Laos? Do you remember the hospital tent and the flies on those bloodied bodies?

I will never let those feelings run out; they will be the fuel, and a guide, for the rest of my life."

In the tent, the Vietnamese soldiers lay—some wanting water, a cigarette, something for their pain—and no Vietnamese army doctors came. It was March in 1971, during Operation Lam Son 719 when twenty thousand South Vietnamese were sent into Laos to cut the supply lines of the North Vietnamese, which the Americans always called the Ho Chi Minh Trail. The operation was intended to prove that the Saigon army, pupils of the Americans, could now fight the war by themselves. The northern army waited for them and knew everything.

It was a rout, a debacle, a defeat emphatically denied by those in Saigon and Washington. But, coming out of Laos, the survivors did not lie. A private said to me, "The whole brigade ran down the hill like ants. We jumped on each other to get out of that place. . . . It was quick, quick, quick or we would die." One man, then another, then a dozen needed to speak.

In the hospital tent the heat made all our faces wet, so it did not matter who was weeping. These men might have been called lucky for they had flown out by helicopters, not left behind in Laos, but not one could guess how long they would lie in the tent or where the doctors were. There was a private from the Delta with a smashed arm and blood on his trousers who sang out a Vietnamese name, a woman's name, and then stopped. I held his other hand for a while and hummed a child's song to him. There was nothing to use to clean or cool his face and our own water was gone. Once I looked for Tom Fox, but he had left the tent and was standing alone, outside, his eyes closed for a second. It was worse for him, his Vietnamese was so good he could understand every word the wounded were saying in high, thin voices, what they were asking for, the soldiers who now knew no one cared about them.

The thirty-six-year-old history instructor who worries that his eight-year-old daughter may not find a sufficiently enlightened man to love and be loved by when she is grown, sees a deeper danger in what he calls these crazy times. To some, of course, the times are quite calm, things are going well. Many men are talking about what fathers should do for their children, how little Stephen makes cookies and little Lisa kicks a ball. A larger number, who have custody of children and who are bringing them up without a wife, are speaking their minds, have theories and new ideas and no longer need to prove they can be fit or loving.

Having raised his daughter, Christina, by himself since she was fifteen months old, Mr. Jimenez, a widower when he was twenty-nine who now teaches History 304 at Princeton University, a course on Latin America, has this to say: "As we so purposely liberate our daughters and a generation of free women are born, what is to prevent them from rushing into the unfreedom, the confinements, of the still predominantly male culture? If in some measure we believe, as I think we do, that in the deepest recesses of our culture it is the women who are its moral ballast, what will become of our civilization if they become like men?"

When he speaks his mind whole passages roll out. "It will be tragic if the Christinas of tomorrow have no real, effective, strong, caring men in their lives, but it will be even more tragic for the culture as a whole if women are not raised to be fully human but rather like men. I think of my women students and I think of Christina. I think of the parents who may now urge, no, compel, their daughters to compete for wealth and power, and just as we have given our sons instructions to be successful, so too we will ask this of our daughters. And what will become of us?"

When Christina was in the second grade she told her father with unusual emphasis how much she hated boys her age, the ones in school and those in her after-school program at the YWCA. Boys were pushy, loud, noisy, show-offs, mean, she said, among other things. At a meeting of the parents' advisory board of the Y, always sparsely attended, Mr. Jimenez raised the question of the boys' behavior.

"The boys would be very aggressive; the boys would do sports by themselves and the girls would sit on the sidelines and watch, or go off and play hair salon or that sort of thing," Mr. Jimenez said. "At the meeting I suggested that we require all the kids to be in sports, ask the girls to play too; they might not want to at first, but later they will begin to feel a stake in it.

"What was interesting was what some parents said after listening to me: Look, *that* is the way boys are and *that* is the way girls are," he said. "I said no, that is *not* the way they are, that is the way we *allow* them to be."

He did not hold the widely accepted assumption that male children, because of their hormones and different muscular structure, were inclined to be so assertive and were expected or permitted to be frequently unruly since this behavior was considered masculine, manly, manlike, manful, virile.

"It doesn't come out of the biology," he said. "The thing is, you cannot protect your child against the culture. One of the dilemmas is, how can I raise Christina to be able to live in this culture but not to be of it, all its destructive manifestations?"

His own life was often rushed, not only because of his teaching and the attention owed to his students but because Christina had a busy life as well. After school on Mondays there was catechism, creative theater at Trinity Church on Wednesdays, then ballet classes from 6:30 to 7:30, Brownies Troop 606 on Thursdays, swimming and sports at the Y on Fridays. He drove and picked her up. He knew exactly what television programs she watched, and together on Thursday nights they saw "The Cosby Show," which he found interesting, and talked about it.

Shopping and cooking for the two of them every night was more than Mr. Jimenez could manage, so he and Christina ate dinner with undergraduates in one of the university's colleges where he is a fellow. Christina, in the third grade, was not shy and was often quite good at making conversation with her seniors. It was the father's wish that this deeply loved child be curious, and perceptive of the world she lived in, and generous to its other inhabitants. And she already owned a child's telescope and a microscope, not the usual possessions of little girls.

"The male students are more interested in talking to Christina than the women are. The same things was true at Harvard," the father said. "I think that being so near a child raises questions for the women about choices; it brings up all the issues—getting married or not, putting off having a family. The predominant tendency among women these days is to wait, delay. I think it's okay to delay having children. But the problem is that people delay intimacy."

In the small house where the two of them lived, rented from the university, there were often flowers in the dining room and nice place mats on the table, the furniture nice, the child's room unusually neat after he periodically called for a cleanup, her weekly schedule lettered and hung on the door, the whole place tidy and cheerful. It surprised a few people who looked for dishes in the sink, dust, disorder, as if a man on his own was doomed and not much could be expected.

Some women, often with children Christina's age, worried how a man could properly raise a daughter and from time to time stepped in with the loveliest intentions. One Christmas, for example, the mother of one of the child's friends told Christina to ask her father for ten dollars. It was spent for a Christmas present for the father when the mother took the little girls out shopping. Later, the woman saw Mr. Jimenez and asked how he had liked the present, as if by leading the child to a store she had in some way made his Christmas nicer while correcting this odd situation, an imbalance in the universe. His response was polite, but he suspected the woman felt pity and prided herself on accomplishing a kindness. He had quite different ideas about what Christina could give him at Christmas.

The truth is that he had been immensely assisted in all ways while raising the child and said so, there were two pairs of grandparents helping the father and the child. His wife's parents in Florida, Rita and Joe, and his own in California, Betty and Salvador, not only saw Christina every year but knew at all times how her little life was going and the person she had become.

After the death of his young wife, he had not avoided other women, disparaged all normal impulses and needs, or isolated himself. There had been remarkable women in his life, only a few, for he did not hop around, but long after he still spoke of them with affection. To them he owed much. "No one can do it alone," said Mr. Jimenez when sensing he was being slightly too much admired. This made him uneasy.

When Christina was much younger and would from time to time boil over, she used to yell at him, "I hate you, I want my mother!" So much later he recalled those outbursts because it led to this: Christina was coming to an age when, he felt, she wanted him to marry again since she wished for a deep, unchanging intimacy with a woman who would not leave. He thought it an appropriate and sweet longing and knew that if this happened she would begin moving away and their closeness could not stay the same.

It was still so unusual for a man to be a parent on his own that Mr. Jimenez grew accustomed to the attention and interest he and Christina aroused in the community. Among the students he had a certain celebrity because of his daughter, and the young also admired his energy as if here was a man who could not be exhausted or depressed by the demands of the day. But still he had to guard against too great an attachment to this identity, to always being seen as the exceptional father, the unusual man.

He had mastered so much, managed so well, become so self-sufficient, that it sometimes appeared as if he might never remarry. For all his horror of sexism and its complicated and pernicious reverberations, he thought in some ways he was still held by his traditional male upbringing and had not, as yet, completely changed. Talk of the "new man" who was at all times confiding, expressive, sympathetic, and sensitive bored him. "It's all garbage," said Mr. Jimenez. "That is not me." He was not the sort who could bear to have you describe how every inch of your day had gone, to hear each morning what you had dreamed and what it might mean.

Still he appeared cheerful, anxious to get on with each day, do as much as possible, and at no time was he the least bit timid about his beliefs and opinions.

"I think probably the best thing in the world is to let men raise children until they are of a certain age," Mr. Jimenez said. "And then let women raise them. It will make men more aware of the problems of bringing up children and the problems of being a human being. The other side of the story is not what happened to Christina but what happened to me, how transformed I have been by the experience."

Once, both of them in her room, Mr. Jimenez told Christina she must buckle down and learn her multiplication tables. The child began to cry and was not instantly consoled, although he tried. Don't cry, he said. Don't. Afterwards he repeated her response to his friends.

"Everybody has the right to cry," the child told the father.

She made him happy. His theories on raising children, hardly commonplace, grew more distinct.

Here is his argument: "I think, in America, boys have always been favored. Boys were always treated more protectively. It's just that we didn't understand what the consequences of such protection were. Yes, girls were treated protectively, too, but the deep and important thing is that boys were always, in a sense, favored. Yes, boys were asked to go out and confront the cruel world, but girls were required to bear emotional burdens and to have much more control than boys. We ask girls to take on extraordinary psychological burdens, to be much more supple emotionally than boys are ever required to be. And the issue is we don't ask boys to be complicated, to reflect. I know this to be so: I am not, in many ways, a reflective person.

"Women are being taught to be more assertive, but we may also be teaching women to be less supple emotionally while not teaching men to be more. There is so little cultural drive for men to change. That is the great terror we all confront."

Steven Trimm, who protested the last war, who always thinks of which men went to prison rather than be part of it, which of his high school friends died in it, and who went and came back never to be themselves again, sees it differently.

"I don't think it is a matter of protection; it is a matter of being more confined," Mr. Trimm said. "Males are trained to stay within more narrow limits when it comes to expressing emotion, but this protects them only in the sense that a straitjacket protects. Sometimes confinement can serve a good purpose, but it usually fosters a kind of dependence—a kind of twisted innocence."

His best friend was a marine in Vietnam. "The guys who enlisted in the marines—he among them—were innocents and dreadfully dependent. They tried to 'do what men do' and 'feel what men feel.' My friend feels like a failure. He has seen himself that way ever since he came home from that war." He thought the other man had over the years been obsessed with helping other veterans because he needed to prove that he remains a good marine, which is to say, a good man. For two years—one man just back from Canada, one just back from Vietnam—the two saw each other nearly every day, each man keeping the other on his feet, but never inclined to say so.

"One of the things that is distinguishing about the children of the middle and upper classes is that they are highly educated but very ignorant. They are ignorant of the pain, the suffering from bad choices that the working class daily must contend with, and that ignorance gets reflected in their politics and, finally, their ability to be sensitive about anything. Working-class guys are accustomed to suffering in one way or another."

Going home from Canada under the amnesty program of President Gerald Ford, he mingled with students at Skidmore College in theater groups and saw them as almost another race, so expensively groomed and sleek, he would say. With their assumptions about life, their higher notions of themselves, the students made him feel foreign.

"What boys have to confront is a terrible mixture of fantasy and brutality," Mr. Trimm said. "I don't think anyone is equal to that, to successfully mastering that. An eighteen-year-old might get all choked up when he watches the flag going by in a parade, and he sees the next logical step, after that emotion, is to a battlefield. But the battlefield he imagines is a fantasy; the real one is a place of unending brutality."

For seventeen years he had not been able to free himself from the war, and did not know if it was possible for any of them. "One of the things that leads me into my depressed phases is the memories, and I get so tired of them, over and over. It is just a great weariness. I wish I had different memories."

His pursuit of Pamela Trigg was brash, clumsy, amusing, and endearing. Nothing remarkable about it, anyone's story, endlessly familiar and touching. Michael Jimenez, whose grandparents emigrated from Spain and whose own hair and skin and eyes made it unlikely he would be seen as a Californian or the child of an old New England family, was at Trinity College in 1967. With college friends he drove one winter weekend to Mount Holyoke, a women's college, for Oktoberfest, a "mixer." As was the custom among young men, he and his friends, setting out on such an adventure, would take whiskey sours to drink on the way, or beer, or gin and tonic, in the conviction that by being drunk they would be brave enough to ask girls to dance, brave enough to kiss and to love if they were so lucky. Mr. Jimenez set eyes on Miss Pamela Trigg, asked her to dance and then, slightly crocked, entertained both of them with totally fraudulent stories, such as his life as the son of a Russian count. It was pure game and she laughed.

When she attempted a retreat, he held her arm and made an announcement: "If you walk away right now, you are going to be missing the most beautiful thing that could every happen to you in your life." Daughter of a doctor in St. Louis, a senior taking what he calls all "the upper-class course stuff," preparing to do a thesis on "Urban Space in Classical Athens," Miss Trigg then led him to a room where people were playing guitars and sitting on cushions on the floor, an ambiance gaining great vogue in those days.

It was his chance and he attempted to overwhelm her. "She kept resisting, she kept on smoking cigarettes and blowing smoke in my face. She had on long underwear because the mixer was outdoors, so I said, 'What do you have, some sort of skin disease?' I tried to get underneath all those clothes, that's what she always said afterwards."

He refused to let her go; he did not see when he was balked and so had his victory. Invited to meet her family, who were in Florida, he appeared so peculiar to the father that Dr. Trigg consulted his son on this stranger: "Bud, what do you make of him?" Bud answered, "Dad, I think he is a Red." Mr. Jimenez had not tried to ingratiate himself.

"I did nothing but argue with them and told them that when the revolution comes we are going to turn your country club into an orphanage for black children," he said. "I was outrageous." Stuffed with such visions, he could not have guessed that in the hard years ahead it was the parents of Pamela Trigg who would become so close to him, such generous and loving friends.

His background and hers did not touch or connect at any point. His own father, whose working-class Spanish parents had settled in Santa Barbara, plunged into business, becoming an executive for Texaco who specialized in labor relations. The family was sent to Bogotá, Colombia, where Michael grew up until he entered a Presbyterian boarding school in the East.

He and Pamela Trigg married in June 1969 and were to have only eight years together.

She was more proper, very shy, not so political in the beginning, while her husband knew no timidity, was eager for the world, forceful and stubborn. The pushing and pulling between them came from his attempts to make her bolder, more coherent, and respectful of her own gifts. When the transformation came he could not take the credit: other women by their writing, their actions, the new attitudes they held made her see there was no time to lose. She changed; he loved it.

At Stanford University he wrote a thesis on the history of Colombia for a master's degree. The two of them traveled through

South America—Salvador Allende's Chile, Peru, Argentina—on a Watson fellowship and headed for Harvard University, where he earned another master's degree to be admitted into the university's doctoral program in history. Pamela Jimenez, as she was known, taught first grade in a school in West Bridgewater, south of Boston. A new section of the library was named for her after the death, Mr. Jimenez said.

So the two of them, not just he, became resident tutors at North House, at the far end of the Radcliffe quadrangle, a house he chose because of the students' reaction to his wife. Here, so different from the older, male, Harvard houses, she was of consequence, for the young immediately saw her worth and asked her to be staff liaison with the Student House Committee. The couple was in charge of a dormitory of nearly sixty students, both sexes, mostly juniors and seniors. They lived in the building, they ate with the students, listened to them, gave counsel and succor, and had fun.

"We were trying to teach them to be responsible democratic citizens in an environment which was teaching them to be corporate, future members of a corporation," Mr. Jimenez said.

In this community, liking the students so much, they knew happiness, being not much older than the undergraduates. She started a women's collective and was the one who did not indulge or coddle students if they seemed to be lagging. "Whereas I would never say anything, I would be the nice guy," Mr. Jimenez said. "She used to say, Michael, the difference between you and me is that you always want to be loved and I want to be respected."

Nothing suggested their lives might topple, that he was to lose her in a way a young man could not dream of, that what was ideal for them was soon to end.

Ten days after the lump in her breast was discovered, by him, she had a radical mastectomy; this was the spring of 1975. Women from the North House collective came to the hospital, where she showed them the scar, explained all that she knew about the disease and how it could be treated. Nothing changed her beauty for him; he too insisted on seeing what surgery had done, finally saw, and reassured her. In two weeks she went back to teaching, commuting three hours a day, and working as a volunteer for the American Cancer Society, teaching poor Hispanic women in Boston how to detect the signs and how to accelerate recovery. When

Pamela said to her husband she wanted to have a child, there were no arguments he could marshal, even a suggestion they adopt a child in Colombia was rejected, so in the end it was she, once so obedient, who prevailed. The doctors were not pleased, some suggesting that hormonal changes could be dangerous. Others were not so certain, suggesting with caution that pregnancy might strengthen her metabolic system. But she had gone beyond the doctors and knew her mind.

It was going well—there was no reason to believe otherwise— when, visiting her parents in Florida, she suffered a seizure and was met at the Boston airport by her husband, so weak she did not attempt to walk. Then he knew: this is it, this is the long haul, get ready. The cancer had crossed the brain blood barrier, he was told, radiation essential, so it began, a lead shield placed over her belly.

The night that they invited students to watch President Gerald Ford debate the Democrats' candidate Governor Jimmy Carter of Georgia on their television set, September 1976, the baby inter- fered. When the amniotic sac burst, Pamela wanted to go to the hospital. It was a comedy, the kind most men deeply dread, the helpless woman going into labor as the car fails and a wrong turn is taken. Arriving at the hospital he was told to drive to the emer- gency room, thought he was doing this, missed an exit, found himself circling in a parking lot, and saw, in his mirror, a nurse running, shouting, pushing a wheelchair behind the car. "You are such a fool," his wife said, almost laughing. "I can't believe I am going to have a child in a used Toyota."

It was before midnight, the cesarean section a few hours off, so he went home, called their two mothers, put on a three-piece suit—homage to the child waiting for him—got the tape recorder and the tapes of the music she liked, and went back. In the hos- pital room, they were listening to a Brandenburg Concerto when the time came for her to be taken to surgery, and he remembered, always, how she kept her hands moving to the music as she was taken away, conducting until she was out of his sight.

When a nurse came out with the baby, born seven weeks premature but in good health, he began to cry, so immense were the feelings that seized and lifted him. The baby was perfect. Just this once he went to pieces and was happy to do so.

"Mr. Jimenez, will you please get hold of yourself," the nurse said, and he made an effort to obey, barely succeeding.

That very day his wife lost all of her hair; it came out in huge bunches as the nurses combed and showed kindness. They went home to North House, where she would often say to a young man, "Come over here, I want to teach you how to change a diaper. It's not going to be just women who do this."

"If we had been graduate students living in some Cambridge apartment it would have been devastating, but we lived in this wonderful community," Mr. Jimenez said. "And at North House she was loved."

Told she was going to die not by her own doctor but by a resident in the hospital, after she had suffered another seizure, the headaches more frequent and cruel, Pamela Jimenez wished for a house by the ocean. She wanted her parents to be near. The last six weeks she was in bed in the Holyoke Center at Harvard when a psychiatrist named Elisabeth Kübler-Ross suddenly appeared to see her. They had heard of her work with the dying, her extraordinary ability to comfort in ways that were not realized by most physicians. His wife, with the irony he had always loved, merely said, "Oh gosh, I have to do my hair," when she had no hair at all. She put on a pretty scarf and the visitor came in, an unusually small woman who did not hesitate.

"Kübler-Ross spoke to us both for about fifteen or twenty minutes, asked me to leave, and got into the bed with Pam," Mr. Jimenez said. "She spent an hour with her, holding her in her arms. She told Pam stories and what she said to children whose parents were dying, that their parents would be going into a coma, weaving a cocoon around themselves and when they die, become butterflies. From that day on Pam knew complete relief."

Two weeks later, in December, after midnight, in a darkened room as his tape of *Camelot* ended, she died. He stayed with her for ten or fifteen minutes, peaceful now that her long siege had ended. Then his mother and more than two dozen students crowded in to grieve and to celebrate the life of Pamela Jimenez.

"They kissed her, they said prayers, and they sang," Mr. Jimenez said. "It was incredible." Some students wanted to cancel the Christmas Ball two days later at North House, but he would not hear of such a thing, went to the ball, and danced until 3 A.M.

In time he left North House, aware that some students who had loved his wife felt resentful or sad when he began to go out with other women. He was only trying to make himself well.

At fifteen months Christina Jimenez entered a day-care center in Cambridge where racism, sexism, and sugar were considered odious and harmful. Parents were required to be on committees, and almost two-thirds of them were raising a child alone. He was the only single male parent.

"Probably the most disadvantaged people in America are single women with children," Mr. Jimenez said. "But these women I met at the center taught me how to be a parent. I think probably the most important thing they taught me was not to worry. They taught me not to be scared, that I could do it, it wasn't something awesome. There is no course you take, nobody gets trained to be a parent."

One of the black women whose child was in the center appeared distressed, Mr. Jimenez said, because the kids were using bad language and nail polish had been applied to the fingers and toes of both little boys and girls. The woman, aghast, said, "You're making my boy into a fag!" As it happened, one of the fathers was at the center that day and attempted to calm the mother by saying, "Don't worry about it." The man was wearing sandals and his own toenails were painted.

He knew very well that a good many people had such fears, so he felt some sympathy for this woman who was so convinced her son was being warped for life, hopelessly damaged. But these were not his fears, he sided with the founders of the day-care center who wanted children to be free of repressive sexual stereotypes and inhibitions.

The meetings went on and on, he rather liked them. Once he was criticized by another parent who said, "Michael you are so obsessed with Christina saying please and thank you. It is such a bourgeois affectation." No, he replied, it is important because it is respectful.

In the winter months when the children played indoors, he always put Christina in nice dresses, brushing her hair every morning and braiding it. The children from wealthier families looked disheveled, wore old clothes—their parents clearly opposing consumerism—while Christina looked the immaculate, pretty little girl. (Perhaps he wanted to show the others that a man could take care of a little girl and be attentive to her appearance. It counted for very little in the day-care center.) Christina had a child's necklace, too, small colored beads which he let her wear.

When a boy wanted to bring his toy gun to the center, the question was discussed at a parents' meeting and the vote was staunchly against any child bringing any make-believe weapon. But a woman raised this point: If guns are the accoutrement of the masculine culture and are now banned here, should we let girls wear the accoutrement of the feminine culture, which is jewelry? He begin thinking about it, and then changed, not buying the dresses for Christina he thought were so charming on her.

"The ideology of the place was always consistent, boys and girls treated equally, boys taught to be gentle, girls to be assertive," Mr. Jimenez said. "There was a real and thoughtful effort when boys began to act up, the realization that this wasn't natural, that it was not a biological requirement or urge."

What he loved, and so needed, was the new community the day-care center in Cambridge provided, many parents taking turns having the children in their houses on different weekends, the discussions and committees, the sense of what he calls "a democratic, participative culture."

The summer Christina was seven she went to the Appel Farm Arts & Music Center, a summer camp that does not emphasize competition among its campers, although the children are encouraged to create, experiment, and perform. The food eaten is often homegrown, the children helping with the care of the farm animals and working in a vegetable garden. It was here she learned that boys could be nice, worthy of friendship, even of affection. "She began to feel comfortable around them; she was less afraid of them," the father said.

He went few places without her, so while still so young she took part in demonstrations of different kinds, against nuclear arms, against apartheid in South Africa and the intervention of the U.S. in Central America. On the great peace march in New York in June 1982, when half a million gathered in Central Park, Christina and her father walked forty blocks in the immense, peaceful, cheerful parade of people streaming through the streets to reach the park. The last few blocks the little girl walked with a delegation of survivors of Hiroshima and helped the Japanese fold the white paper cranes, a symbol of peace.

"What she is being taught is not necessarily a single issue, whether it's Central America or nuclear arms," Mr. Jimenez said. "One of the things that has traditionally happened to men and women raising children is that they don't raise their young in communities. So what Christina is learning is that there are people who live in a community, that it is not a question of a father and daughter alone in the world, not she and I *against* the world, but rather that life is like a seamless web, as the Archbishop of Chicago often says. What she sees is that her father is connected with other people, with other men and women in something which is a struggle but it is not an unhappy struggle."

His course History 304 was very popular, hard work, twenty-one lectures in one semester and a good deal to read. Quite a few students thought of him as a friend, or wished to. In ways he did not himself see, he gave them hope for their own lives. He was never a sad man, appearing the victim of an injustice or a vicious fate.

At the end of April in 1985, when students across the country were demonstrating to protest the holdings of universities and colleges in those companies with investments in South Africa, the Reverend Jesse Jackson came to speak at Princeton University after visiting protestors at Rutgers. Nearly twenty-five hundred students, despite the coldness of the day, crowded Cannon Green to hear him speak. Three faculty members addressed them first; a professor of political science spoke of "complicity that denies it is implicated in the cycle of power." It was the first time in many years that a considerable number of undergraduates at Princeton and other schools were making known their opinions, this time their opposition to apartheid and the collaboration of American businesses and its beneficiaries.

It was Michael Jimenez who gave a speech to introduce the Reverend Jackson.

"In a sense Jesse Jackson and the Princeton Coalition for Divestment, which is a large and growing committee of the whole, are teaching us not just to debate apartheid but to act on our knowledge of its horror, to participate as citizens," Mr. Jimenez said. For many years he had kept a paragraph from a magazine article that quoted the Greek essayist and biographer Plutarch, and now he spoke the words he knew so well. The struggle against apartheid would not end tomorrow, he told the students, but it would go on, for, as Plutarch wrote: " 'They are wrong who think that politics is like an ocean voyage or a military campaign, something to be done with a particular end in view, something which leaves off as soon as that end is reached,' " Mr. Jimenez read.

Later a student asked him if he had not put himself in jeopardy. Since he had not yet completed his doctoral dissertation, Mr. Jimenez had yet to be considered for tenure.

He sought to reassure her. By that time a faculty petition with more than 220 names called for immediate withdrawal of university investments in banks loaning funds to the government of South Africa and withdrawal of investments in companies that conduct business there.

He was hardly in peril and knew it.

"The worst thing in my life has already happened," he told her. "What is there to be scared of?"

It surprised her that he spoke so openly, not taking refuge in a vague declaration of principle or a self-serving and magisterial statement, as she felt so many men tended to do. Although Michael Jimenez was under no obligation to speak of his own life, of the old and immense sorrow, to a twenty-two-year-old senior, this is exactly what he did. It startled her. That day the student, who speaks so often of how the lives of women were changing but of the thousands of nails still holding them down, was reminded that some men were changing too. Although she refused to count on such hope, she saw the possibility that many more men were capable of change and that someone her age might just live to see it.

ABOUT THE AUTHOR

Gloria Emerson, a New Yorker, is a former foreign correspondent for The New York Times whose coverage of the Vietnam war won a George Polk award. *Winners and Losers,* her book on the war and its effects on Americans, won a National Book Award and a Matrix. She has received other honors, including a Penney-Missouri award for magazine writing. She has held teaching fellowships at Harvard and Princeton.